Boris Popivanov

CHANGING IMAGES OF THE LEFT IN BULGARIA

The Challenge of Post-Communism
in the Early 21st Century

ibidem-Verlag
Stuttgart

Bibliografische Information der Deutschen Nationalbibliothek
Die Deutsche Nationalbibliothek verzeichnet diese Publikation in der Deutschen Nationalbibliografie; detaillierte bibliografische Daten sind im Internet über http://dnb.d-nb.de abrufbar.

Bibliographic information published by the Deutsche Nationalbibliothek
Die Deutsche Nationalbibliothek lists this publication in the Deutsche Nationalbibliografie; detailed bibliographic data are available in the Internet at http://dnb.d-nb.de.

Cover picture: Protest in Sofia against the Oresharski cabinet, 8 July 2013. © Luchesar ILIEV. Source: Wikimedia Commons. Licensed under CC-BY-SA 3.0 (s. http://creativecommons.org/licenses/by-sa/3.0/deed.en).

∞

Gedruckt auf alterungsbeständigem, säurefreien Papier
Printed on acid-free paper

ISSN: 1614-3515

ISBN-13: 978-3-8382-0667-7

© *ibidem*-Verlag
Stuttgart 2015

Alle Rechte vorbehalten

Das Werk einschließlich aller seiner Teile ist urheberrechtlich geschützt. Jede Verwertung außerhalb der engen Grenzen des Urheberrechtsgesetzes ist ohne Zustimmung des Verlages unzulässig und strafbar. Dies gilt insbesondere für Vervielfältigungen, Übersetzungen, Mikroverfilmungen und elektronische Speicherformen sowie die Einspeicherung und Verarbeitung in elektronischen Systemen.

All rights reserved. No part of this publication may be reproduced, stored in or introduced into a retrieval system, or transmitted, in any form, or by any means (electronical, mechanical, photocopying, recording or otherwise) without the prior written permission of the publisher. Any person who does any unauthorized act in relation to this publication may be liable to criminal prosecution and civil claims for damages.

Printed in Germany

Soviet and Post-Soviet Politics and Society (SPPS) Vol. 145
ISSN 1614-3515

General Editor: Andreas Umland,
Institute for Euro-Atlantic Cooperation, Kyiv, umland@stanfordalumni.org

Commissioning Editor: Max Jakob Horstmann,
London, mjh@ibidem.eu

EDITORIAL COMMITTEE*

DOMESTIC & COMPARATIVE POLITICS
Prof. **Ellen Bos**, *Andrássy University of Budapest*
Dr. **Ingmar Bredies**, *FH Bund, Brühl*
Dr. **Andrey Kazantsev**, *MGIMO (U) MID RF, Moscow*
Prof. **Heiko Pleines**, *University of Bremen*
Prof. **Richard Sakwa**, *University of Kent at Canterbury*
Dr. **Sarah Whitmore**, *Oxford Brookes University*
Dr. **Harald Wydra**, *University of Cambridge*

SOCIETY, CLASS & ETHNICITY
Col. **David Glantz**, *"Journal of Slavic Military Studies"*
Dr. **Marlène Laruelle**, *George Washington University*
Dr. **Stephen Shulman**, *Southern Illinois University*
Prof. **Stefan Troebst**, *University of Leipzig*

POLITICAL ECONOMY & PUBLIC POLICY
Prof. em. **Marshall Goldman**, *Wellesley College, Mass.*
Dr. **Andreas Goldthau**, *Central European University*
Dr. **Robert Kravchuk**, *University of North Carolina*
Dr. **David Lane**, *University of Cambridge*
Dr. **Carol Leonard**, *University of Oxford*
Dr. **Maria Popova**, *McGill University, Montreal*

FOREIGN POLICY & INTERNATIONAL AFFAIRS
Dr. **Peter Duncan**, *University College London*
Dr. **Taras Kuzio**, *Johns Hopkins University*
Prof. **Gerhard Mangott**, *University of Innsbruck*
Dr. **Diana Schmidt-Pfister**, *University of Konstanz*
Dr. **Lisbeth Tarlow**, *Harvard University, Cambridge*
Dr. **Christian Wipperfürth**, *N-Ost Network, Berlin*
Dr. **William Zimmerman**, *University of Michigan*

HISTORY, CULTURE & THOUGHT
Dr. **Catherine Andreyev**, *University of Oxford*
Prof. **Mark Bassin**, *Södertörn University*
Prof. **Karsten Brüggemann**, *Tallinn University*
Dr. **Alexander Etkind**, *University of Cambridge*
Dr. **Gasan Gusejnov**, *Moscow State University*
Prof. em. **Walter Laqueur**, *Georgetown University*
Prof. **Leonid Luks**, *Catholic University of Eichstaett*
Dr. **Olga Malinova**, *Russian Academy of Sciences*
Prof. **Andrei Rogatchevski**, *University of Tromsø*
Dr. **Mark Tauger**, *West Virginia University*
Dr. **Stefan Wiedekehr**, *BBAW, Berlin*

ADVISORY BOARD*

Prof. **Dominique Arel**, *University of Ottawa*
Prof. **Jörg Baberowski**, *Humboldt University of Berlin*
Prof. **Margarita Balmaceda**, *Seton Hall University*
Dr. **John Barber**, *University of Cambridge*
Prof. **Timm Beichelt**, *European University Viadrina*
Dr. **Katrin Boeckh**, *University of Munich*
Prof. em. **Archie Brown**, *University of Oxford*
Dr. **Vyacheslav Bryukhovetsky**, *Kyiv-Mohyla Academy*
Prof. **Timothy Colton**, *Harvard University, Cambridge*
Prof. **Paul D'Anieri**, *University of Florida*
Dr. **Heike Dörrenbächer**, *DGO, Berlin*
Dr. **John Dunlop**, *Hoover Institution, Stanford, California*
Dr. **Sabine Fischer**, *SWP, Berlin*
Dr. **Geir Flikke**, *NUPI, Oslo*
Prof. **David Galbreath**, *University of Aberdeen*
Prof. **Alexander Galkin**, *Russian Academy of Sciences*
Prof. **Frank Golczewski**, *University of Hamburg*
Dr. **Nikolas Gvosdev**, *Naval War College, Newport, RI*
Prof. **Mark von Hagen**, *Arizona State University*
Dr. **Guido Hausmann**, *University of Freiburg i.Br.*
Prof. **Dale Herspring**, *Kansas State University*
Dr. **Stefani Hoffman**, *Hebrew University of Jerusalem*
Prof. **Mikhail Ilyin**, *MGIMO (U) MID RF, Moscow*
Prof. **Vladimir Kantor**, *Higher School of Economics*
Dr. **Ivan Katchanovski**, *University of Ottawa*
Prof. em. **Andrzej Korbonski**, *University of California*
Dr. **Iris Kempe**, *"Caucasus Analytical Digest"*
Prof. **Herbert Küpper**, *Institut für Ostrecht Regensburg*
Dr. **Rainer Lindner**, *CEEER, Berlin*
Dr. **Vladimir Malakhov**, *Russian Academy of Sciences*

Dr. **Luke March**, *University of Edinburgh*
Prof. **Michael McFaul**, *US Embassy at Moscow*
Prof. **Birgit Menzel**, *University of Mainz-Germersheim*
Prof. **Valery Mikhailenko**, *The Urals State University*
Prof. **Emil Pain**, *Higher School of Economics, Moscow*
Dr. **Oleg Podvintsev**, *Russian Academy of Sciences*
Prof. **Olga Popova**, *St. Petersburg State University*
Dr. **Alex Pravda**, *University of Oxford*
Dr. **Erik van Ree**, *University of Amsterdam*
Dr. **Joachim Rogall**, *Robert Bosch Foundation Stuttgart*
Prof. **Peter Rutland**, *Wesleyan University, Middletown*
Prof. **Marat Salikov**, *The Urals State Law Academy*
Dr. **Gwendolyn Sasse**, *University of Oxford*
Prof. **Jutta Scherrer**, *EHESS, Paris*
Prof. **Robert Service**, *University of Oxford*
Mr. **James Sherr**, *RIIA Chatham House London*
Dr. **Oxana Shevel**, *Tufts University, Medford*
Prof. **Eberhard Schneider**, *University of Siegen*
Prof. **Olexander Shnyrkov**, *Shevchenko University, Kyiv*
Prof. **Hans-Henning Schröder**, *SWP, Berlin*
Prof. **Yuri Shapoval**, *Ukrainian Academy of Sciences*
Prof. **Viktor Shnirelman**, *Russian Academy of Sciences*
Dr. **Lisa Sundstrom**, *University of British Columbia*
Dr. **Philip Walters**, *"Religion, State and Society", Oxford*
Prof. **Zenon Wasyliw**, *Ithaca College, New York State*
Dr. **Lucan Way**, *University of Toronto*
Dr. **Markus Wehner**, *"Frankfurter Allgemeine Zeitung"*
Dr. **Andrew Wilson**, *University College London*
Prof. **Jan Zielonka**, *University of Oxford*
Prof. **Andrei Zorin**, *University of Oxford*

* While the Editorial Committee and Advisory Board support the General Editor in the choice and improvement of manuscripts for publication, responsibility for remaining errors and misinterpretations in the series' volumes lies with the books' authors.

Soviet and Post-Soviet Politics and Society (SPPS)
ISSN 1614-3515

Founded in 2004 and refereed since 2007, SPPS makes available affordable English-, German-, and Russian-language studies on the history of the countries of the former Soviet bloc from the late Tsarist period to today. It publishes between 5 and 20 volumes per year and focuses on issues in transitions to and from democracy such as economic crisis, identity formation, civil society development, and constitutional reform in CEE and the NIS. SPPS also aims to highlight so far understudied themes in East European studies such as right-wing radicalism, religious life, higher education, or human rights protection. The authors and titles of all previously published volumes are listed at the end of this book. For a full description of the series and reviews of its books, see
www.ibidem-verlag.de/red/spps.

Editorial correspondence & manuscripts should be sent to: Dr. Andreas Umland, DAAD, German Embassy, vul. Bohdana Khmelnitskoho 25, UA-01901 Kyiv, Ukraine. e-mail: umland@stanfordalumni.org

Business correspondence & review copy requests should be sent to: *ibidem* Press, Leuschnerstr. 40, 30457 Hannover, Germany; tel.: +49 511 2622200; fax: +49 511 2622201; spps@ibidem.eu.

Authors, reviewers, referees, and editors for (as well as all other persons sympathetic to) SPPS are invited to join its networks at
www.facebook.com/group.php?gid=52638198614
www.linkedin.com/groups?about=&gid=103012
www.xing.com/net/spps-ibidem-verlag/

Recent Volumes

137 Kristin Schreiter
Stellung und Entwicklungspotential zivilgesellschaftlicher Gruppen in Russland
Menschenrechtsorganisationen im Vergleich
ISBN 978-3-8382-0673-8

138 David R. Marples, Frederick V. Mills (Eds.)
Ukraine's Euromaidan
Analyses of a Civil Revolution
ISBN 978-3-8382-0660-8

139 Bernd Kappenberg
Setting Signs for Europe
Why Diacritics Matter for European Integration
With a foreword by Peter Schlobinski
ISBN 978-3-8382-0663-9

140 René Lenz
Internationalisierung, Kooperation und Transfer
Externe bildungspolitische Akteure in der Russischen Föderation
Mit einem Vorwort von Frank Ettrich
ISBN 978-3-8382-0751-3

141 Juri Plusnin, Yana Zausaeva, Natalia Zhidkevich, Artemy Pozanenko
Wandering Workers
Mores, Behavior, Way of Life, and Political Status of Domestic Russian Labor Migrants
Translated by Julia Kazantseva
ISBN 978-3-8382-0653-0

142 Matthew Kott, David J. Smith (eds.)
Latvia – A Work in Progress?
100 Years of State- and Nation-building
ISBN 978-3-8382-0648-6

143 Инна Чувычкина (ред.)
Экспортные нефте- и газопроводы на постсоветском пространстве
Анализ трубопроводной политики в свете теории международных отношений
ISBN 978-3-8382-0822-0

144 Johann Zajaczkowski
Russland – eine pragmatische Großmacht?
Eine rollentheoretische Untersuchung russischer Außenpolitik am Beispiel der Zusammenarbeit mit den USA nach 9/11 und des Georgienkrieges von 2008
Mit einem Vorwort von Siegfried Schieder
ISBN 978-3-8382-0837-4

Contents

Abbreviations of political parties and organizations		VI
Preface		IX
1	Contextualizing the Bulgarian Left: The Communist Successor Parties in Central and Eastern Europe	1
	1.1 The Post-Communist Left in Central and Eastern Europe	1
	1.2 Programmatic and Structural Change within CEE Communist Parties	16
	1.3 Programmatic and Structural Transformation of BCP	43
2	The Complex Historical Pathways of the Bulgarian Socialist Party	57
	2.1 A Proletarian Party with no Proletariat	57
	2.2 BCP in its Attempt to be Party of the Entire People	77
	2.3 The Party in the Transition and the Transition in the Party	91
3	Leftist Elite and Leftist Supporters: An Emerging Divide	113
	3.1 Has the Socialist Leadership been Sliding 'Right'?	113
	3.2 Has the Socialist Electorate been Sliding 'Left'?	127
4	The Bulgarian Post-Communist Left in Crisis. Is a New Left on the Way?	145
	4.1 The Challenge of New Leftist Projects	145
	4.2 The Challenge of New Leftist Groups	160
	4.3 The Challenge of the 'Protest Year' 2013	177
In Lieu of a Conclusion		193
Bibliography		195

Abbreviations of political parties and organizations

Abbreviation	Full name of the organization in the original language	Full name of the organization in English	Country of origin
BCP	Balgarska komunisticheska partija	Bulgarian Communist Party	Bulgaria
BSP	Balgarska socialisticheska partija	Bulgarian Socialist Party	Bulgaria
BZNS	Balgarski zemedelski naroden sajuz	Bulgarian Agrarian National Union	Bulgaria
DPS	Dvijenie za prava i svobodi	Movement for Rights and Freedoms	Bulgaria
FSN	Frontul Salvării Naționale	National Salvation Front	Romania
GERB	Grajdani za evropejsko razvitie na Balgarija	Citizens for the European Development of Bulgaria	Bulgaria
KSČ	Komunistická strana Československa	Communist Party of Czechoslovakia	Czechoslovakia
KSČM	Komunistická strana Čech a Moravy	Communist Party of Bohemia and Moravia	Czech Republic
KSS	Komunistická strana Slovenska	Communist Party of Slovakia	Slovakia
MSzMP	Magyar Szocialista Munkáspárt	Hungarian Socialist Workers' Party	Hungary
MSzP	Magyar Szocialista Párt	Hungarian Socialist Party	Hungary
OSD	Obedinenie za sozialna demokracija	Union for Social Democracy	Bulgaria

PCR	Partidul Comunist Român	Romanian Communist Party	Romania
PD	Partidul Democrat	Democratic Party	Romania
PDS	Partei des demokratischen Sozialismus	Party of Democratic Socialism	German Democratic Republic
PES	---	Party of the European Socialists	European Union
PRM	Partidul România Mare	Greater Romania Party	Romania
PSD	Partidul Social Democrat	Social Democratic Party	Romania
PZPR	Polska Zjednoczona Partia Robotniczej	Polish United Workers'Party	Poland
SDL'	Strana demokratickej l'avice	Party of the Democratic Left	Slovakia
SdRP	Socjaldemocracja Rzeczypospolitej Polskiej	Social Democracy of the Republic of Poland	Poland
SDS	Sajuz na demokratichnite sili	Union of the Democratic Forces	Bulgaria
SED	Sozialistische Einheitspartei Deutschlands	Socialist Unity Party of Germany	German Democratic Republic
SPD	Sozialdemokratische Partei Deutschlands	German Social Democratic Party	Germany
SPS	Socjalistička partija Srbije	Socialist Party of Serbia	Serbia
SSRNJ	Socjalistički savez radnog naroda Jugoslavije	Socialist Alliance of Working People of Yugoslavia	Yugoslavia

Other important abbreviations

Abbreviation	Full name
CEE	Central and Eastern Europe
Comecon	Council for Mutual Economic Assistance
CSP	Communist Successor Party
GDR	German Democratic Republic (East Germany)

Preface

It is now 11 years since Bulgaria became a full NATO member, and 8 years since the country acceded to the European Union. Yet Bulgaria is still receiving relatively weak coverage in the annals of the European and global social sciences—a situation evident both from the limited number of special editions devoted to the country, and from the gaps in the literature to which scholars often explicitly refer. There are diverse reasons for this state of affairs. The socialist period of Bulgaria's history is not to be remembered for an impressive resistance against the regime or for strong expressions of discontent against the Soviet domination. Later, in the processes of transition to democracy in Central and Eastern Europe, Bulgaria did not come to present a success story or model for emulation. On the other hand, there was no dramatic failure, such as, say, a triumph of authoritarian trends, to be observed in the country, either. In the context of the Balkans, Bulgaria happily avoided the fate of neighbouring Yugoslavia and did not get tangled in the quagmire of civil wars. Markedly positive or resolutely negative cases usually tend to attract greater attention. Bulgaria's case did not fall in either of those categories. Nevertheless, unique historical experience could be found here. It is an experience which relates to the peculiarly intertwined roles of Europe and Russia in the national development as well as to the anti-fascist resistance and the social struggles of the contemporary world.

Those introductory remarks are needed as initial steps to motivate interest in one of the important manifestations of the Bulgarian political process for many decades: the functioning of the Bulgarian left. This interest can be positioned in a twofold context. The first aspect of this context is the background of the transition to post-socialist democracy and the specific role of the principal organizational agent of the Bulgarian left, the former Communist Party. In contrast with its counterparts in the other former Eastern Bloc countries, the party maintained its unity and influence in a pluralist political model from the very start of transitions, and remained the only one among them to maintain emotional closeness to Russia. The second aspect of the context is the perspective of the current situation, in which the Bulgarian left can become the object of interest given the serious crisis it is now experiencing—an organizational, moral, political, and ideological crisis that has significantly affected its image.

The issue of the adaptation and transformation of the communist successor parties in CEE has received a significant place in the scholarly debate. A cursory glance on the amassed literature—which is impressive even in its sheer volume—already shows that what we have at hand is a number of different strategies and trajectories of development. We cannot construct some general scheme claiming to be valid for all former socialist countries, and then apply it to Bulgaria to fill it with the required factual content.

That is why two central questions are facing us here. First, which are the factors that can help explain the transformation of the Bulgarian Communist Party in the new democratic situation—factors which, in addition, have contributed to its success, at least in comparison with all other former Eastern Bloc counterparts? Second, which factors in the course of that transformation led to the crisis trends that found their most distinct expression in the early 2010s?

The context of the Eastern Bloc system, marked by its belonging to the Soviet sphere of influence, constitutes a starting point and basis of comparison. This is the necessary background against which the differences in the roads walked by leftist parties in different countries can be put into clear relief. From here the need follows to look for those differences not only in the general system features of the Bloc but also in the different historical legacies of each country. This, broadly put, is the subject of the first chapter of this study.

When tracing the place of the Bulgarian Socialist Party in the modern Bulgarian politics, I am interested above all in the connection between its messages and actions, on the one hand, and the expectations of certain parts of the Bulgarian society, on the other. In this way, the problem of the different images of the Bulgarian left comes to the foreground. It is on those images that I place the focus of my discussion, leaving a secondary role for issues such as organizational development, policies, leadership, and institutions. A look back into history reveals a string of metamorphoses and different political agents that can be viewed as comprising parts of the dynamics of the leftist spectrum in Bulgaria. Within those processes, there is a specific organized political actor of indubitable leading importance because already at its creation some 125 years ago it ambitiously defined the potential and specific nature of the left in Bulgaria and delineated the space in which a political left must find its place. In the second chapter, I offer an attempt to briefly present the programme and ideological role of that party which for a long period of time ruled the country as a communist party.

In the public and political debate regarding the direction of democratic change after 1989, the Bulgarian left was naturally featured as a post-communist left, and it was this fact, with all of its advantages and disadvantages, that marked its search for a place in the newly forming political life of the country. Together with its post-communist status and its references to the past, the Socialist Party had to also delineate a forward-looking horizon for the left in that new situation. In the end of the day, the Bulgarian left accepted the interpretation that the transition has an essentially rightist liberal character, thus failing to find an adequate leftist image for its own actions and in many respects starting to drift away from the attitudes and expectations of its supporters. I present this divergence between leaders and electorate in the third chapter.

In the fourth chapter, which leads us into the present-day situation, I analyze the consequences of this evolution which have found an expression in a crisis of image and of identity, in new opportunities for alternative left-wing actors, including grassroots movements, and in the crossroad on which the traditional Bulgarian left is now finding itself. The widest and most obvious road is leading down. But are there really no other roads for the leading Bulgarian leftist party? And is this a road down not only for that party but also for the Bulgarian left as a whole? I am aware that I am not able to give categorical answers to those future-oriented questions. I have taken the risk of analyzing events that are literally happening as we speak. But I am convinced that without making sense of the past we can hardly orient ourselves in current processes and make a relatively accurate assessment of the options in this crossroad.

In this sense, this book is not a study of the history of one party but rather an interpretation of the historical processes connected with that party. In other words, my goal is to offer an interpretation of the leftist trend in the modern Bulgarian politics and its changing political and ideological coordinates. Today's situation is the result of the interaction of diverse historical factors. There is a constant change of variables stemming from the specifics of changing situations. Due to that fact, I am employing a number of methods in this study. A large part of the processes that I am going to delineate can hardly receive an adequate quantification. That is why qualitative methods have pride of place in the discussion. At different points in the course of the study, I am employing historical reconstruction, analysis of documents, ideological critique, and secondary analysis of empirical data. I hope that this diversity does not sound confusing, and that it is presented in apt combinations. The goal I am setting for myself is not to prove but rather to show.

Several other preliminary points are in order. I am working with concepts such as 'communist successor parties', 'Eastern Bloc', and 'Central and Eastern Europe' for which I have endeavoured to specify the meanings I am employing. A somewhat graver issue is posed by concepts such as 'socialist' and 'communist' which are often used interchangeably in the literature. Insofar as societies built under the Soviet control in that part of the world called themselves 'socialist', and insofar as the dominant Marxist-Leninist doctrine viewed socialism as the first stage of the future, not yet achieved communist society, I believe that the concept of communism should not be used to denote the social and political situation in Bulgaria and its 'fraternal' countries in the period between the 1940s and 1980s. Due to this, I am talking about a socialist period and a socialist state but also about a communist regime, meaning a regime of the Communist Party. Analogously, after 1989, in my reading, CEE countries underwent a post-socialist transformation, while the transformation of the ruling parties was 'post-communist'.

As far as sources are concerned, I have attempted to use as far as possible international studies and English language research literature, in order to facilitate the reader in their possible search for references and additional information and analyses. Of course, where I have found it that studies in Bulgarian are of crucial significance for the interpretation of processes, I have made use of them, too. Guided by the same motives, I have limited as much as possible my use of mass media sources.

Finally, it is my pleasant obligation to extend by sincere gratitude as an author to a number of people who have significantly contributed to my work. Even one-man studies are born in an environment of discussion and exchange of opinions. I am indebted to all my colleagues in the Political Science Department at the St. Kliment Ohridski Sofia University for the creative working atmosphere I have been privileged to enjoy among them. I would especially like to mention Maria Pirgova, to whose advice and lessons on Bulgarian politics and the Bulgarian left I owe more than words can express. I am grateful to Vassil Penev who attentively read each section of this text and offered important criticism and advice. Petar-Emil Mitev, Goran Goranov, Iskra Baeva, Antony Todorov, Dobrin Kanev, Andrey Raichev, and Valeri Jablyanov have all offered valuable ideas and proposals for the work. The help and stimulation by Georgi Karasimeonov (Sofia University), Peter Bajomi-Lazar (Budapest Business School), and Elena Genova (University of Nottingham) were strongly motivating. On the topic of new left groups in Bulgaria, I highly valued the cooperation offered by Georgi Medarov and Madlen Nikolova. Parts of this book were presented as talks at conferences in London (February 2014), Sofia (September 2014) and Warsaw (November 2014). I am grateful to the participants in the discussions after my presentations for their observations and comments. There are certainly still other people that I am forgetting to mention. Yet, last but not least, there are two persons to whom I am most indebted. Those are my editor Max Jakob Horstmann, who showed trust in me and encouraged me to develop the theses from a conference paper into a full-fledged monograph study, and Ognian Kassabov, without whom this study would have hardly come into existence.

Of course, there are probably some errors in this book. There might be some unjustified digressions, arguments showing some degree of partiality, or imprecise formulations. The liability for them remains entirely mine.

1 Contextualizing the Bulgarian Left: The Communist Successor Parties in Central and Eastern Europe

1.1 The Post-Communist Left in Central and Eastern Europe

The question regarding the new dimensions of the political left in Bulgaria is firmly situated within the more general discussion about the development of the political process in Central and Eastern Europe (CEE) and the post-Soviet space after the democratic changes in the late 1980s and early 1990s.

The Cold War period that followed the victory over the Axis forces in World War II was a time of antagonism between two blocs. This period has its distinct and relatively clear geopolitical and ideological coordinates. In the USSR zone of geopolitical influence, political regimes were established that were directly and closely committed to a communist ideology, more precisely to the Soviet version of the extreme left—an overarching commitment that took on specific shapes in the USSR and the different CEE countries (especially after Stalin's death in 1953). This process had its variations and nuances, sometimes forming a quite broad range of individual cases, yet it can be seen as one abiding by some important shared characteristics that give good reason for all those countries to be considered under the common denominator of the so-called Eastern Bloc.

Comparative studies of the post-communist left have traditionally employed two approaches to defining the geographical and geopolitical boundaries of their object of investigation. The first one is to consider the group of countries that were in the past ruled by a communist regime (which also includes the former Soviet republics in Central Asia as well as those of former Yugoslavia). The other approach, which is more restrictive, is to treat CEE countries—which, in spite of their character as sovereign states, were previously officially allied with the USSR (i.e., the Eastern Bloc). In this study, I will be reviewing literature that uses both approaches, but I will opt for the second approach in my own interpretation of the Bulgarian case.

The countries of the Eastern Bloc—one of which is Bulgaria—formed a political, military, and economic alliance under the leadership of the Soviet Union within two important structures: the Organization of the Warsaw Pact and Comecon. In each of those countries, there was a power monopoly reserved for the respective Communist Party, which presupposed a rejection of liberal democratic political pluralism. Their economies functioned (in varying degrees) on the basis of the mechanisms of central planning and the domination of public property over the means of production. The development of social structures was subordinated to the then ruling interpretations of so-called Marxism-Leninism, which in effect modelled all spheres of public life.

Those key characteristics of the Eastern Bloc disappeared in the course of its dissolution during the tumultuous times of 1989–1991. The reason for their rejection and dismantling was the decision of the separate CEE countries to undergo a geopolitical transformation (by leaving the Warsaw Pact and Comecon and terminating their special relationship with the USSR) and to start a transition to political democracy and market economy, generally following the models established in Western Europe after World War II. Marxism-Leninism, however understood, interpreted, or upgraded, was repudiated and ceased to provide an explanatory framework for ongoing events. Influential social forces for which Marxism-Leninism's applicability remained unshakeable were found to be lacking.

Previously, communist parties in the countries of the Eastern Bloc had played the role of 'avant-garde' bearers of a social and political project that in the end failed, a project that came to be broadly and firmly associated with the left—in its Soviet version, as already mentioned. That is why the question regarding the left after the democratic changes has to a large extent taken the shape of a question regarding the organizational and ideological fate of the communist parties, which had lost their monopoly on power. Considered as a group of ideologies, values, practices, and approaches, the left is of course a much broader concept. Yet, at least during the first years of transition in the CEE region, the debate on the post-communist left was structured as a debate on CSPs. In the course of those initial social changes, other possible versions of the left did not possess weight and significance sufficient to give impetus to alternative directions of study. Interest in the post-communist left started to wane only later, in the post-9/11 world, in the face of new challenges for collective security, after the more resolute introduction of the issues of European integration, and with the crisis of representation and the ascent of populism. Nevertheless, even today, this remains an influential area of research in the social sciences that places the development of processes in CEE in a historical perspective and in a much needed regional comparative context.

When critically assessing CSPs,[1] I will be following one of their most widely used definitions, namely the one given by Ishiyama. According to this author, CSPs are those parties "who were formerly the governing party in the pre-1989 communist regime and which inherited the preponderance of the former ruling parties' resources and personnel" (Ishiyama 1998: 62). The definition has the advantages of succinctness, clarity, and a potential of encompassing the wide diversity of phenomena under study.[2] It is often used as a reference point of analysis in the subsequent debate on CSPs (see, e.g., Hough, Paterson and Sloam 2006; De Waele and Soare 2011).

In the literature on the fate of CSPs, a groundwork study has been delivered by Kitschelt, who to a large extent has derived the formation and characteristics of those parties from the structures of the former communist regimes. According to the author, those regimes exhibit at least three different configurations based on differences: (1) in the degree of pluralism and opportunities for contention in decision-making within the communist elite; (2) in the freedom of expression of public disagreement with the party; as well as (3) in the degree of bureaucratic professionalism, or, on the opposite side, of patronage as a mode of functioning of the state apparatus. Thus Kitschelt (1995: 452–453) has distinguished among three

---

1 I will limit my very short review of the literature to key texts in the comparative political analysis of CSPs. Of course, the issue of those parties has been investigated in many other contexts, such as those of post-communist party systems, of constitutional and institutional transformations in the region, of political culture, of nationalisms and populisms, of economic reforms, etc. Some of the works in those areas have been useful for this study. But in order not to unduly extend this initial review, I will not be discussing them at present, but will be using them later in the book, at the places where they can be of help to clarify specific questions regarding the Bulgarian left.

2 Another widely used definition has been given by Grzymala-Busse, according to whom we should understand CSPs as "the formal descendants of the communist parties—that is, the main political parties that arose from the ruling communist parties in 1989 and that explicitly claim their successor status" (2002: 14). Such an approach however excludes the Romanian case, in which there is one party that indubitably succeeded in many respects the former communist party, but did not claim, and even denied, that it did so.

types of communist regimes. The first one is patrimonial communism, under which there are weak preconditions for division within the elite and for expression of mass public attitudes as well as low to medium rational bureaucratic institutionalization. This type of regime is distinguished by a solid degree of entrenchment within society. It functions on the basis of hierarchical chains of personal dependence amongst leaders and their associates, while the opposition has been crushed or co-opted in a system of patronage. The tendency during transition here is for the model to be reproduced in the new conditions through a preservation of the networks of influence of the former communist elites, often in the guise of a strongly personalized government. As examples for patrimonial communism, the author has singled out a large part of South-Eastern Europe (Serbia, Romania, "to a considerable extent also Bulgaria"), Russia, Ukraine, Belarus, and in the type's most extreme forms—the former Soviet republics of Central Asia. A second type of regime is bureaucratic-authoritarian communism. Here political divisions and the interest articulation are also weakly exhibited, but the degree of rational bureaucratic institutionalization is high. Elites in this case are not capable of adaptation faced with the crisis of the communist bloc. They break down completely and cannot negotiate the guise of future institutions, which are then constructed following the will of the anti-communist opposition on a depersonalized basis, i.e. in the shape of parliamentary rule. East Germany, the Czech Republic, and, with many qualifications, Slovakia, are given as examples for bureaucratic-authoritarian communism. A third type of regime is the national or national-consensus communism, under which medium levels of political divisions, interest articulation and bureaucratic professionalism appear. It is distinguished by a strong desire for national autonomy from Soviet hegemony, a lasting influence of the pre-World War II past and of the Catholic Church, a capability for flexibility and negotiation with different social and political communities. The latter also applies to the course of transition to democracy. The most prominent examples for national-consensus communism are Poland and Hungary, but also, to some degree, Slovenia and Croatia.

Kitschelt explains the different types of regimes with two fundamental factors: the historical periods of industrialization in specific societies, as well as the manifestations of political mobilization representative of each of them (1995: 455–458). For instance, the earlier before the inception of the communist regime industrialization took place, the greater the probability that the regime itself will bear the characteristics of bureaucratic professionalism. The later industrialization took place and the weaker the tradition of civic mobilization in support of public causes, the greater the possibility of entrenchment of a patrimonial communism. According to the author, the type of regime that came to be established bears a direct influence on the programmatic structuring of party cleavages in post-communist party systems. The type of regime can explain those cleavages and at the same time creates the preconditions for the place and role of former communist parties in the new environment. This role is significantly influenced by the variations in the weight and capabilities of communist elites during the former regime (1995: 461–462).

Kitschelt's work offers important reference points allowing an initial orientation in the manifestly complex picture of the post-communist problem area. Firstly, the post-communist left should not be regarded as some unified ideological wave, trend, direction, or character of the left in the given region but rather as a set of political forces and elites with specific traditions of action and thinking. Secondly, the successors to communist parties have their conditions for existence and development that were not expected or foreseen at the time of collapse of the given regime. Thirdly, the character of the former regime is to a large degree decisive for the character of CSPs, which requires employing historical approaches in the interpretation of current processes. And finally, the efforts at building typologies of the diversity of post-communist left phenomena are a tool for their better understanding.

Actually, there was an expectation that the death of communist regimes will also bury their ruling parties. Many authors studying the post-communist left do not fail to express the surprise that this did not transpire. I will provide some quotations by way of illustration. Thus, Bozoki and Ishiyama comment that: "Contrary to early expectations that the organizational successors to the communist parties would disappear into the ash can of political history, the successor parties have proven quite durable" (2002: 3). Similarly, Curry and Urban note that: "The year 1989 seemed to be the end in Eastern Europe not only for communist rule but for any political party ever associated with Marxism-Leninism" (2003: 1). Equally, Hough states that: "Post-1990 it was widely believed that central European communist movements would die a swift and sudden death, and very few people expected them to be playing any role at all in political life come the twenty-first century" (2005: 254).

Given these expectations, it is only natural that two central questions would start making rounds in the literature: (1) Why did those parties survive?; and, (2) Having once survived, what course would they take to ensure their preservation?

Different factors have been mustered to explain the survival of communist parties in the new situation. In the spirit of Kitschelt's (1995) analysis, Bozoki and Ishiyama single out, in the first place, the characteristic traits of the former regime and the preconditions created within it. Additionally, they argue that a special significance is to be seen in the presence or absence of competition from other leftist parties within the developing postcommunist party systems. The lack of serious competitors of that kind provides, in most cases, good opportunities for successor parties to build a monopoly of the left political spectrum and to gain a solid hold of it. Since no other actor expresses a desire to occupy that space, it is left for the successor parties to take, even when sharply negative attitudes against their preservation are present in society. These parties often get the chance to capitalize on topics considered important for the public, such as the issue of social rights, and the like. The loss of many social benefits gained during the former regime and the shrinking of others during the transition to market economy inevitably gave rise to dissent and discontent in certain social strata and fuelled the propaganda engine of postcommunist leftists. The latter could also take advantage of the existence of social groups cherishing a lasting biographical or emotional commitment to the times of the former regime. Of course, the most significant among them are the members of older generations (2002: 3–5). Other studies mention still other potential groups[3].

Grzymala-Busse (2002: 19–20, 265–267) underscores the importance of the social psychological and social mobilization inertia of the past. According to her, an important factor for the survival and new strengthening of the

---

[3] For example, Lubecki (2004) argues that the ballots cast for CSPs may depend not only on the social and economic situation of countries after the transitions, and on the anti-communist forces' success or failure in government, but also on whether before World War II in those countries there were masses of agricultural proletarians and impoverished peasants who experienced an unprecedented social advancement during the communist regime, and who entirely owe their higher social status to that regime and the then ruling party.

successor parties are communist legacies, understood as public norms, models of political behaviour, and organizational networks. The transformation of those parties was a process dominated by elites who managed to effectively use the political and administrative resources already available to them, in order to develop successful strategies for adjusting to the new political environment. The past is a hindrance but also an opportunity. The central argument of the author is that the successful successor parties were those that find ways to redeem the lost communist past. The change in their identities, e.g. in the direction of social democracy or social liberalism, was the more needed, the more strongly discredited the communist system is in the eyes of public opinion. Conversely, a preserved prestige and a positive attitude among the population towards the party's results automatically legitimized those parties and deprived them of a motive to change. They remained true to the ideas because of which and actually *only* because of which part of their voters supported them.

Curry and Urban (2003: 245–248) bring forward some consequences of the shared communist legacy of successor parties that allow them to find their place in the new post-socialist environment. The first one is the initial ostracism under which they were placed after the end of the regime: a broad spectrum ranging from accusations and wholesale rejection on the part of political opponents, through governmental revanchism, to criminal prosecution against party figures or legal procedures for forfeiture of party assets. All of these helped build mechanisms of cohesion, a peculiar siege thinking, a self-styled 'united we stand, divided we fall' ethos, as well as fears that the disappearance of the collective party agent would leave its individual supporters at the mercy of the opponents' revenge. The second consequence that emerges is the specific organizational skills applied in seeking resources within an environment that has now become competitive. Those skills inherited from the past were lacking in most newly created competitive anti-communist formations, constituting a political advantage not to be underestimated. They were evident everywhere in CEE, except in countries such as Russia or Ukraine, where the opponents of the post-communist left also turn out to be connected with the formerly ruling communist party.[4] Finally, there comes the opportunity (already mentioned

---

4 An interesting quantitative study of the parliaments of countries traditionally viewed as hostile to Soviet type communism, such as Poland, Lithuania, Latvia and Estonia, has found out that, within the 20-year period since the start of transitions, the

by Bozoki and Ishiyama in the wok cited above) for successor parties to capitalize on the palpable achievements of the old regime, in particular—the guarantee of minimal social protection for everyone.

The course of development of ideas upheld by CSPs after the end of communist regimes has also become the subject of many studies. The cracking of Marxism-Leninism's dogmatic shell required—at least as official programs are concerned—a re-evaluation within each of those parties. The new orientation of CEE countries towards West European models of political democracy and market economy revived the significance of historical divisions in the left that had been long suppressed in the former Eastern Bloc by the hegemony of the Marxist-Leninist version of the left. In a way, the varieties of the West European left became models against which successor parties had to be measured, taking into account the specifics of national traditions and culture. The division between moderate and radical left in post-communist conditions has become established in the literature among the most widely held interpretations of the trajectory of development of the post-communist left.

According to Curry and Urban's (2003) key argument, the line of demarcation among CSPs is the division between social democrats and neo-Leninists. Serious variations among parties and specific roads of development for each single country notwithstanding, successor parties in the end reproduce the above division. The criterion for the course taken is mostly historical. Where Marxism had its own roods and social basis before World War II, neo-Leninism became dominant (the Czech Republic, the former East Germany). Where Marxism was imposed by Soviet military force in the absence of domestic preconditions for its growth, the arrow of change pointed towards social democracy (Poland, Hungary).

According to Ziblatt (1998), former communist parties adapt to the post-socialist environments in two ways, which he calls 'leftist-retreat' and 'pragmatic-reform', and which he illustrates, respectively with PDS in Germany and MSzP in Hungary. Studying the diversity among courses for

---

number of representatives of ex-communist nomenklatura among MPs remained stable and even higher than the number of former dissidents. With time, the first number indeed begins to dwindle, but the decrease in the number of former dissidents is much faster. The latter as a whole are found to display much weaker organizational skills and capacities to adapt to the dynamics of the current political situation (Matonyte 2009).

change, Hough (2005) extends Ziblatt's typology to a broader area on the map. According to Hough, processes in Poland led to an establishing of social democratic ideals, whereas processes in the Czech Republic led to a reformed communism. Processes in Hungary led to a social liberal interpretation of Blair's Third Way, while those in Slovakia—to a turbulent development in which the messages of the leftist party did not come to achieve a stable ideological consistency. In spite of this, the options of party adaptation, just as offered by Ziblatt, can be reduced to two. The leftist retreat is illustrated by the example of the Party of Democratic Socialism in Germany and the Communist Party of Bohemia and Moravia. The starting point of this retreat is the scepticism and even the rejection of individualism and market economy, motivated mostly by the damages they inflicted on the welfare systems of those societies. Paradoxically, it turns out that these parties, drawing their arguments from the achievements of so-called Real Socialism[5], have come close to the radical messages of the West European radical left. The veritable change within them came to pass organizationally rather than ideologically. In contrast with the strict centralism characteristic of Marxist-Leninist parties, these parties came to orient themselves towards a broad party democracy under which the attitudes, views and nostalgia of members and supporters became the driving force of the parties' political behaviour. Consequently, as organizations, they were less flexible and more dependent on the opinions of their local structures than on the decision of their leaders. The second option—pragmatic-reform—follows the route of West Europe social democratic parties. It is usually characterized by a centralization of decision making on the part of a reformist elite, which also allows much greater flexibility in surmounting the complex challenges of the democratic political process. Party elites strive to adapt to the changing environment without being slaves to the past, and they impose their views on the whole party, even in opposition to the expectations and hopes of their more left leaning supporters.

---

5   Real Socialism is an ideological concept that refers to a particular phase of development of the CEE societies during the Brezhnev era and shortly afterwards. It was described as creating the 'immediate prerequisites' for a transition to communism.

This typology of CSPs as parties of leftist retreat and pragmatic reformism has been adopted as a leading reference point in some of the literature[6]. Bozoki and Ishiyama[7] also employ this categorization in their study, but they argue it needs to be elaborated in order to be precise. According to them, the processes in the Balkans, especially in the former Yugoslavia, as well as in the former Soviet space, gave rise to an additional "national-patriotic" vector of change of the post-communist left, stemming from the different type of development and the different tasks to be solved by those societies, in comparison to the Central European cases, which have traditionally been more favoured as subject of analysis. That is why the authors introduce two dimensions of successor parties' adaption strategies after the end of the communist regimes: (1) reformed/non-reformed parties, dependent on their movement towards social democracy, and (2) transmuted/non-transmuted parties, dependent on their movement towards nationalism (2002: 6–8). Individual instances should be considered in both dimensions in order to yield a more precise assessment of the nature of their adaptation to the new situation.[8]

Another approach argues that attempts at constructing a typology of CSPs are wholly dependent on the division between the Soviet Union and its satellites, between the 'inner' and 'outer' circle of empire, and always tend to view them separately. Kuzio (2008) develops a typology generalization with the intention to cover the whole range of countries from the former Eastern Bloc and to relate the type of their post-communist statehood with their type of post-communist left. According to him, the course by states after the dissolution of the bloc is to a large degree decisive for the transfor-

---

6 Another important study, that of Nagle and Mahr, contends that there have been three alternatives for new left politics in the first wave of disillusionment with the economic difficulties in CEE: (1) an unreformed Leninist politics, as exemplified by KSČM; (2) a Western-sponsored or imported Social democracy, as partially presented in Slovakia; and (3) a reformed but authentically domestic democratic left, as the case stands in Poland and Hungary (1999: 179). It is easily seen that CSPs belong to options (1) and (3). Thus Nagle and Mahr's typology is close to the 'leftist-retreat'-'pragmatic-reform' division elaborated by Ziblatt (1998).
7 The earlier mentioned study of Ishiyama (1999) also makes a significant contribution to the research on CSPs, but I will not discuss it here, given the fuller and richer conceptual and interpretative framework in Bozoki and Ishiyama (2002).
8 This triple typology of leftist-retreat, pragmatic-reform and national-patriotic adaptation strategies has been subsequently taken up by Webb and White (2007) and others.

mation of CSPs. That is why the factors influencing the specific country are of foremost significance: its pre-communist historical heritage, the nature of its communist regime, its type of nationalism and presence of national minorities, the existence of anti-regime opposition during communism, and the influence of the European Union in giving incentives for democratization. Using such instruments, it can be for instance shown that countries such as Russia or Serbia are much closer together in their post-communist transformation due to sharing similar imperial projects in the past, than Russia is with countries from the former USSR or than Serbia is with Bulgaria. On the basis of a detailed analysis of factors influencing change, Kuzio argues that post-communist countries can be classified into four groups: (1) Central and East European democracies or "rapid reformers", including Poland, the Czech Republic, Hungary, Slovenia, the Baltic countries; (2) Central and East European half-democracies, or "reform laggards", including Romania, Bulgaria, Slovakia, Croatia, Albania, Ukraine, Georgia; (3) post-imperial pseudo-democracies or "reform obstructionists", among them Russia and Serbia; and (4) Eurasian autocracies, or "reform stiflers", including Belarus, Armenia, Azerbaijan and former Soviet republics in Central Asia. According to Kuzio, this typology of countries is capable of also explaining transformations in the respective successor parties. Correspondingly, in the first case communist parties transformed quickly into parties of a West European social democratic type; in the second case, the same effect is to be observed, yet significantly slower and with bigger twists and tensions; in the third case orthodox communism found many points of contact with nationalism and fostered the 'marriage' between the two in the parties' political messages and actions; in the fourth case we have non-reformed communist parties operating in an environment of dominating 'centrist' formations that too were built and that too are being guided by the former communist nomenklatura (2008: 415–416).

Independent of the differences in approach, the specific character of separate countries in the course they took in post-communism and the considerable variety of cleavages in the respective societies across the region are something generally acknowledged (Whitefield 2002). Of course, every author is ready to admit that classifications are always conditional and marked by different qualifications. The difficulties to produce a sufficiently working typology indeed stem from the completely different starting points at the end of the regimes, as well as from the exceptionally rich variety in that seemingly monolithic unity that we are used to call 'communist regimes'. This way, 'communist regime' actually serves as an umbrella term encompassing the rather different trajectories not only of the countries in the former Bloc but of CSPs themselves. For instance, what are the shared traits of successor parties' transformation in countries like Poland and Serbia? In Poland, after the fall from power and the triumph of Solidarity, the former communists started to build a party from scratch under ostracism and isolation from other actors in the social and political space. They started downplaying their 'leftist' label, flexibly avoiding the identification with 'leftism', 'post-communism' and 'socialism', and shaping their strategy using a side route. For years, they claimed not so much to be a 'left' alternative to the new power but something much more general and vague, namely that they represent the intelligentsia or the social forces of pragmatism, professionalism and competence, that they are much more an expert community than a political party ideologically belonging to the left spectrum (Zubek 1994). The situation in Serbia could hardly be more different. The falling apart of Yugoslavia was preceded by the deep divisions and collapse of the ruling League of Communists of Yugoslavia. Its Serbian section, the League of Communists of Serbia, decided to unite with the satellite mass organization of SSRNJ and to create SPS. There was no ostracism in this case. On the reverse, SPS had the confidence of flying on the wings of popular approval due to the so-called anti-bureaucratic revolution, resolutely looking forward to its imminent victory at the first democratic election. Moreover, there were no attempts at covering the leftist identification of the party and replacing it with pragmatic values. At its very creation, SPS declared in its first post-communist programme that it would work for Serbia as a "socialist republic based on the rule of law and social justice." "Solidarity", "equality", and "social security" were among the boldly stated principles of that programme (Brankovic 2002). I do not mean to comment the issue of putting the words to practice in Poland and Serbia. My intention is not to assess the practical side of the Polish and Serbian cases. Conversely, my aim is to point out, in Kitschelt's (1995) spirit, how the different types of communist regime can reproduce radically different starting positions for successor parties and influence their trajectories of democratic development in ways obstructing all-embracing attempts to erect a typology.

In the picture of the post-communist left, Bulgaria provides one of the manifest difficulties for classification. As things stand however, comparative studies have devoted limited and insufficient attention to the Bulgarian case. The key texts on CSPs reviewed here give a good illustration for this observation.

Curry and Urban's (2003) study does not mention Bulgaria at all, either in a separate chapter (separate chapters are devoted to Poland, Hungary, Lithuania, Germany, Russia and Ukraine), or even in the introductory review of the general context or the conclusions. The situation is the same in Hough (2005). The main thesis of the study, which posits a division between social democrats and neo-Leninists, is illustrated nationally only with the differences between Poland, Hungary and Slovakia, on one hand, and Germany and the Czech Republic, on the other.[9] There is an exceptionally detailed and useful anthology on communist and post-communist parties in Europe (Backes and Moreau 2008), in which for some 700 pages the parties of the four regions of the continent are discussed according to a geographical arrangement. The section on Eastern Europe offers chapters on post-communist parties in the Czech Republic, Slovakia, Poland, Romania, Serbia, Ukraine, Belarus and Russia—again nothing on Bulgaria. The Bulgarian case is mentioned only once and, what is more, this happens in the conclusion, where the editors formulate their thesis that the Czech Republic and Bulgaria are the only post-socialist EU members in which orthodox communism has not disappeared and still continues to play a role (2008: 562). Unfortunately, the arguments given for that thesis do not attest to a good acquaintance with the situation in Bulgaria.[10] We can mention also a

---

9 Later, using Hough's (2005) methodology on successor parties, and with his personal participation, a project was developed which resulted among other things in the collection Hough, Paterson and Sloam (2006). It includes separate chapters on Poland, the Czech Republic, Slovakia, and Germany. Parts of the book treat more general problems of European integration or parties' programmatic development, but again Bulgaria's case evades the academic scrutiny of the authors (which is also true for South-East Europe as a whole).

10 More precisely, the editors remark on the presence of one Communist Party of Bulgaria, led by Alexander Paunov, in the composition of Coalition for Bulgaria, as well as on the first place of the Coalition at the 2005 parliamentary election with 30.95% of the vote. From those facts they conclude that the Communists won the vote using a coalition. However, everyone familiar with Bulgarian politics would know that election results of the Coalition for Bulgaria are essentially equivalent to the results of the senior partner in the Coalition—the Bulgarian Socialist Party—

study of the role of CSPs in the European integration processes in the former Eastern bloc. Dauderstädt (2005) pays no attention to Bulgaria although it is partly explicable by his focus on the 2004 Wave of Accession countries.

In an attempt at providing a classification of successor parties, Kuzio pedantically gives some attention to practically all of them. On the issue of the Bulgarian post-communist left he mostly uses two sources to delineate the following picture. In Bulgaria, like in Romania, the communist regime enjoyed a strong legitimacy. There was in effect no opposition against it; in Bulgaria such appeared only at the time of Gorbachev's Perestroika. In contrast to other countries, in Bulgaria society did not view the ruling party as an agent for Soviet imperialism but rather as a protector of national sovereignty. The emergence of nationalism in the country had to do with the communist elite's adaptation to the gradual delegitimizing of the regime close to the end of the Cold War. All of this explains why the former communist party retained strong positions in the first years of democratic development and to a large degree implemented status quo—type policies. Election defeats for Romanian and Bulgarian successor parties, respectively in 1996 and 1997, drove them to re-orient their programs and policies towards upholding social democracy, accepting the market economy, and supporting Euro-Atlantic integration. It is in those processes that their social democratic transformation took shape (2008: 408–409).

Grzymala-Busse does not consider Bulgaria separately (her case studies are the traditional Central European examples, Poland, Hungary, the Czech Republic and Slovakia), but she at least takes Bulgaria into account in her analysis and also underscores the initial legitimacy of the regime and its leader party. The author remarks that in Bulgaria, Romania and Albania, unlike in the Central European cases, the transition towards democracy did not consist in a collapse of the old regime but rather in changes in the political conditions for the ruling parties' functioning. According to her, the Bulgarian post-communists did not experience a significant transformation due to the lack of incentives to do so (which means a lack of pressure on the part of society), and also due to a lack of left alternatives. Their course of maintaining the status quo was further bolstered by the privi-

---

while the other formations, including the above mentioned Communist Party, have only a peripheral significance and taken on their own do not give a sufficient justification for the claim that orthodox communism has any electoral weight in Bulgaria.

leged access to patronage, state resources and media they managed to retain (2002: 267–269).

Bozoki and Ishiyama's (2002) edited volume brings to the front the distinctive features of the Bulgarian case. In the chapter on Bulgaria and Romania by Murer (2002), it is explicitly stated that the Bulgarian post-communist left fits well neither in the category of 'leftist-retreat', nor in that of a pragmatic ideology, and even not in that of a national-patriotic turn, which are the three categories that shape the typology division of CSPs. The Bulgarian post-communist leftists are found to contain elements of all three. According to the author, in the Bulgarian case, we have a peculiar combination of historical and contemporary factors contributing to the presence and achievements of the party. He argues that of special significance among the historical factors is the long tradition of an egalitarian peasant political movement in Bulgarian society, while among the current factors he places special significance on the formation of forces directed against globalization and neo-liberal capitalism. In this sense, the stability of the Bulgarian party suggests not so much a certain type of post-communist politics but rather a set of attitudes from the age of communism and earlier, which live on together with new fears for the future and the rend underpinning it.[11]

Thus, a paradox seems to arise from the diametrically opposed approaches of comparative political scientists to the Bulgarian post-communist left. Part of them have entirely ignored the country, perhaps thus suggesting that it does not hold great significance for the explanation of the successor parties' transformation, or else they have almost automatically put Bulgaria under one of the types of successor party they have formulated. Another part of researchers have explicitly underscored the Bulgarian case's distinctive character and the infeasibility to easily subsume it under a given common denominator. In short: a peculiar case that however has far from been widely investigated in a comparative perspective.

Taking into account the danger of excessive generalization, from the comparative studies one can conclude that the Bulgarian post-communist left: (1) has a serious tradition and draws its legitimacy from a regime that has

---

11 The same author, Jeffrey S. Murer, also wrote the chapter on Hungary, Bulgaria and Romania (1999) in the earlier comparative study by Ishiyama on CSPs. Since however his main theses and conclusions overlap with those in his 2002 text, I shall not discuss the older one separately.

not been entirely rejected by society; (2) managed to retain its positions after the democratic changes due to the lack of strong traditional alternatives; (3) underwent a very slow transformation away from its initial Marxist-Leninist confines; (4) manifests some quite similar traits to processes in neighbouring Romania.

In order to better clarify this specific character of the Bulgarian left, it would be useful to look in more detail into the history of the former communist parties' transformation in the dawn of democratic changes in the region. Against this backdrop, and thanks to the factual basis for the programmatic and structural transformations in Central and Eastern Europe, we will be able to more adequately explain what distinguishes the Bulgarian case from other CSPs.

1.2 Programmatic and Structural Change within CEE Communist Parties

I must first make several remarks regarding the span of the review I am about to offer. When we are about to investigate changes within the CEE communist parties effected under the pressure of the heady transformations of the 'year of miracles' 1989, we are due to first clarify three issues that only apparently pose no problems: which countries we are talking about, which parties we are having in mind, and what types of changes exactly we are going to consider.

As I have already pointed out, two approaches are present in the literature on the post-communist left: a broad one, encompassing all countries which have passed from a communist regime during the Cold War on to a post-communist stage of development (this includes USSR's CEE allies, the Central Asian Soviet republics and the republics from Tito's Yugoslavia); and a more limited approach, focusing on the so-called Eastern Bloc (i.e. just the USSR and its satellites). I will here follow the second approach, and will limit it further. I will not be touching on the consequences of the Soviet Union's collapse, which led to a painful and often bloody building of new statehood in a situation of a completely different role of the former communist parties and their elites. In order to delineate the context of transformation in Bulgaria, I will be reviewing the countries whose common starting point is the Comecon and Warsaw Pact system, and the featured

geopolitical domination by Moscow: namely Poland, Hungary, Czechoslovakia, the German Democratic Republic, and Romania.
With respect to the second question pointed out above, it appears that CSPs are easy to identify. However, it turns out that this is not always so. In some cases, the identities of the successors are beyond doubt (e.g., it is well known that in Germany PDS succeeded SED, while alternative candidates for this role have played only a marginal role in public life). Yet in other cases, researchers are not certain whether to name one or several parties as contenders for the legacy, or to identify parties that do not contend to be successors, but bear clear ties to the former communist parties (e.g. in Romania, where Ishiyama (2001) and Grzymala-Busse (2006) unequivocally name Ion Iliescu's PSD as the successor, yet Pop-Eleches (2008) also names as additional successors Petre Roman's PD and even Corneliu Vadim Tudor's PRM). There are various criteria to be employed in the search for continuity with former communist parties. They include similarities in ideology and symbolism, continuities in leaders and members, as well as legal succession, and so on. In order not to diverge in a discussion that is peripheral to the object of this study, I will follow the dominant position, which recognizes the following successor parties at the start of democratic changes: SdRP in Poland, MSzP in Hungary, KSČM and KSS in the former Czechoslovakia, PDS in Germany, and FSN in Romania.
Regarding the third issue, the question as to the type of transition under consideration, I will remark that the common denominator of changes within communist parties is the loss of monopoly on power which was constitutionally grounded and geopolitically guaranteed by the countries' belonging to the Eastern Bloc. From there on, changes took place in various directions. They include implemented policies, decision making mechanisms, the ways party functioning was organized, the relations between leaders and members, the party's ideology in the broadest sense of the term, as well as many other factors. My interest will be devoted to two variables—programmatic and structural change. They are important because it is those two variables that make the most significant contribution to shaping the image of the respective parties in a domestic and international perspective. Those two types of transformations took place chiefly in 1989 and the first years after, with transformations in the following two decades up to now more limited and rather showing a desire to follow and modify a

political pathway that has already been chosen.[12] The significance of those changes and their concentration within a relatively short period stem from the circumstance that through them, parties achieved a stable form in which to appear in front of citizens in the new democratic situation (after a re-founding, renaming, splitting up, etc.), and forged the official messages that helped them find their best positioning in the political spectrum (as social democratic, neo-communist or some other type). On this basis we can get a clearer understanding of the election results of each of those parties, which I have illustrated with tables below.

Poland. This is the CEE country where changes in the political system started out earliest, and the ruling PZPR had to respond to them without being able to rely on precedents or historical examples. In fact, among all other ex-communist countries, it is Poland in which power was weakest in the 1980s. The 1981–83 period of martial law had limited—without completely obliterating—the field of action for the independent Solidarity trade union. With the lifting of martial law, the anti-communist opposition acquired additional social force and weight further eroding trust in official institutions and party power, which had been low to start with.

At PZPR's 10th plenum in December 1988 the party decided to start negotiations with Solidarity. This amounted to admitting that it was no longer able to gain command of the situation in the country. Talks took place at the so-called Round Table, between February and April the following year, and became an institutional model for subsequent withdrawal from power of communist parties in other Eastern Bloc countries. PZPR's monopoly on rule in Poland suffered its first blow with the agreement for new elections in June 1989, which guaranteed 65% of seats in the Sejm (the lower chamber of the Polish Parliament) to the communists and their allies. The party lost all other Sejm seats and did not get any representatives in the Senate (the upper chamber). The head of state Wojciech Jaruzelski's unsuccessful attempts to draw Solidarity into a big coalition with PZPR by nominating Czesław Kiszczak for Prime Minister led to a second blow on the party's

---

12 Grzymala-Busse, for instance, makes the point: "[W]hile enormous differences could arise between the communist parties of 1989 and of 1991, efforts after this period had far less impact. Party programs and organizations continued to evolve, but there was no possibility of a dramatic turnaround of the sort that was feasible in 1989–91. Efforts by reformists-come-lately... had far less chance of success" (2002: 8).

power monopoly—the communists had to step back from the executive. August saw the election of Poland's first non-communist Prime Minister for the preceding 40 years, Solidarity's candidate Tadeusz Mazowiecki. PZPR's power monopoly was to be terminated in December 1990, when President Jaruzelski was forced to resign, and Solidarity leader Lech Walesa went on to win subsequent presidential elections.

There can be no question that the Polish opposition threaded determinedly on its course to power. PZPR made attempts to reform facing growing social hostility and a dramatic outflow of party members. A step towards internal democratization, which however did not produce substantial effects, was the end of July 1989 decision to separate state power from party power. At that time, Jaruzelski retained his position of head of state, but withdrew from the position of PZPR first secretary, which was taken up by the reformist Mieczysław Rakowski, with his earlier reputation of a nonconformist journalist. Months later, it was to become evident that, in that guise, the party was not able to efficiently meet the challenges of political change. The notion that a disbanding of PZPR is needed came to be almost consensually shared among senior party executives. Its implementation started with preparations for the creation of a new party to follow a social democratic course, yet without denouncing the past or the positive legacy of the former ruling formation.

A difference of views, however, arose regarding the last issue. Unlike what happened in other Eastern Bloc countries, disputes within PZPR regarding the profile of its future political shape were not a clash between conservatives and reformists but rather a clash between reformists and radical reformists. Even before the January 1990 final PZPR congress, part of its leaders, including most of the party's Sejm MPs had decided for building a Polish Social Democratic Union. They made a point of refusing to work with local party structures and to seek their support, instead starting a partnership with the 'July 8 Movement', uniting opposition intellectuals. This Union stood up for the establishment of a welfare state, thoroughly distancing themselves from PZPR's history and practice, and, perhaps not inadvertently, came to elect as leader Tadeusz Fiszbach, former party chair of Gdansk, who was known for his close contacts with Solidarity since the early 1980s.

The majority of the party elite, grouped around Mieczysław Rakowski and Lezsek Miller, acted much more moderately. The concluding PZPR congress was held and the party was disbanded. SdRP, subsequently created by that group, can be considered as a successor to the communist party since it inherited PZPR's assets and liabilities. When in November 1990 the new Sejm passed a law for the forfeiture of assets of the former ruling party, it was SdRP that this law affected. And it was SdRP that participated in suits regarding those assets in the following 10 years.

SdRP entered the political stage as a largely mechanical aggregate of reformist PZPR leaders, a small group of party MPs, as well as local party structures that had nowhere else to go. At least initially there was no common ideology involved. The role of binding glue for the diverse camps within the party was played by the fierce anticommunism then prevalent in Poland, which brought those camps together. It was not shared political values but rather the fear of revanchism that made them one entity. The policy offered by SdRP did not matter so much (for all it was worth, that policy could even be radically liberal). What mattered was that the organization remained the sole possible political defender of its members and supporters. This comes to explain the swift decline of the Social Democratic Union, a formation initially designed as an alternative. Its supporters and leaders were considered to be communists, without however actually benefitting at all from their communist past, and without differing from the new democratic formations in their position regarding that past.

SdRP made huge efforts to avoid isolation and ostracism. Looking for a coalition had been a chief goal for the party ever since 1990. In July 1991, different structures of various sizes, among which the former communists played the leading role, formed the Democratic Left Alliance. SdRP was to enter elections in that shape for years, until in 1999 a decision was taken for the Alliance to become a party in its own right and incorporate its member organizations within itself. But the left—and still less the communist left—was far from being an overtone of the party and of the coalition's public presence. The 1991 coalition platform did not offer an alternative to the notorious 'shock therapy' introduced by deputy PM and neo-liberal financier Leszek Balcerowicz, or to the social effects of that doctrine, but rather voiced a soft spoken critique of the anti-communists for allegedly throwing into the dustbin the hard work and achievements of the Polish people accumulated during the preceding 40 years. The expressions 'communist party' and 'communist rule' however were not used at all. Social services were made conditional on future growth of the economy. The ideas in the platform sounded extremely general and could be understood only against the backdrop of the messages issued by then dominating anti-communist formations. When the Alliance called for equal weight of the types of property (state, private or cooperative), that was because Solidarity had brought private property to the front. When the Alliance called for freedom of religious confession, that was because Solidarity had embarked on a campaign of imposing Catholic norms and rituals in public life.

The platform for the 1993 election, which was to send the Democratic Left Alliance in power, was not teeming with leftist ideas either. The word 'workers' was absent, the ones who lost from the reforms were not mentioned, the new expression 'people who work' was introduced, support was declared for the middle class and for entrepreneurship. It seemed that SdRP insisted on presenting itself as a 'party of winners', as a party of those with knowledge and know-how, as a party of those who work—and not as a 'party of losers', or of those adversely affected by rightist policies. Overall, ideology was little covered in the party's messages. It is an important fact that the development of ideology took place not via the party and its forums but rather via the coalition and its election platforms. That is why it has been an oft formulated conclusion that the Polish left did not represent any separate group of society or any clear social ideal but rather functioned as a stable and homogeneous entity in the fragmented Polish political world—and that it was successful precisely as such an entity.

The paradox has been noted long ago that SdRP carried out its post-communist transformation by emphasizing economic rather than social, cultural, or moral issues, while the party electorate voted for it due to ideological, moral or cultural rather than social or economic reasons. It is unusual for a leftist party to initially enjoy a quite feeble support among industrial workers. And still, in that specific case this was expected, given that Solidarity had appeared precisely as support for workers—against communists. On their part, party leaders geared their political course towards businesses and young city professionals, with many pensioners and devout communists also among their voters. It is understandable why they did not change their electoral behaviour through the years. The other political forces retained their strong reserves towards those voters. It could be that the former communists did not support them, but they at least did not isolate them. SdRP was in the favourable situation of having an electoral core who would have accepted almost any policies of their leaders.

Many of the peculiarities of SdRP's initial political positioning can be understood in the context of PZPR and Poland's political development. The difference between PZPR and the other ruling parties in the Eastern Bloc can help explain its path of development after 1989. As a party, it had not experienced a heavy Stalinization. There was never a concentration of absolute power in its leader that, in some other cases, reached levels of a personality cult. In contrast, a more or less collective leadership was present, in which for instance the First Secretary and the PM each had his own position of significant political weight. PZPR displayed great political flexibility in a string of crises that were part of its entire rule from 1948 to 1989. The party governed practically recognizing the presence of a social (not political) alternative to it in the powerful Catholic Church, and of an economic (not political) alternative in private property, which was dominant in agriculture. With the democratic change, the party could take advantage of its own flexibility in order to pursue two chief goals—demonstrating its democratic nature (which was adversely affected with the introduction of martial law) and its economic efficiency (which was unconvincing due to the failure of all attempts at reform in communist Poland). Historically speaking, PZPR had no reasons to demonstrate its leftist nature. What is more, the successor party was from the start populated by young leaders who had joined the old party during the 'pragmatic' 1980s. Those people were not politically socialized by communist ideals or the struggle for social justice. Their driving force was the conviction that change was needed to economically revitalize the country. A new edition of the dogmatists—revisionists conflict could not take place, in contrast to the situation in other countries. In Poland, this conflict had been lived through some decades before. The historical problem that PZPR had to solve while in power was seen as having been dealt with (with some success, or, more probably, with lack thereof). After 1989, the political horizon was completely different (see, e.g., Zubek 1994; Szczerbiak 2001; Markowski 2002; Curry 2003).

**Table 1.2.1.
National parliamentary representation and participation
in power of the communist successor party in Poland**

National parliamentary elections	Name under which the party ran (alone or as part of a coalition)	% of received votes	Number of MP seats (out of 460)	Place at the elections	Participation in government (as single ruling party or as senior partner in a coalition)	Monopoly on leftist political space
1991	Democratic Left Alliance	12.0	60	2	no	yes
1993	Democratic Left Alliance	20.4	171	1	yes	no
1997	Democratic Left Alliance	27.1	164	2	no	no
2001	Democratic Left Alliance—Labour Union	41.0	216	1	yes	yes
2005	Democratic Left Alliance	11.3	55	4	no	yes
2007	Let and Democrats	13.2	53	3	no	yes
2011	Democratic Left Alliance	8.2	27	5	no	yes

Source: Adapted from http://www.pkw.gov.pl/
Note: The results above are from the elections for the Sejm, the lower chamber of the Polish Parliament. The table does not reflect the 'half-free' 1989 elections that were conducted under reserved quotas for the representatives of PZPR. Under 'monopoly on leftist political space', here and in all other tables in this and the following section, I mean the absence of other leftist parties in parliament.

Hungary. This country is in many ways different from its Eastern Bloc partners. Having experienced the bloodiest violence against an anti-communist uprising (the crushing of the 1956 Hungarian Revolution), after that the country built what was perhaps the most liberal among former communist regimes[13]. MSzMP led by János Kádár slowly and methodically carried out a course implementing partial market mechanisms in the planned economy, as well as granting certain freedoms within the limits of the party monopoly on government and public life. The crisis in the 1980s however raised the question regarding the character of reforms and their implementation. In contrast with the comparatively unified PZPR, MSzMP was heavily fragmented in separate reformist and non-reformist wings. The same also applied to the emerging opposition grouped in different structures around different ideas regarding the country's political agenda.

Towards the end of the 1980s, Kádár's team clearly realized that the model of rule it aptly managed had come to the limits of its potential. Having achieved some significant results for a long period of time, that model no longer brought positives or gave answers to any of the looming issues. Kádár's resignation at the May 1988 party conference and the removal of the vocal opponents of liberalization from Politburo expressed an understanding that MSzMP had to take a new road, revising the parameters of 'goulash communism', which had become ineffective. New Secretary General Károly Grósz had some strong reformist ambitions. However, he did not belong to the party's most radical wing, which gradually began to see it as a future actor in a new liberal democratic system. If Kádár was not able to go beyond his New Economic Mechanism, then Grósz wanted to change the 'model'—but not the 'system'—by structuring democracy around the socialist choice for public development, while figures such as Miklós Németh and Imre Pozsgay openly called for marked economy and a multiparty system.

The February 1989 MSzMP plenum acknowledged the need for a multiparty system. In the period from June to September 1989, Round Table negotiations were held with the opposition. The situation became even more complex with the disputes regarding the past that culminated with massive rallies on occasion of the re-burial of Imre Nagy, Hungary's leader during the most dramatic days of the 1956 Revolution. In contrast with its Polish counterpart, the party faced serious internal strife. The dispute regarding the past did not take the simplified shape of a conflict between communists

---

13 The Hungarian communist regime is frequently referred to as "Goulash communism", as an analogy with the apparently unlikely mixture of ingredients in that famous local dish.

and anti-communists because the Hungarian Revolution itself had been organized by communists and crushed with the help of communists. Not only 'the bad' but also 'the good' in that game were communists, so to speak. If part of the party elite led by general secretary Grósz stood up against Nagy's legacy and made available to the public documents showing Nagy's collaboration with Soviet secret services, another part of that elite, including PM Németh, insisted on a democratic renewal in the spirit of the Nagy cabinet positions from the bloody days of November 1956. The search for a balance among different camps received its organizational expression in the June 1989 statute reform, which handed the party's helm to a 4-member collective chairmanship. Yet, it became clear that party unity could not be retained. It became clear that MSzMP had to step down from the stage, not only or even not so much because of pressure on the part of the anti-communist opposition as because of its own incapability of resolving internal conflicting trends that expressed its controversial historical sojourn in power.

Finally, in October 1989, MSzMP officially disbanded. The successor party—MSzP—held its founding congress, at which Rezső Nyers was elected at its helm. Unhappy with the programme tenets of the new party, Károly Grósz's supporters took their own path and in December founded a new communist party under the old MSzMP moniker. Having changed four appellations and gone through two internal splits in the years leading to 2014, this formation preserved and deepened its extreme neo-communist messages, but did not succeed in even getting past the election threshold, remaining comparatively isolated and unrecognized by the European radical left family.

MSzP inherited the ruling positions and party assets of MSzMP but not its pool of members. Former MSzMP members did not automatically enter into MSzP, but had to register anew. However, the intention to make a 'clear' new start again clashed with rear-guard battles for the communist left's past. Having given up its monopoly on power, the party's successor would lose the positions of President and PM with the party's defeat at March 1990 free elections. But the road to those elections and the party's behaviour after them reflect a dramatic and tense process of reassessment of MSzP's place and role in political life.

The first MSzP congress, which took place in October 1989, witnessed the discontent of the more radical neo-communist wing. However, the resolution passed by the congress seemed to try to reconcile the different camps and balance among them. MSZP determined itself as a party "with roots in Marxism and establishing a synthesis of socialist and communist fundamental values." Its leading commitments were to: (1) democratic socialism, (2) the protection of private property in a mixed economy, and (3) the free competition among political parties. There was a rejection of Marxism-Leninism as a political doctrine but not of Marxism as a set of values and a political vision. In the election campaign, the party chose to place its stakes on distancing itself from the past (by issuing the assessment "that was not socialism" and presenting itself as "a party of reformed communists and democratic socialists"), as well as on coming closer to pragmatism (by emphasizing skills in statesmanship, political stability, democracy, European integration, and economic liberalization). We could hardly speak of a clear ideological profile here. Marxist, social democratic, patriotic, moderately liberal, and technocratic motifs were all present.

March 1990 brought with itself election defeat. MSzP ranked fourth, with little above 10% of votes. Two months later, the new party congress declared a programmatic change, which would come to be implemented as a turn to the right. The congress resolution presented MSzP as a "social democratic party that does not dogmatically adhere to Marxism." As far as the party's political positions are concerned, they were defined in the space between 'conservatism' and 'liberalism'. The party saw itself as "a party of experts, technocrats and pragmatics." In its range and depth, the party's rightist orientation surpassed that of MSzP's 'rightist' opponents. What remained leftist was not so much the party's view of the social sphere, as those in the areas of culture, everyday life and religion. MSzP's slogan in the 1994 election campaign—"Power to professionals"—was completely natural given this transformation of the party.

At least two factors played a key role for the programmatic change in the Hungarian post-communist left. Those are the axis of the split from the end of 1989 and the structuring of the political spectrum from the very start of the democratic period in Hungary. The old MSzMP ruptured not simply on the basis of alternative points of view regarding the party's future but rather on the basis of already shaped and long-lived political currents. In the successor party the upper hand was gained by the circles which had resolutely called for the continuation of market reforms during the 1980s. They viewed their new political project as a chance for putting to work their ideas that were rejected because of Hungary's membership of the Eastern Bloc and the resistance of their less reformist fellow party activists. Splitting was for them an opportunity to comparatively quickly leave behind the battle for the past. In effect, executive positions in MSzP came to be filled with cadres who gravitated around the entrepreneur and market oriented nomenklatura of the former MSzMP. (This tradition would be strikingly continued and illustrated by personae such as Péter Medgyessy and Ferenc Gyurcsány and their teams). They accepted as their inheritance the de-ideologization of the late Kádárism and the relative social stability of those times. Part of the voters was inclined to identify them precisely in the light of those achievements. The choice of a social liberal road for transformation was also dictated by the context of the shaping of the new party system. The MSzP elites were biographically and mentally alien to the left in the Károly Grósz version. They also had to respond to the challenge of the Hungarian Social Democratic Party, a radical wing in the anti-communist front, which also aimed for the social democratic niche. The ambition for a pragmatic self-presentation is part of that response. Even the best of efforts cannot unambiguously place MSzP somewhere fixed along the axis between market-liberal and social-protectionist forces. In the course of the economic crisis in the 1980s the then ruling party resorted to austerity measures that limited the social protection of the population. Hence it was on social issues that the Hungarian society had no trust in the socialists—and the socialists, on their part, did not look for such trust, either. Having rejected conservatism as part of their own party's past, they embraced and strengthened the liberal trend inherent in Kádárism. In this way their party, having started out quite differently, would come close to its Polish counterpart in the public adherence to entrepreneur-like pragmatism and expert knowledge in a social democratic framework with a liberal twist (see, e.g., Tóka 1998; Ziblatt 1998; Körösényi 1999).

Table 1.2.2.
National parliamentary representation and participation in power of the communist successor party in Hungary

National parliamentary elections	Name under which the party ran (alone or as part of a coalition)	% of received votes	Number of MP seats (out of 386)	Place at the elections	Participation in government (as single ruling party or as senior partner in a coalition)	Monopoly on leftist political space
1990	MSzP	10.9	34	4	no	no
1994	MSzP	33.0	209	1	yes	no
1998	MSzP	32.9	134	1	no	no
2002	MSzP	42.1	178	2	yes	no
2006	MSzP	43.2	186	1	yes	no
2010	MSzP	19.3	59	2	no	no
2014	'Unity' Coalition	26.8	38 (out of 199)	2	no	no

Source: Adapted from http://www.electionresources.org/hu/

Czechoslovakia. KSČ has become famous among researchers as hardliners who opposed serious reform in the 1980s and were poorly prepared for the challenges of democratic reforms in the course of the so-called Velvet Revolution. If after the 1956 Hungarian Revolution, MSzMP oriented itself towards slowly and consistently liberalizing the regime, after the 1968 Prague Spring KSČ actually stood on more hard-line positions. A strong informal opposition had developed in Czechoslovakia, grouped around the figure of playwright Václav Havel and the Charter 77 authors. In response to the palpable dissident moods, the 'left' advocated by the party went through an organizational and ideological hardening. But the awareness that change is needed was not absent there, either. This has to do not only with the efforts of PM Lubomír Štrougal to develop a strategy of reform but also with the resignation of the long-term party and state leader Gustáv Husák from the position of party Secretary General (December 1987), motivated by the desire to open the door to younger political generations. Husák was succeeded by Miloš Jakeš, who at least in theory was a supporter of reforms and Gorbachev's Perestroika.

In effect it turned out that, some separate expressions of discontent notwithstanding, protests in Czechoslovakia erupted almost unexpectedly for the ruling party, whose reactions were defensive and haphazard. From the beginning of November 1989 on, KSČ practically no longer dictated the agenda in the country, which is even more surprising, given that the organized opposition—the Czech Civic Forum and the Slovak Public Against Violence—were formed in the course of mass unrest, and not before. In contrast with the Hungarian or Polish cases, Czechoslovak party leaders had to make exceptionally swift decisions regarding their party's future. Mass protests started November 16. Just 8 days later KSČ's entire executive echelon, led by Miloš Jakeš, resigned; with a more moderate Karel Urbánek elected as Secretary General. On the following day, Urbánek declared his readiness to negotiate with the opposition. Key party hardliners also resigned, including the chair of the party's Prague unit, Miroslav Štěpán. The party paper *Rudé právo* published articles critical of the slow motion of reforms. On November 28, KSČ declared it was going to terminate one-party state rule in Czechoslovakia. At this early point of time, the supporters of change among party activists articulated their own faction, named Democratic Forum of Communists. On November 29, the parliament swiftly repealed the articles of the Constitution that granted the Communist Party a monopoly on power. On December 10, President Husák appointed the first cabinet not featuring a majority of communists in the country's history since 1948. The President then also went on to resign. KSČ started planning an extraordinary congress for before the end of the year.

The lack of publicly influential camps in the party during the years before the Velvet Revolution came to be compensated with the quick appearance of different factions in the few weeks before that congress. Those included orthodox communists, a Democratic Left of social democratic tendencies, and the already mentioned Democratic Forum of Communists, among others. The December congress legitimized decentralization by officially permitting fractions and tracing the autonomization of two separate national parties, one Czech and one Slovak. The position of Secretary General was abolished, and the supreme power in the party was divided between a chair and a first secretary. At the personal level, the change was radical: only four of the 200-member Central Committee were re-elected. At the programmatic level, however, the direction does not seem unambiguous. KSČ stood up in support of multi-party system and issued an apology for its role in the crushing of the Prague Spring. But outside of those general assessments, an ideological course was not delineated. The party even borrowed general calls for democratization from the opposition, or even the wordings of the Prague Spring itself.

KSČM was first created as a territorial unit of KSČ and Czech partner to the Slovak Communist Party in the federalized KSČ. It became an independent party at its first congress in March 1990, in spite of a declared full continuity with the structures from the past. During the following three years, a leading place was occupied by the debate on the party's past and identity focused mostly (though not exclusively) on the fight for the party name. KSČ's two sections were put in a defensive position. The party began to distance itself from its history, recognizing only two positive moments in it: the times around the party's founding 70 years earlier, including the foundational activities of the social democrat Bohumír Šmeral, as well as the party leaders' liberal moves during the Prague Spring. The name was also made the subject of reassessment. The Czech reformists discussed different options, among which Party of Democratic Socialism, Party of the Democratic Left, and Party of the Radical Left. In Slovakia, the Party of the Democratic Left surfaced as the leading proposal. The victory of anti-communist forces at June 1990 free elections led to diverging political reactions. The Czech communists declared an end to "national understanding" and the start of a "relentless political fight." In contrast, their Slovak partners put forward the thesis that they would defend pluralism, democracy, and social market economy rather than communist ideas.

The fight among different groups in KSČM continued. Its leader Jiří Svoboda proposed a new name—Party of Democratic Socialism—putting it to internal party referendum in September 1991. 76% of party members voted for keeping the prior name. This resulted in the departure of the Democratic Left faction, which founded a social democratic Democratic Party of Labour, which however did not succeed in making a breakthrough in political life, given the anti-communist social democrats' hegemony. From the other end of the left spectrum, a challenge was posed by the For Socialism faction, newly created by Štěpán and other compromised KSČ figures—a group that directly called for a return to the pre-1989 regime. In this dilemma, described by Svoboda as a choice between neo-Stalinism and democratic socialism, the middle road of the neo-communist current happened to be the winner. This group defended a modern way to combine communism and democracy, and achieved majority at the June 1993 congress. The formal powers of factions were terminated, the For Socialism leaders were expelled, while the defenders of a more centrist line were stimulated to split in a Party of the Democratic Left, which also remained without subsequent electoral success. At the same time point, the will of Slovak communists towards social democracy seemed more resolute, yet more short-lived. As early as October 1990 they accepted the temporary name KSS-SDĽ, and in January the following year officially assumed the name Party of the Democratic Left, adopting left-centrist programme principles. The ensuing wavering of their political messages was due to the party's unconvincing showing at elections. SDĽ partially lost part of its electorate without succeeding in efficiently winning a substitute for it. On the one hand, the party continued to be seen as 'the former communists', while on the other, it did not manage to mobilize its traditional supporters, who had found a political harbour in other formations, including their executive organs.

Probably the structural and programmatic change within KSČ could be presented as a choice between two scenarios: leaning on the hard core of its voters and establishing itself as politically isolated, anti-system party, or opening to a broader social democratic community, losing part of its traditional supporters. A string of factors made that choice not so free and, to a large degree, predetermined. In the first place among them was the presence of both a strong communist and a strong social democratic tradition in pre-war Czechoslovakia. There communism was not regarded exclusively as a result of the fact that the country turned out to be part of the Eastern Bloc. That fact was seen to have resulted in the adoption of Marxism-Leninism's Soviet version, which had actually been swiftly abandoned by Czech and Slovak communists. Within the Czechoslovak regime of the 1980s no influential party wing emerged that supported liberal and market reforms. The many factions that fragmented KSČ right after the Velvet Revolution were mostly bearers of a pro-communist drive and did not exert a decisive influence on the attitudes of the party members. Once restored after the changes, the Czech social democratic movement swiftly won supporters—on an anti-communist basis. With the 'Velvet divorce' that divided the former state into the Czech Republic and Slovakia, KSČM turned up in a political system significantly deflected to the right, a system that opened up ample space for a left counterpoint. In Slovakia, on the other hand, anti-communism was weaker, and opportunities for social democratic political behaviour were more strongly expressed. The political logic of struggle among factions within KSČM led to the elimination of opposing poles and a preference for the so-called neo-communist option. The neo-communists themselves saw their strategy as being both more principled and more realistic because responding to the attitudes of the majority of party members and because not risking a vanishing into the social democratic spectrum. The instability of the new Slovak party system, originally loaded with both rightist and leftist populism, on its part stimulated the now social democratic SDĽ to leave more open doors for itself and to not put its bets on a categorically expressed ideological course. KSČM looked for the road of modern neo-communism, while SDĽ, that of centrist social democracy (see, e.g., Hanley 2002; Fisher 2002; Strmiska 2002).

Table 1.2.3.
National parliamentary representation and participation in power of the communist successor party in the Czech Republic

National parliamentary elections	Name under which the party ran (alone or as part of a coalition)	% of received votes	Number of MP seats (out of 200)	Place at the elections	Participation in government (as single ruling party or as senior partner in a coalition)	Monopoly on leftist political space
1990	KSČ	13.6	23 (out of 150)	2	no	yes
1992	KSČM	9.7	19 (out of 150)	3	no	no
1996	KSČM	10.3	22	3	no	no
1998	KSČM	11.0	24	3	no	no
2002	KSČM	18.5	41	3	no	no
2006	KSČM	12.8	26	3	no	no
2010	KSČM	11.3	26	4	no	no
2013	KSČM	14.9	33	3	no	no

Sources: Adapted from http://www.electionresources.org/cz/
Note: The elections in 1990 and 1992 were for a parliament of the then still existing Czechoslovakia. Results after 1992 are for the Chamber of Deputies, the lower chamber of the Czech Parliament.

Table 1.2.4.
National parliamentary representation and participation in power of the communist successor party in Slovakia

National parliamentary elections	Name under which the party ran (alone or as part of a coalition)	% of received votes	Number of MP seats (out of 150)	Place at the elections	Participation in government (as single ruling party or as senior partner in a coalition)	Monopoly on leftist political space
1990	KSČ	13,6	23	2	не	да
1992	KSČM	9.7	19	3	no	no
1994	'Common Choice' coalition	10.4	18	2	no	no
1998	SDĽ	14.7	23	3	yes	no
2002	SDĽ	1.4	0	10	no	no

Source: Adapted from http://www.electionresources.org/sk/
Note: The elections in 1990 and 1992 were for a parliament of the then still existing Czechoslovakia. In 2004 the Party of the Democratic Left disbanded and merged in to the SMER party, due to which I do not include later election results here.

German Democratic Republic. East Germany is similar to Czechoslovakia in that in both countries changes transpired quite rapidly and practically took the leaders of the ruling communist parties by surprise. On October 6, 1989, at the celebration of the 40th anniversary of the creation of GDR, state and party leader Erich Honecker expressed with great pathos his firm belief that GDR would enter into the 21st century with pride and dignity. Less than one year later, GDR was to be no longer in existence. But even a few days after that declaration, on October 16, amid brewing mass protests throughout the country, Honecker was brought down from power by a classic 'palace coup' and his position taken up by Egon Krenz, who had been considered his close ally. That act did not mean exchanging a hardliner with a more moderate or reformist politician. Krenz did not give any signals that he intended to significantly transform East German politics. The heady events that followed, however, put into serious question all hopes for stabilization. On November 7, the cabinet of long-term PM Willi Stoph had to resign. On November 8 he was joined by the entire Politburo of the ruling SED, after which the executive organ was filled by 10 much more moderate figures, who were outsiders to Honecker's first power echelon. As it is well known, November 9 is the date of the tumbling down of the Berlin Wall, which had been dividing not just a city and a country but also two hostile political worlds. On November 18, the PM seat was taken by Hans Modrow, popular for his critical attitude towards Honecker. For the first time in GDR's history, the cabinet included people who did not belong to the communist political establishment. On December 1 the East German Parliament abolished the constitutional texts granting SED a monopoly on power. On December 3 the entire Central Committee of the party resigned, giving it a course towards calling an extraordinary congress, with Honecker and his allies expelled from the party. Legal proceedings were initiated against Honecker himself. Krenz was replaced at the helm of the party by Gregor Gysi, who was even more reformist than Modrow and ready to immediately acknowledge that the rule of his own party had led the country to failure.

This short chronology of events illustrates the fact—something that was also publicly acknowledged by SED leaders—that the German communist party entered the democratic transition with the clear awareness that it was not able to control ongoing processes. The party was almost facing its collapse. Just for the period before the end of 1989, some 900,000 members, or 40% of the party's membership pool, left. The 16–17 December congress was exclusively devoted to the issue of the party's survival. The question was not what direction the party would take, but how to make it even possible for it to continue to exist. The name SED-PDS was adopted, and a month and a half later the party leadership decided to establish as sole name the new PDS. All that happened against the background of overt calls from various party circles for the party to disband. Those calls found expression, among other things, in public declarations from intellectuals, grouped around Humboldt University in Berlin, according to whom there was no future for the party in the new political configuration. Gysi's team was convinced that SED must stay, under its new appellation. One of the motives included the understanding that the impressive party apparatus and the assets of the former rulers were crucial resources in the political fight that was to follow—a fight that would be lost following a dissolution and subsequent re-founding. This is the way in which PDS stepped into the first (and last) free elections in GDR, where it ranked third.

Even with its first programme, that from January 1990, PDS singled out the renewal of socialism as direction of its transformation. This general formulation was to be gradually rendered more specific by means of references to the pre-war communist tradition in Germany, in particular Rosa Luxemburg's legacy. The initial view of GDR's historical experience as unsuccessful was qualified: the achievements of the old regime in the social sphere were acclaimed, while its political authoritarianism and economic dogmatism were rejected. PDS's first election platform tried to achieve the maximum with respect to keeping the faith of SED supporters. The platform touched on many aspects of the political left and was based on the ideas and messages of an extremely varied range of left thinkers and theorists, starting with Lenin and ending with Bernstein. Marxism-Leninism was left behind but Marxism, as such, retained its stable presence, as did other, non-Marxist strains of the global left. And that was something normal. As early as the first half of 1990, parallel to that of reformist wings, factions such as the Communist Platform or the Marxist Forum had started to play an active role in the party. After the unification of Germany and PDS's entry in the political life of the Federal Republic, the renewal of socialism came to be interpreted as looking for ways beyond the classical postulates of social democracy. PDS saw itself as a broad profile socialist party left of SPD. The leading role of the working class was replaced by an emphasis on vulnerable social strata in general. PDS stood up against capitalism and the social relations it gives birth to, without however formulating a specific alternative and without explicitly rejecting the market.

Another tendency in the programmatic change of the former East German communists was their orientation towards the defence of specific regional interests, such as the interests of eastern Länder. In spite of the huge funds invested east by Bonn, the standard of life there started to drop, a number of industries went out of business, the economy was restructured at an excruciating social price. The huge part of the PDS electorate in the 1990s was concentrated precisely in the eastern Länder. In 1994 the party launched an election platform with a special section devoted to the alleged "Strategy for Destruction of East Germany," which pointed out the consequences the so-called *Kohl-onisation*[14] after 1990, forging the diagnosis

---

14 It was named after the then German Chancellor Helmut Kohl who was considered by PDS to be the sole responsible person for the allegedly improper and unjust way of incorporating GDR into the Federal Republic.

that East German culture, industry and agriculture had fallen into ruin. The desire to neutralize PDS's public image as the party of the past supported by elderly voters, emerged as the third prominent tendency in the political changes in the early 1990s. The party stimulated the career growth of young leaders sporting views close to those of the so-called new left. Semi-anarchist structures were also created within the party, which had the character of 'bottom up' social movements and preached direct democracy, extra-institutional resistance to current German capitalism and even the calling of an 'alternative parliament' that was to stay free of the stringent norms of liberal democratic politics.

The manifold variety of ideas and movements within PDS after the fall of the Honecker regime is to some extent surprising. Nevertheless, it can be explained by the intensive search for answers to a situation in which the stakes were higher than they were elsewhere. Under question was not only future of the party but also that of the country it ruled. In the first weeks after the fall of the Wall, the party elite overestimated the resistance of the Soviet Union, France and the UK against German unification, assuming that what was on the agenda was the transformation of the 'totalitarian' GDR into a 'democratic' one. It became relatively quickly clear that if PDS wanted to have a political perspective of its own, then it had to find one in the political system of the unified republic. On the one hand, the party initially was strongly relying on its large party apparatus (over 44,000 officers), which formed something of a hard core in the shifting sands of the transition. On the other, the comparative advantages of former communist parties in new conditions—such as better administrative experience and management skills—did not work in an institutional configuration dominated by the political technologies of West German parties. If it wanted to exist as a self-standing formation, PDS could not take the road of rejecting the past and going social democratic. The former SED had built a state in GDR. State-building, in contrast with other CEE cases, had been a primary political goal of the party. That is why a denial of the past would mean rejection not only of the shortcomings or crimes of a former rule but of the very meaning and goals of its own existence as a party—the first attempt at erecting a non-capitalist order in Germany. PDS's political presence in the unified country was not only an expression of a persisting ideology that had outgrown the vicissitudes of the times, but also, at least to some degree, an expression of identity.

Being one among the parties in the Federal Republic, PDS could not become social democratic also due to another reason: there was already an established SPD that occupied that electoral and political space. PDS naturally oriented itself towards the niche left of SPD. But this was not just a nostalgic formation dreaming of the irretrievably gone age of Honecker. When GDR was no more, one could not just be looking back into the past. The past could not be reconstructed when the country of that past was not subject to reconstruction. PDS grew stronger as a radical leftist party with social libertarian positions, and not as much as a traditional socialist party. That was the foundation that helped it blaze a road to new groups of voters in the country's western Länder, including people who had been earlier attracted by the initial radical impulse of the West German Greens. Structurally preserved thanks to the energy and will of its new leaders, building bridges to young people, intellectuals, and new social movements, PDS transformed its programme in into a form of modern neo-communism (see, e.g., Betz and Welsh 1995; Ziblatt 1998; Hough 2001; Olsen 2002; Hough, Koss and Olsen 2007).

Table 1.2.5.
National parliamentary representation and participation in power of the communist successor party in Germany

National parliamentary elections	Name under which the party ran (alone or as part of a coalition)	% of received votes	Number of MP seats	Place at the elections	Participation in government (as single ruling party or as senior partner in a coalition)	Monopoly on leftist political space
1990	PDS	16.4	66 (out of 400)	3	no	no
1990	PDS	2.4	17 (out of 662)	5	no	no
1994	PDS	4.4	30 (out of 672)	6	no	no
1998	PDS	5.1	36 (out of 669)	6	no	no
2002	PDS	4.0	2 (out of 603)	6	no	no

2005	The Left Party.PDS	8.7	54 (out of 614)	4	no	no
2009	The Left	11.9	76 (out of 622)	4	no	no
2013	The Left	8.6	64 (out of 631)	3	no	no

Source: Adapted from http://www.electionresources.org/de/
Note: The first elections (1990) were for the then still existing GDR parliament, the People's Chamber. Later data are from elections for the Bundestag, the lower chamber of the German Parliament.

Romania. Change in Romania was undoubtedly the most radical and dramatic. It took the form of a revolution and was the sole case among socialist countries in which events did not follow constitutional norms. The regime of PCR led by Nicolae Ceaușescu was the last Soviet satellite to fall. The strongly repressive nature of that regime practically to its very end hindered the formation of alternative political currents and visions of change within the party. With the exception of the so-called Letter of the Six from March 1989, which criticized the nationalist austerity policies implemented by Ceaușescu from leftist positions, there were almost no strong examples of internal party dissident activity. On November 24 that same year, while changes were under way in all other CEE countries, PCR's 14th congress unanimously re-elected Ceaușescu and reconfirmed his political course, without hinting at any idea of reforms. World public opinion followed with alarm and compassion the bloody events in Romania that were to become known as the Romanian Revolution or Romanian Christmas, and that for a very short period of time, from 16 to 27 December, swept down the Ceaușescu regime literally *ex nihilo* and led to the physical execution of the dictator and his wife Elena. PCR's power collapsed in the entire country within just a few days. In early January 1990, PCR actually became the first former ruling communist party in the Eastern Bloc to be legally banned (the second and last being the Communist Party of the Soviet Union in August 1991).

The ban on the party is to be seen foremost as a symbolic act. The party's structures throughout the country had in effect terminated their activities as early as the days around December 20. In what then sense can we speak of a CSP here? On December 22, it was announced that a FSN was created to unite all forces of society against the Ceaușescu regime. 5 days later the Front abolished the one-party system, called parliamentary elections, and instated a temporary cabinet, with Ion Iliescu and Petre Roman taking the functions of, respectively, President and PM. Both of them were representatives of the middle PCR echelon. This applied not only to them but also to a great part of FSN executive figures. A FSN Council was created. On the one hand, there was formally an ostentatious parting with the past—out of the 39 initial council members, only one had been a member of the 466-member Central Committee elected by the 14th PCR congress. On the other hand, the majority of the council had to do with the former PCR, notwithstanding that as a whole the council was diverse, featuring professors and students, liberal intellectuals and technocrats. Within a short period of time, local structures of the Front were created, many of which reproduced former PSR structures. The debate on FSN's future was controversial. Many saw the Front as a broad popular movement that had to carry out the institutional and cadre dismantling of the former dictatorship and open the door to new democratic parties. In January, Iliescu, on his part, envisioned FSN as a fundament for an "authentic democracy" based on the competition among different political groups in the movement rather than among different parties. In February, the position that FSN should register and run in May elections came out winning. That was the first signal of disunity in the organization's ranks. Part of FSN activists, especially those unaffiliated under the old regime, opposed the decision, expressing fears that it would lead to a return to the one-party PCR monopoly in new clothes. Student rallies were held, only to be however dispersed with force. FSN resorted (in January and March) to calling large groups of miners from outside of the capital, mobilized to fight with protesters. In this way, criticisms that, rather than being a political product of the anti-communist revolution, FSN was actually a successor to the communist party, gained further weight. FSN won a resounding victory at elections without declaring a specific programme and without leaving other formations the opportunity to gather public support.

Formally seen, no one inherited the membership pool of the banned PCR. The status of its successor was officially claimed by the Socialist Party of Labour, created in November 1990 and led by former PM and close relative to Ceaușescu, Ilie Verdeț. Without inheriting any structures or influence, the party was not much more than a peripheral phenomenon in Romanian politics. FSN was the true successor, both as executive team, and as its own stated political identity. The formation sought the support of the working class and civil servants, and adhered to softer forms of Ceauşescu-style nationalism. Division however transpired within the Front itself. Iliescu entered into a conflict with Roman, split and created a Democratic National Salvation Front, later renamed PSD. Roman remained at the helm of the FSN, which later received the name PD and started to move to more rightist and liberal positions. It is not by chance that the party cooperated with the anti-communist opposition. The left conservative and pro-nationalist line was maintained by Iliescu's party, which also not by chance oriented itself towards cooperation with openly nationalistic parties such as the Party of Romanian National Unity and PRM. Between 1990–92 FSN rejected the idea of privatization because in the views of its leaders market reforms meant selling out the country to foreigners, a line that was to be maintained by Iliescu's party, even if in a softer version and with a number of qualifications. That was the party which to the greatest extent preserved parts of the PCR party core. It would aim to maintain the status quo in large state enterprises and to follow a course of minimum changes with the intention not to lose key groups of its voters. The lack of a significant leftist tradition in Romania before the Cold War and the nationalist tendencies reproduced in different garments by all ruling regimes almost inevitably determined the ad hoc character of the leftist elements in FSN's and then PSD's political presence. Yet, in spite of those qualifications due to local peculiarities, this was the niche that most of the representatives of the former PCR oriented themselves to, in order to shape the political and programmatic transformation of Romanian communism into a stable left conservative and left populist tendency (see, e.g., Mungiu-Pippidi 2002; Siani-Davies 2005; Pop-Eleches 2008; and, out of the many works of an undisputed authority in the academic field, a concentrated formulation in Tismăneanu 1999).

Table 1.2.6.
National parliamentary representation and participation in power of the communist successor party in Romania

National parliamentary elections	Name under which the party ran (alone or as part of a coalition)	% of received votes	Number of MP seats	Place at the elections	Participation in government (as single ruling party or as senior partner in a coalition)	Monopoly on leftist political space
1990	FSN	66.3	263 (out of 395)	1	yes	yes
1992	Democratic FSN	27.7	117 (out of 341)	1	yes	yes
1996	PSD	21.5	91 (out of 343)	2	no	yes
2000	PSD	36.6	155 (out of 345)	1	yes	no
2004	National Union PSD—Romanian Humanist Party	36.8	113 (out of 332)	1	no	no
2008	Union PSD—Conservative Party	33.1	114 (out of 334)	1	no	no
2012	Social-Liberal Union	58.6	273 (out of 412)	1	yes	no

Source: Adapted from http://www.nsd.uib.no/european_election_database/country/romania/
Note: The data are from elections for the Chamber of Deputies, the lower chamber of the Romanian Parliament.

This brief outline of the structural and programmatic change in CEE communist parties in the first months and years after the collapse of the Eastern Bloc has demonstrated that those parties took several different trajectories. Parties viewed as organizationally and ideologically quite similar to one another at times met radically different fates in the light of new democratic circumstances (ranging from modern neo-communism to social liberalism, with diverse liberal, conservative or nationalist twists, however without a return to the initial Marxism-Leninism). It has become clear that the road to transformation for CSPs was not predetermined by the dismantling of the old regimes, but it rather branched out depending on different factors. Without claiming to exhaust them or rank their weight, I would point out among them: the relative strength or weakness of the communist and social democratic traditions in the pre-war history of the respective country; the unity or diversity of the communist party elite during the period of existence of the Eastern Bloc; the presence or absence of an influential reformist or pro-liberal wing in the decade before the changes; the significance or marginal nature of anti-communist opposition forces around the end of the regime; the intensity or limited range of anti-communism latent in society before the changes; the type of positive features of the communist system for public consciousness after the system's collapse; the character and ideological configuration of the emerging democratic party system, and so on.

Many of those factors have found their place in the literature, but here we can see them active in the very transformation experience of the different parties. The inevitable conclusion to make is that the notion of CSPs in CEE is a highly heterogeneous one. The fate of communist parties in each country significantly depended on that country's specific national historical road of development (Orenstein 1998). The tables in this section demonstrate that, with the exception of the Slovak case, the parties under consideration had their lasting presence in the political life of their countries, but this presence was irregular, it waxed and waned, and was influenced by many circumstances in current political life, however generally leading to a reduced electoral turnout in recent times.

Therefore, in order to place the Bulgarian political left in the context of change in the former Eastern Bloc, we have to scrutinize the specific national context. First and foremost, let us see what is specific of structural and programmatic change in the Bulgarian Communist Party. Can we assess its stability against the backdrop of its counterparts? Can we distinctly place it in the spectrum from social liberalism to neo-communism as a starting point of the interpretation of its social and political weight? Finally, how can we interpret its political image in the eyes of the Bulgarian society?

1.3 Programmatic and Structural Transformation of BCP

After 1948, BCP, like its 'fraternal' parties from the Eastern Bloc, was a ruling political force in a regime based on a total monopoly on political power and on domination—sometimes almost exclusive—of state property in the economy. BCP's program, published in 1971, defined the organization as a "mature Marxist-Leninist party" that guides public development. In the same year, a national referendum adopted a new Constitution for the country, in which that role was formally institutionalized: „The leading force of society and the state is the Bulgarian Communist Party" (Art. 1, Par. 2). Programmatic change within BCP had actually started even before the first serious symptoms of collapse in the Eastern Bloc. In 1987 party leaders published a document entitled *Fundamental Principles of the Concept for Further Building of Socialism in the People's Republic of Bulgaria* that would become known as the "July Concept." Without formally revising the existing party program, in effect the document did just that by laying down a direction of development that rejected the state economic monopolism. The goal of the Concept was unfolding of self-governance, to be implemented by granting relative independence of labour collectives and territorial communities in property management. The document also spoke of "socialist pluralism," which was to be understood as the party's abandoning the status of a 'level' in state hierarchy and assuming the position of the principal agent of power. A plenum in December 1988 launched the idea of "company organization based on a shareholding principle," and in early January 1989, Decree 56 was promulgated, which mandated that the company would now be the main unit of the country's economic structure, this providing an opportunity for new economic entities, including private ones.[15] The decisions taken, albeit only partially and inconsistently imple-

---

15 I need to stress out that economic entities in Bulgaria worked in accordance with Decree 56 until 1999. Therefore, to a large degree, privatization in the country was carried out on the basis of that normative framework. It was a whole decade after the beginning of democracy, during the second term in power of rightist anti-communist forces in Bulgaria, that a Trade Law was passed to replace the socialist legal framework effective until then. This fact provides a further argument for my

mented, can be interpreted as manifest signs of an attempt at going beyond the confines of the ruling ideology (Kandilarov 2010: 126–149). Those decisions did not come from reformist groups within BCP. Inclinations towards liberalization were to be observed in some party circles even as early as in the mid-1960s. The fundament, so to speak, was present; what was not present was a political drive from the highest party level. The structure of the regime in Bulgaria was such that all proposals for reforms and changes could publicly come only from the person of the long-time party and state leader Todor Zhivkov[16]. It was he who initiated the new ideas in national economy that comprised the Bulgarian answer to the impulse for change launched by Gorbachev's Perestroika in the Soviet Union.

The end of Zhivkov's rule came to a large extent unexpectedly, taking into account the relative stability in the country. At the end of the 1980s there were no significant opposition movements. There were acts of discontent and dissent throughout the socialist period, but they were not many or organized at least until the end of 1988 (Detrez 2006: 150–151), when the so-called Club for the Protection of Glasnost and Perestroika was founded, to be followed by Ecoglasnost and the independent trade union Podkrepa. In contrast with similar opposition activities in other socialist countries, the Bulgarian Club in effect did not attack the power of the communist party or the country's belonging to the USSR's geopolitical orbit. On the contrary, the Club called for a speeding up of reforms in the spirit of socialism and according to Moscow's model. It was not pressure from 'informal structures' that led the ruling communists to reform. The repressive measures against representatives of the emerging quite fragile and predominantly intellectual opposition however demonstrated that even at the end of its rule BCP did not see the changes it undertook as leading to a subsequent loss of political monopoly. Those measures were introduced in a situation that was politically stable, but could hardly be called entirely peaceful. The social climate in Bulgaria was dominated by the perception that an economic crisis had already started and was heading for new lows. The crisis had to

---

thesis that BCP's programmatic and practical reorientation towards market economy started in effect before the fall of the regime.

16 Todor Zhivkov (1911–1998) was the longest-serving communist leader in the Eastern bloc. He was BCP's chair for 33 years (1956–1989) and formally head of state for 18 years (1971–1989).

do with negative processes within the Comecon, a decrease of Soviet subsidies for Bulgarian agriculture, as well as an insistence on Moscow's part for an equal trade exchange. Additionally, the campaign for the forceful change of the names of ethnic Turkish Bulgarian citizens and the attempts at their 'Bulgarization' resulted in social tension in Bulgaria (Crampton 2005: 204–211)[17]. Those actions led to some international isolation for Zhivkov's regime, including from the USSR.

Todor Zhivkov fell from power on November 10, 1989 in a 'palace coup' of sorts, after senior BCP executives, unhappy with his leadership, organized themselves to exert pressure for him to resign, using, among other instruments, Soviet support for their actions. Petar Mladenov replaced Zhivkov, and the cabinet was soon to be taken over by Mladenov's close ally, Andrey Lukanov. Both Mladenov and Lukanov, who came to be recognized as the key people involved in what happened on November 10, were longtime members of the Zhivkov regime's senior nomenklatura[18] and were not known for their critical or alternative views. They were to acquire the label of 'reformists' a bit later, under the pressure of the stormy events in Bulgaria, and the Eastern Bloc as a whole.

The statements issued by Bulgaria's new party and state leaders before the end of 1989 bear witness to the fact that they did not envision a deeper change than the continuation of Zhivkov's reforms by new people, as well as a rehabilitation of those repressed under the communist regime, hand in hand with a decrease in the role of the state's repressive apparatus. They were far from questioning the BCP's leading role in society or the dominant socialist character of the economy (Spirova 2010: 404). Initially, the transformation was not directed against the party's communist nature but rather

---

17 This was the so-called Revival Process which took place between 1984 and 1989. Arguably, it was aimed at avoiding the formation of a Turkish national consciousness among the Bulgarian Turks in a period of a political, cultural and economic ascent of neighbouring Turkey. Also, BCP was probably trying to maintain its diminishing legitimacy by means of a strong nationalist appeal. The campaign led to various acts of violence and eventually to the 'Big Excursion'—the forceful departure of the country on the part of some 300,000 Bulgarian Turks in the summer of 1989. The Revival Process registered one of the most lamentable instances of violation of human rights in Europe during the Cold War.

18 At the time of Zhivkov's ousting, Petar Mladenov (1936–2000) was a Politburo member and had been a Minister of Foreign Affairs for some 18 years; while Andrey Lukanov (1938–1996) was a Politburo candidate, anad had been a vice-PM and a Minister of Foreign Economic Relations, also for more than a decade.

against the deficiencies of its leaders. Zhivkov and his entourage were personally blamed for the crisis events and problems of the preceding decade. A distinction was made between 'true' reforms (those undertaken by the new leaders), and an 'imitation' of reforms (in which Zhivkov was accused). The day of Zhivkov's deposition was elevated to the status of a key historic date—not with respect to some change of direction but with respect to the implementation of socialist development. As per Mladenov's wording from the party plenum from December 11–13, 1989, November 10 "put the beginning of the actual transformation and renewal of socialism in Bulgaria" (quoted in Kandilarov 2010: 151–152). An echo of this attempt at concentrating problems around the persona of the former chief was his expulsion from BCP. Moreover, legal proceedings against him began in January the following year.

The need to give a new assessment of the change and to strengthen party support for the new leaders found an expression in the calling of an extraordinary BCP congress in late January and early February 1990. The congress elected for party leader Alexander Lilov[19]. Petar Mladenov retained the position of President of Bulgaria, while Andrey Lukanov formed a new cabinet entirely composed of Communist Party representatives. The congress also voted a programme document entitled *Manifesto for Democratic Socialism*. The manifesto set as the party's current task its 'de-Stalinization' and transformation in a "new type of contemporary Marxist party" to lead the building of a "society of democratic and humane socialism." The stated intention was to make a step forward in the development of socialist society, which was described as "more humane" than capitalism. The assessment for the preceding period was also positive. According to the text, that time was a period of creation of "material and spiritual assets, of a national economy, education, healthcare, culture, and a standard of living that brought Bulgaria out of its backwardness." A negative twist to the picture in the manifesto came from the "deformations and perversions" of Zhivkov and his close associates, who allegedly gave birth to what the text called 'a command administrative system'. By overcoming those problems BCP would be able to become "a party of democratic socialism," inspired by "the ideals of scientific socialism" based (among other people) on

---

19 Alexander Lilov (1933–2014) was also a close associate of Zhivkov that had however been removed by him from Politburo membership in 1983.

the ideas of Marx, Engels and Lenin, and fighting for the "socialist choice." As can be seen from those quotations, any talk of hegemony of a social democratic trend would be out of place here. In contrast with other communist parties that criticized their totalitarian period with the thesis "that was not socialism," BCP placed a negative evaluation of the past almost only on the persona and behaviour of its former leader. Lenin was put in a positive light—a figure whose authority many transforming communist parties quickly abandoned in order to step on the 'more democratic' soil of classical Marxism. Another significant figure presented positively was Georgi Dimitrov, the first chief of communist Bulgaria and, according to many critics, the one who has to bear large part of the blame for the Stalinization of the Bulgarian political process in the late 1940s. What is more, the document repeatedly stresses that Bulgaria was continuing to walk the path of socialism, not of capitalism, and surely not by distancing itself from the Soviet Union (BSP 2008a: 11–30). At that point of time (early February 1990) BCP was the sole one among communist parties in the USSR allies of the Eastern Bloc to defend such a view[20]. In Poland and in Hungary, the socialist system had been abandoned months ago. In GDR first on the agenda was the survival of the party itself and not that of the already collapsed Honecker socialism. In Czechoslovakia the Velvet Revolution triumphed. In Romania the communist party was banned and together with it all socialist perspectives for society. In Bulgaria the communists indeed gave up their political monopoly, after on January 15, 1990 the old communist parliament repealed Art. 1 of Bulgaria's Constitution,[21] and they

---

20 The Manifesto was undoubtedly elaborated by the Bulgarian party leadership and reflected its own positions for the specific moment. Simultaneously, certain Soviet influence should not be excluded. The very term "democratic socialism" had appeared shortly before in the USSR as a key concept in Gorbachev's new understanding of Perestroika. According to the Soviet leader in his famous article "The Socialist Idea and Revolutionary Perestroika", Perestroika should be perceived as a movement towards "humane, democratic socialism", which is based on the achievements of the contemporary civilization and the all-human values, and which combines the "socialist choice" with market mechanisms in order to fight the bureaucratic system (Gorbachev 1989). Gorbachev himself recommended his views to the new Bulgarian chief Mladenov during the latter one's visit in Moscow on December 5 the same year (Fakel 2004: 330).

21 At one of the first free democratic rallies in Bulgaria, on December 14, 1989, the multitude gathered in front of Parliament called for the abolition of the Constitution's Art. 1. However, this can hardly be recognized as organized opposition pressure because opposition entities at that point were still too weak to efficiently exert a de-

sent signals that they were ready for a broad dialogue by starting talks with the just officially founded opposition at the so-called Round Table starting January 3, but at the programmatic level they continued to think that the return of political pluralism would not go beyond the confines of socialism.

Similar to the situation with the Czech communists, who were consolidated and homogeneous in the years before the end of the regime, only to see the quick formation of alternative internal currents at the very beginning of the political transformation, different factions appeared in BCP just weeks after November 10 (Kandilarov 2011: 353–363). Some of them put forward a very broad leftist programme (Alternative Socialist Union), others were of a social democratic strain (the Bulgarian Road to Europe platform, DEMOS Movement for Democratic Socialism, Social Democratic Initiative in BSP, etc.), still others declared more moderate socialist views (Socialist Unity), while a fourth group stood behind more radical neo-communist positions (Marxist Platform). Taken together, the separate factions expressed the whole range of roads for development of the party within the left spectrum. Ever since the 14th congress, party leaders sought a political course that would balance among those entities. Both radical and conservative options appeared to be, at least temporarily, left to the side.

The situation however was changing very quickly. The opposition gathered confidence, among other things due to increasing international support. If initial expectations for the opposition had been that it would limit its activities to an anti-nomenklatura course based on a rejection of Zhivkov and the privileges of his entourage, then such expectations turned out unjustified, and the anti-nomenklatura course grew into an anti-communist one, rejecting BCP *tout court*. Around February or March 1990, BCP leaders had to accept the fact that socialism as a social and political system in CEE was gone. In February, Mladenov spoke with fear about the fate of socialism, while in April, the new leader Lilov was already explicitly referring to his fears about the fate of the party. The congress had already opened the discussion for a change of the party's name, as a token of taking into account the new situation. Different options had been discussed:

---

cisive influence on the political agenda. The BCP elite succeeded in gaining acceptance for its argument that the abolition of Art. 1 can happen only in accordance with the constitutionally prescribed procedure, with a 1-month period of tabling and voting in Parliament, and did not allow the change to acquire the character of a violent revolution destroying institutional norms.

Party of Democratic Socialism in Bulgaria (Communists), Communist Party for Democratic Socialism, Bulgarian Socialist Party, Reformed Bulgarian Communist Party, Bulgarian Democratic Communist Party, etc. The party elite chose Bulgarian Socialist Party, and put that name to a party referendum at the end of March. Out of some 984 thousand BCP members (according to party records), 726 thousand voted, with 626 thousand (87% of them) voting in support of renaming to BSP and 92 thousand (13%) against. BCP adopted the name BSP in full organizational and programmatic continuity. BCP members automatically received the status of BSP members, with no re-enrolment procedure involved.

An opposition with anti-communist motivation, Round Table with agreements for democratization and liberalization, a tendency of the former Communist Party's leaders towards making concessions—all of this can to some extent bring to mind the situation in other countries from the crumbling Eastern Bloc. Nevertheless, BSP was the only successor party to win the first free elections in its country. At the June 1990 vote in Bulgaria, the party achieved an absolute majority (211 out of 400 MPs) in the Grand National Assembly[22]. The former communist party was also the only one to form a one-party cabinet of its own (again chaired by Andrey Lukanov) after democratic elections. Contrary again to the cases of former 'fraternal' countries, the Bulgarian ex-communists played a leading role in the drafting and adoption of the country's new democratic constitution (July 1991)[23].

BSP was reorienting itself extremely slowly, against the backdrop of a growing anti-communist radicalism in Bulgaria. Such radicalism was evident in the August 1990 torching of the BSP head office, as well as in a string of rallies, strikes and blockades in the following months. In Septem-

---

22 The Grand National Assembly is a special legislative body in Bulgaria to which historical tradition has assigned the responsibility to adopt new constitutions or major constitutional amendments.

23 This "early" constitution can be assessed in various ways. Without delving into a discussion of its advantages and deficiencies, I should mention the hypothesis that BSP's eagerness to make it happen in the very first stage of democratic changes reveals a way of thinking close to that of Gorbachev and his Perestroika: the transformation of the political system should precede the transformation of the economy.

ber the party held a new congress[24], which passed a new programme document entitled *Platform for Further Renewal and Transformation of the Bulgarian Socialist Party into a Modern Leftist Party of Democratic Socialism*.

The platform outlined a programmatic development different from that of other former communist parties. As we have already pointed out, change in some of them started radically, with social democratic positions that were to further develop in the direction of pragmatism and pro-market tenets. In others, there was initially a stepping back from the former course, which was to be comparatively quickly replaced by a return to a neo-communist identity, of course backed by new, modern arguments. If we are to judge based on its Platform, with BSP we have elements both of re-affirmation of certain neo-communist views, and of a certain movement towards the West European socialist and social democratic value fundament. Here is a curious detail. When it referred to World War II anti-fascist resistance, the Manifesto stated: "The contributions of the party to the struggle against fascism and capitalism are unquestionable." The Platform, 8 months later, stated on the same occasion: "We are proud with the contribution of our party to the struggle against fascism and reactionary forces." BSP had already accepted that it would have to work in the conditions of a capitalist society and that the "socialist choice" had been left far away back in the past. The issue of the place and role of the Socialist Party under capitalism was being dealt with the maximum possible continuity, including adherence to the principal tenets of the Manifesto.

The ties with the past and the party's tradition were explicitly noted. It was stated that the socialism built in Bulgaria under the leadership of the party after World War II was an "alternative to the general backwardness of the country." As before, the working class was pointed out as the leading element in BSP's societal basis. The party presented itself as having arisen

---

24 That congress acquired symbolic significance due to the change in congress numbering. The party itself was founded in 1891, but it turned communist in 1919 and underwent bolshevization according to the model established in the Soviet Union. From then on, party congresses were counted from the moment of bolshevization, rather than the moment of founding. BSP decided to reinstate numbering congresses from the very start, in order to demonstrate responsibility for and continuity with its entire party history, in all of its stages. In this way, after the party's 14th congress from January and February 1990 came the 39th congress in September the same year

"under the influence of Marx's and Engels's teaching." The influence of the October Revolution in Russia and Lenin's theoretical legacy was valued positively. In this sense, the party's renewal was presented as necessary not because of some refutation of Marx's method but rather because of the new tasks that faced the left—tasks for which no ready solutions could be found in the classic authors of Marxism.

At the same time, the leading concept of the party's self-identification—democratic socialism—received a somewhat Bernsteinian interpretation. 'Democratic socialism' was no longer seen as a desired state of society (or a completed mode of social reality, as in the Manifesto) but rather as a movement actualizing the potential of the humanist, social and democratic tendency in the left. The transition from thinking of socialism as the first phase of communist society to thinking it as constant development and perfection is argued in the Platform by no other means than referring to the authority of Marx and Engels. BSP set itself the goal to become "a contemporary leftist party." Theoretical constructs from the Socialist International were for the first time included in the ideological arsenal of the party, while the value fundament promulgated by the party consisted of the triad freedom—justice—solidarity. In the area of international politics, the document called for "close partnership" with the Communist Party of the Soviet Union but also for a "broad opening" towards the parties of the European left (BSP 2008a: 31–67).

Lilov's team emerged as truly devoted to the ambition to neutralize polar positions within the party and to balance among factions. This role was partially compromised by the party leader's behaviour around the putsch against Gorbachev in August 1991, when BSP was the only European leftist party that refused to denounce the perpetrators from the so-called State Committee on the State of Emergency. In spite of that, in a programmatic perspective it was Lilov's line which was to dominate during the following years and which was at the foundation of the new party programme adopted in 1994 under the title *New Times, New Bulgaria, New BSP*.

The political debate regarding BSP's role in the post-socialist situation was structured to the greatest degree around the discussion regarding the new party programme and was carried out with the intensive participation of two factions—OSD and the Marxist Platform. OSD was created in late 1991 with a manifesto regarding the need for a social democratic transformation in BSP and united in itself many of the party's famous figures, among which the then already former PM Lukanov. Marxist Platform, on their part, drew their resources from conservative circles among party members and increasingly called for a denunciation of social democracy and an adoption of an orientation towards what was in effect a neo-communist ideological course with nationalist overtones.

OSD's project for party programme saw BSP as a 'party of social democracy' that was to act within the political system as a 'parliamentary party'. That draft had a mostly, though not entirely, critical stance towards the communist past. The project by Marxist Platform saw in BSP a 'contemporary Marxist party' functioning as a 'mass political organization'. It avoided the very mention of the then key concept of democratic socialism, and displayed a markedly positive stance towards the former regime, which had allegedly crumbled due to the "treacherous and destructive actions of part of the party elite." Priority was given to the vision, supported by the moderate project of the Centre for Strategic Studies chaired by Lilov. The document saw BSP as a "modern left party" that was both a "mass" and a "parliamentary" one and that aimed neither to reject, nor to idealize its past. It is true that Lilov's and OSD's projects were closer together than they are with the one by Marxist Platform, and that they both declared a desire for BSP membership in the Socialist International (which would mean international affiliation with the family of socialist and social democratic, and not that of communist parties). However, simultaneously the party committee on the drafting of the new programme explicitly forewarned: "We can assess as positive the efforts of the Alternative Socialist Union, Road to Europe and OSD for a revival of social democratic ideas among socialists, but among party members the prevalent view is that social democracy cannot exhaust the party's constant renewal" (all quotes in BSP 2008a: 68–98).

The self-identification with which BSP stepped forward in its 1994 programme ran as follows: a modern socialist party, party of the Bulgarian, European and world left, party of the self-renewing democratic socialism (BSP 2008a: 227). This cannot be seen as a completion of the party's process of going social democratic at the programmatic level. Yet another feature is to be mentioned. During the 1990s, BSP suffered splits (by the Civic Union for the Republic in 1993 and the Bulgarian Euroleft in 1997) ideologically motivated by the perceived insufficient social democratization of the old party. It was as social democrats that many people who left identified themselves, not as communists or socialists. In an international context, the Socialist International gave the full member status not to BSP but to the anti-communist Bulgarian Social Democratic Party. Subsequently, an observer status was given to the Euroleft. It was only after BSP's forming an alliance with some small social democratic formations in the format of the New Left at the end of the 1990s that was to unlock processes of international recognition that would reach completion with the party's becoming part of the International in 2003. In the first decade of transition, BSP also had strong reservations towards Bulgaria's possible NATO membership. It was only in 2000 that the party would formulate an approval of the Alliance. This contributed for the removal of some of the then still existing barriers for the party's international recognition.

In the early 21st century one can speak of a certain trend to social democratization at a programmatic level, partially manifested in the new party programme *For Bulgaria—Free Citizens, Just State, Solidary Society* (2008), even though this document also meticulously avoided the uncomfortable expressions 'social democracy' and 'social democratization'. The reference to Marxism and class theory has disappeared, although the direction of "historical transcendence of capitalism" has remained. The general task of the party has been specified as the need for a "social alternative of the neoliberal model." The goal sounds to a large extent in social democratic terms—the building of a welfare state on a West European model, which would help decrease inequality. The defined social basis of the party—all strata of society, of course with priority of the working people, the poor and vulnerable groups—corresponds to the programme postulate of BSP being a "people's party" (BSP 2008*b*). One could think that at many places the party uses the concept of democratic socialism with a meaning equivalent to that of social democracy in contemporary European societies. However, the fact that social democracy is not present at the conceptual level could hardly be fortuitous. Rather, it manifestly demonstrates the difficulties experienced by the former Communist Party to identify itself clearly and unambiguously for many years after democratic changes.

Table 1.3.1.
National parliamentary representation and participation in power by BSP

National parliamentary elections	Name under which the party ran (alone or as part of a coalition)	% of received votes	Number of MP seats (out of 240)	Place at the elections	Participation in government (as single ruling party or as senior partner in a coalition)	Monopoly on leftist political space
1990	BSP	47.20	211 (out of 400)	1	yes	no
1991	An election alliance of BSP and other small parties	33.40	106	2	no	yes
1994	An election union of BSP and other small parties	43.50	125	1	yes	yes
1997	Democratic Left	22.07	58	2	no	no
2001	Coalition for Bulgaria	17.15	48	3	no	yes
2005	Coalition for Bulgaria	30.95	82	1	yes	yes
2009	Coalition for Bulgaria	17.70	40	2	no	yes
2013	Coalition for Bulgaria	26.60	84	2	yes	yes
2014	BSP—Left Bulgaria	15.40	39	2	no	no

Source: Adapted from data by Bulgaria's Central Election Committee

This short review of the structural and programmatic transformation of BCP allows for some conclusions in a comparative perspective.

One of the most prominent features is that the party has demonstrated a high level of unity: it did not disband or dissolve under the pressure of democratic transformation—it only changed its name, without undergoing organizational disturbances and without giving up its past.

Next, the party has also succeeded—with the qualification of some small 'breaches' for short periods—to preserve its monopoly on left political space in the country for quarter of a century up to 2014. The separate groups that left it throughout the years did not manage to create a long-lived viable alternative to the successor party's political presence. The possible 'external' alternative in the person of the reborn Bulgarian Social Democratic Party was initially part of the anti-communist and growingly rightist camp, and then underwent marginalization and lost public influence.

Also, the party has sustained a serious internal organizational and ideological pluralism encompassing the domain of the entire modern left—from neo-communist to social democratic factions with their messages and policies. With respect to its program, the party has gradually come closer to contemporary West European social democracy, without however identifying with it. The Bulgarian Socialists have positioned themselves neither in the social liberalism of some former communist parties (Poland, Hungary), nor in the neo-communism of others (Czech Republic, Germany).

Additionally, the party won the first democratic elections after the socialist period and retained a stable presence in the Bulgarian political process from then on. With one exception (2001–2005, when it was third largest political power, but with just 3 MP seats below the second), it has not fallen below the second place at national parliamentary elections. Its electoral weight has varied, but prior to 2014 never dropped below 17–18% of votes at general elections, and on this index it has fared better than all other former communist parties from the collapsed Eastern Bloc, except the Romanian one—which, let us recall, however rejected its ties to its communist past.

Finally, the party has participated several times in the executive, both on its own and as part of different coalition formats. No matter whether it was ruling or in opposition, the party's official positions (e.g. regarding Bulgaria's NATO membership) have had a central and decisive significance for all major changes in Bulgarian politics.

We observe a slow transformation of BSP coupled with problems in self-identification—but also high public support for the party. How was that made possible? And how does it reflect the country-specific fate of the Bulgarian left?

2 The Complex Historical Pathways of the Bulgarian Socialist Party

2.1 A Proletarian Party with no Proletariat

The present Bulgarian Socialist Party likes to often refer to its long history. In all of its programme documents and in various declarations, the party has been underscoring the continuity of its development and the zigzagging but still uninterrupted line that connects the party with its beginnings in 1891. Each year in early August, BSP members and supporters assemble on Buzludzha Mount in the Bulgarian Stara Planina, where the party was founded, in order to solemnly mark its new anniversary. Their pride is inspired by the fact that the party is the oldest left Marxist organization in the Balkans. In a comparative perspective, it is also significant that in the interwar period it was the workers' party of biggest public weight in the region (Penev and Popivanov 2012).

On August 2, 1891, 15 people from 6 Bulgarian cities assembled on Buzludzha in order to discuss the statute and program of the party they envisioned. The documents were passed (mostly thanks to the drive of two figures, Dimitar Blagoev and Nikola Gabrovski) with 12 to 3 votes, and the delegates declared their assembly the foundational congress of the Bulgarian Social Democratic Party. In many respects, their programme was close to the documents of the French and Belgian Marxists, with few original moments. The event itself initially did not receive any powerful publicity in Bulgarian society. At that time, this was a society of a predominantly rural population (80%), with a small degree of industrialization in town areas (Crampton 2005: 113)—i.e., it was far from harbouring the prerequisites for a mass workers' movement that had been observed by Marx and Engels in England and other West European countries half a century earlier. The enterprise of the 'pioneers' of the organized Bulgarian left has been described by an author as an 'experiment' to create "a Bulgarian proletarian party in a country with no working class, no trade unions, no spontaneous workers' movement" (Guentchev 2008: 34–35). It is all the more odd that this 'experiment' was in the end successful.

How has this fact been explained by international scholars of Bulgarian history and politics? I have already pointed out that Bulgaria cannot be said to enjoy a significant interest within social sciences around the world. Yet, it can be hardly by chance that some of the best studies of Bulgaria's modern history have been devoted to the Bulgarian left. In one way or another, all of them have attempted to interpret not only the Bulgarian left's social and political role but also the preconditions for its birth, in order to argue for their interpretation of its emergence and the soil it came to grow upon.

In his analysis, Rothschild (1959) argues that a principal factor in the history and development of the Bulgarian socialist tradition is its provenance from the Russian socialist tradition rather than the German or French ones. The author remarks that the majority of Bulgarian socialists had ties with Russia, and most often studied at Russian universities. In contrast to the situation in Western Europe, and like the one in Russia, the Bulgarian left did not correspond to locally existing class structures. According to the author, its representatives were initially concentrated in narrow closed circles, alienated from the societal and political structures of their times, and deeply convinced in the power of ideas to change the world. In such conditions, dogmatism and fanaticism started to breed. In spite of that—and to a larger degree even because of it—the communist left became a leading intellectual tradition within the Bulgarian intelligentsia. The left, more than other trends, became able to exert an influence on politics and to view politics as the most certain road to radical social change. The inclination of the Bulgarian communists in favour of a 'superstructure'-type education: law, history, and politics, deepened that tendency.

According to Rothschild, the growing influence of the communist movement in Bulgaria during the first decades of the 20th century was due to the specific and unexpected concurrence of the attitudes about the present entertained by the communists, on the one hand, and the rural population, on the other. The Bulgarian peasants' traditional fond feelings for the national liberator Russia were one of the prerequisites for that. But other factors also played a role. They included the country's bureaucratic legacy, dating from the times of Ottoman rule. The intelligentsia in Bulgaria tended to despise the rural population, where it had come from, and tended to reject all types of professional occupations, except public office. Corruption had become established as a tradition. The civil servant taught the peasant that bribe can set into motion the artificially bloated administrative apparatus. Public funds were siphoned off to politicians. In their despair from that sorry situation, idealistically minded young people turned to communism. From their completely different starting point, peasants were also disgusted. They came to know better and better that the state is something external and even hostile to their interests. On the one hand, says Rothschild, communists sounded the drum of social justice and social revolution. On the other, the Bulgarian rural population preferred a radical agrarian rule, but was not ready to resist the communists taking power, especially after they did so after a Russian intervention. The Russian card acquired key significance. When it was so to speak played with determination, resolution, and loyalty, it could win the whole deal. According to the author, "Language, sentiment, irredentism, and the tradition, established by Blagoev and his colleagues, of particularly close relations between the Bulgarian and Russian Marxist movements, explains this unique trust reposed in the Bulgarian communists by the Russian leaders. Among the most backward of European countries, Bulgaria produced international Communism's best Bolsheviks" (Rothschild 1959: 301–302).

Himself a student of Rothschild, Oren (1973) works out further his thesis about the specific relationship between the left and the rural areas in Bulgaria. In a book that has been often criticized for its excessive caution in generalization and its, at times, too literal chronological reading of processes, he focuses mainly on the inter-war period, where he argues that explanations for the growth of trust in the communists are to be sought. During that period, three contrasting political models came to be effectively articulated in Bulgaria: Alexander Stamboliyski's agrarian chiliasm, Tsar Boris III's bureaucratic dictatorship, and the communist vision of a party-state. What was common among them is that they all ventured for a sweeping social reform from above, using the mechanisms of political power rather than the gradual maturing of tendencies within society. The communist position started to come closer to the rural masses, not so much in order to help them as to use them. The intensified economic development called for by the communists had its price, and that was the degradation of peasants. In order to achieve their goals, they stepped on two apparently contradictory preconditions—the fanning of nationalist feelings and full subservience to Moscow. In that way, argues the author, their road featured seeking national mobilization in conditions of unconditional faithfulness to a specific foreign political factor.

John Bell (1986) has offered what is perhaps the most thoroughgoing analysis—from an external perspective—of the reasons for the birth and ascendancy of the communist left in Bulgaria. He speaks about a predilection for political radicalism that was already present during the age of Ottoman rule in Bulgaria. The late rise of modern national consciousness favoured the flourishing of radical ideas in this backward agrarian country. The creation of its own state did not put an end to the desire for change. Supplementing political independence with social justice started to dominate the thinking of the Bulgarian intelligentsia in the late 19th century. Having entered the world of ideas through the doors of universities in pre-war Russia, Germany, Switzerland, and Austria, many representatives of the Bulgarian intelligentsia were attracted by Marxism, which provided convenient resources by claiming to be systematically and intelligibly integrating and ordering all human knowledge.

Bell presents the ties to Russia more complexly than other authors have done. Since its founding, the modern Bulgarian state had been pursuing one cause, national unification. And since the issue of the identity of the population in different parts of the Balkans was controversial and had continually been the source of conflict between neighbouring states, Bulgaria felt the need to have a defender in the person of at least one among the Great Powers. Before the end of World War I, Russia, Austro-Hungary, and Germany were all seen in such a role. After the war, however, Weimar Germany was weakened, Austro-Hungary fell apart, while Russia, having experienced the Bolshevik revolution, was isolated. With no competition from 'bourgeois' parties, they could exploit on their own the traditional Bulgarian Russophilia to their own benefit.

Bell also gives a critical reading to the third story line—the one concerning the communists' growing influence in the inter-war period. The impoverishment and declassation after 1918 definitely helped spread leftist ideas. The national catastrophes just experienced[25] led many Bulgarians to think there was no way to achieve national goals other than a communist revolution. At the same time, the immense refugee wave from the lost Bulgarian

---

25 In Bulgarian history, the expression 'national catastrophes' refers to the consequences to the heavy defeats in the Second Balkan War (1913) and the World War I (1918).

territories created a social resource for the left in the big cities. In the course of the two inter-war decades, the communists gradually evolved from class positions to more explicitly national ones, but in that respect the policies of the tsar's regime were ahead of them. That is why, during the anti-fascist resistance organized by them during World War II, the Bulgarian communists (in contrast to, e.g., their Yugoslav or Greek counterparts) did not manage to harmonize their efforts with the population at large, which depended to a much larger degree on the national fruits of the Bulgarian-German cooperation. After the triumphant entry of the Red Army in Bulgaria in 1944, the Soviet state leaders learned that in spite of the widespread Russophile sentiments in the country only the communists and none other could be their partners in the country. This is the main drift of Bell's thesis regarding the "special relationship" between the Bulgarian left and Russia.

Let me recapitulate the main points of those interpretations of the generation and development of the Bulgarian left. Firstly, the Bulgarian left has engendered interest among researchers in its communist and not so much in its social democratic branch. Secondly, the left won its own significance in Bulgaria's public and political life even before the Cold War and the creation of the Eastern Bloc, and this fact deserves special attention against the backdrop of the country's overall backwardness and low level of industrialization. Thirdly, the Bulgarian left developed in a complex relationship with Bulgaria's rural population—as its counterpoint, but at the same time as closely related to it. And fourthly, the Bulgarian left gained strength in the shadow of Russia.

Why Russia of all countries? After Bulgaria's liberation from Ottoman rule in 1878, the Bulgarian Liberal Party and its later successors for a long time incarnated the Russophile political trend in the country—not the socialists. What is more, the thesis that the 'pioneers' of Bulgarian socialism were in some shape or form strongly influenced by processes or ideas in Russia (Njagulov 2014: 202–205) is a little exaggerated. Many of them were rather of a West European schooling and mode of thinking. Still, it is justified to argue that events in Russia during the latter half of the 19th century exercised some influence upon the formation and especially upon the practical political behaviour of the Bulgarian left. That was because of the party chief Dimitar Blagoev[26]. For long years, Blagoev was in fact behind all major events for the left: from the idea for the creation of a party, through its programme profile, attitude towards power, politics and processes in society (including its stance regarding the permissible degree of outside influence), to organizational continuity and comportment towards factions and splits.

The formation of the Bulgarian social left is part of two broader contexts, international and national. The first one is characterized by the entering upon the stage of leftist political parties in Europe as defenders of the industrial proletariat, which was intensively growing in numbers during the 19th century. It was a defence chiefly inspired by the Marxist doctrine for explaining history and processes within society. The second context has to do with the creation of the Third Bulgarian State after the liberation from Ottoman rule in 1878 and the discussions for the road of development of the Bulgarian national community using the armamentarium of a statehood of its own.

The question regarding the condition of Bulgarian society after the liberation can be described as a worldview question. It contained, broadly viewed, two foundational questions: "Whither now?" and "Can we find support in the past?" Bulgaria acquired its independence after decades of economic and cultural progress, known under the textbook name of National Revival. A process took place of self-organization and consolidation of trade and economic entities as well as creation of an independent network of schools and churches. In 1870 the Bulgarian Orthodox Church separated from the Patriarchate of Constantinople. The church has been traditionally viewed as a social integrator and the most stable conservative institution in the nation (Penev and Popivanov 2013). In that specific case, however, the church could not serve as a model for future social development since it was restored by the modern drive for self-determination of the Bulgarian people and incarnated the liberal national views of the current Bulgarian elites. Bulgaria had its own tradition of community life, but it was locally limited and did not succeed in unfolding into an all-encompassing social project. In the Bulgarian lands, the Revival played the role of the European Enlightenment by opening the roads to modernity. In contrast to the

---

26 Dimitar Blagoev (1856–1924) was widely considered to be the most important figure of Bulgaria's left in the first decades of its existence.

Enlightenment, however, the Bulgarian Revival did not generate a Bulgarian intellectual and scientific tradition to help the functioning of a Bulgarian state. The Revival borrowed models, examples, and paradigms from West and East and adapted them to Bulgarian economic, social, and cultural conditions. On its part, Ottoman statehood was subject to universal rejection. It possessed no features that the Bulgarian elites wished to see reproduced in a Bulgarian state. Due to those reasons, Bulgaria's historical past did not offer points of support on the basis of which a strategy for post-liberation development could be worked out. The issue of how to use government received predominantly foreign reference points.

In its greater part, the enlightened Bulgarian intelligentsia from that period received their education abroad, and it was only natural for them to become attuned to the newest social and political teachings that shaped the intellectual climates in the countries where they studied and lived. The figure of the clearest and most consistent notion of the meaning and objectives for a leftist party in Bulgaria—Dimitar Blagoev—studied at the University of St. Petersburg. His ambitions were similar to those of many cultured Bulgarians in the years following the liberation—to not allow the exchange of an already rejected political oppression with a new one, and to free the country from the backwardness of a former Ottoman province. That is why Russian autocracy could not become an inspiration. Blagoev, like other Bulgarians who studied in Russia around that time, were sympathetic to the anti-tsarist attitudes of large parts of the Russian intelligentsia. Which strains of the manifold and stormy Russian cultural life could exert an attractive political force for the Bulgarians? For certain, that was not the Russian conservatism that helped support a social and political order widely seen in intellectual circles as unjust and wildly outdated. A liberation from backwardness implied walking a road different from the Russian road, for the Russian Empire itself was perceived as backward. Russian liberalism, which was gaining strength during those years, was focused on private property, but private property was not a problem in Bulgaria. Throughout the entire five-century Ottoman period, the Bulgarians had retained their rights to private property—something that was never denied to them. Russia's *narodnichestvo* was drawing cultural and psychological resources from certain views about the special character of the Russian people and made for poor export overseas. Slavophilia had its many different varieties, but they almost always looked back to the past and were too much Christian Orthodox and anti-Western to be liked by a people such as Bulgarians, who wanted to only look forward, did not experience religion as a mode of social organization, and saw in the European West not a threat but rather an opportunity. The anarchism widespread in Russia, and especially its extreme nihilistic varieties, was also alien to Bulgarian thinking, which welcomed its restored statehood and did not in any way wish to put its future into question.

Only socialism remained among progressive schools of thought. Blagoev took an active part in the work of the emerging Marxist circles and study groups and even became one of the authors of the first Marxist programme in Russia—that of the so-called Party of Russian Social Democrats in 1883. When he returned to Bulgaria, he was to resolutely stand behind the conviction that socialism cannot be immediately implemented in a backward country. Blagoev believed that in such a country, capitalist conditions have to first unfold in their completeness. A large working class and strong class antagonism were needed as prerequisites for social revolution. Capitalism's progress is the most important precondition for socialist transformation, stated Blagoev in his famous book *What Is Socialism and Can It Take Root Here?* (1891), which was to become the most popular Bulgarian Marxist text. In the same spirit, but in the Russian context, was the reasoning of G.V. Plekhanov, 'the father of Russian Marxism', in his 1885 book *Our differences*. An opponent of revolutionary impatience, which had a soft spot for the collectivist traditions of the Russian rural commune (*obshchina*) and saw in it readiness for a leap into a just social order, Plekhanov argued that the rural commune was to make way to bourgeois rather than communist forms of public life, that the communist movement can have no other initiator than the working class, and that power can be efficiently won and used for social change only in a situation of developed capitalist relations.

So let me turn back to the thesis that the establishment of the Bulgarian Marxist party was actually an 'experiment'. Its goals and messages could not be accurately described as 'experimental' or adventurous. What Bulgarian Marxists said was that the country needed policies of modernization through development of capitalism which was the same as the then liberal governmental elite was trying to establish by that time (Njagulov 2014: 279). Final intentions being different, the paths did not seem to be initially diverging. The newly created party was committed to delineate the possibilities of a leftist political thinking in the independent Bulgaria's ideological spectrum, and only subsequently, in these intellectual parameters, locate the possibility of a true leftist political action. Immediate results were given explicitly secondary importance (Damianova 1990: 419).

The Bulgarian Social Democratic Party, founded in 1891, was viewed by its most prominent leader Blagoev as a long-term project that had to devote itself to patient educational activities and help the growth of a Bulgarian proletariat to levels in which it can raise claims for an equitable and justified revolutionary transformation of society. Blagoev's years in Russia were not in vain. But from there he took and transferred to Bulgaria not Russian but rather Western ideas and doctrines. The Social Democratic Party arose as a European party. Let us recall that that was the time of Marxism's upsurge as one of the leading ideologies providing answers to the problems coming from the flowering of industrial production, the concentration of workforce in large cities, and the formation of a radically new social structure in the European countries. The first key names in the Bulgarian left included young intellectuals of European education and experience: Nikola Gabrovski, Christian Rakovsky, Georgi Kirkov, Yanko Sakazov, Vassil Kolarov, and others. In the idea of socialism they recognized the factor that they thought would bring Bulgarian national development forward. Initially, they were convinced that the process of change had to be gradual. The current chief objective was the strengthening of capitalism— and this was the goal the bourgeoisie pursued, using the state. Bulgaria's emergence from its recent peripheral pre-modern stage had to be quickly made irreversible. Changes had to be furthered that would make impossible to turn back. Bulgarian statehood was the last to be created on the Balkans in the 19th century, and had to be preserved. That is why, in contrast to the European political process, only innovative change was considered an acceptable goal. Any restoration of older conditions was not to be admitted. Support and fostering of Bulgarian statehood was thus integrated in the Bulgarian left's initial design[27].

The European processes played a key role not only in the initial course of the Bulgarian left but also in its future controversial development, putting a deep mark on the left's internal discussions and disunities. This was al-

---

27 In this sense, for the Bulgarian early socialists, 'social justice' is not to be seen as an alternative to the 'sovereignty of the people' but rather as its complementary dimension (Njagulov 2014: 279).

ready the case during the first short split in 1893–94, when the dispute flared around the issue whether, given the smallness of the proletariat, there was any sense for the left to exist as a political party, or whether it was better for it to engage in economic, trade union, and educational activities. The influence of foreign events was to be felt even more greatly in the conflict between Blagoev and Sakazov which grew into a clash between the *Novo Vreme* and *Obshto Delo* journals and the final split into 'Narrow' (Blagoev) and 'Broad' (Sakazov) socialists in 1903. A strong motive for disintegration were the tremors that shook the European socialist movement after the release of Eduard Bernstein's book *The Preconditions for Socialism and the Tasks of Social Democracy* (1899) and the beginning of so-called revisionism. Bernstein rejected the chief postulates of Marxist dialectics, the laws of economic development formulated by Marx, as well as the notion of class struggle. In other words, he rejected everything on which Blagoev insisted as the central explanatory framework for the left, applicable for Bulgaria too. Revisionism also turned out to reject the reasons because of which the Bulgarian leftist party announced a commitment to defending the interests of wage labour rather than those of the poor in general, as well as the reasons it delayed solving the issue of coming to power until the stage of full unfolding of Bulgarian capitalism.

In Bulgaria Sakazov took Bernstein's side. Initially, Blagoev leaned on the authority of 'the Pope of Marxism', Karl Kautsky, who had a negative view of Bernstein's theses. The ideas of 'class cooperation' and 'compromise tactics' were, however, to later affect Kautsky himself. The 1900 Fifth Congress of the Second International in Paris already decided that socialist parties were allowed to enter into tactical coalitions with bourgeois parties and in cabinets dominated by those parties if in that way they could more efficiently help the condition of vulnerable social communities, in particular workers. This allowance was, of course, made dependent on the special circumstances in each specific country. In 1902 Kautsky wrote his famous open letter to Enrico Ferri entitled the *The Two Tendencies* in which he explicitly admitted the possibility for the proletariat to unite with some middle class factions against others and also to create common reformist parties with them in order to participate in government. This was entirely in line with Sakazov's vision of socialism as a 'common endeavour' of the productive social strata, which could—and should—unite in one shared progressive undertaking agrarians, craftsmen, merchants, industrialists, and workers (workers were put at the last place!) for the creation of a veritable 'people's state'. Sakazov's motives appear to be completely understandable. Bulgaria's industrialization and the achieving of hegemony for industrial production could take an indefinite amount of time. After all, the chief political strategy with which Bulgarian elites entrusted state government after 1878 was not industrialization but rather an actualization of the national idea under an irredentist reading, i.e., as a unification of all Bulgarians in one country. That is why transcending class barriers was thought by some to be able to produce a much more specific and positive effect on the welfare of many groups of the Bulgarian society than the strict adherence to Marx's favouring of the proletariat.

Blagoev's response is telling of the high self-esteem with which he and the party viewed their role in politics. Sharply disagreeing with Bernstein's course and without Kautsky's support, Blagoev resolutely stood for the Marxist path chosen for Bulgaria's left. Blagoev insisted that class cooperation could lead to a blurring of the party's leftist identity and the loss of its *raison d'être*.[28] The slow but determined efforts for the strengthening of the proletariat in Bulgaria, he argued, were a much more justified way to defend the country's road to progress than broad coalitions around ad hoc social and economic causes, or the ambition for immediate radical action. Blagoev stood up against Sakazov's 'Broad Socialists', but also against 'left communists'; against petty bourgeois reformism and quasi-anarchist revolutionism. This led to the decision to oppose the interference of the European social democracy into the party affairs—on the issue of the 1902–03 party splitting as well as during the 1910 attempts of the emissaries of the International Socialist Bureau to lobby for a new unification. Those events led Blagoev to write, at the very beginning of World War I, the article "Magister Dixit", in which he resolutely argued against the European social democrats' policy with respect to the war and military budgets. The essence of Blagoev's political legacy is the notion of a small but modern parliamentary party to defend the workers' interests in harmony with the

---

28 This point of view is also grounded. As scholars have pointed out, after adopting the ideas for collaboration with progressive bourgeois parties, in 1899 the Romanian left in effect disappeared, merging into a liberal formation. Romania was not to create a significant leftist political tradition before 1944 (Guentchev 2008: 62). In the same vein, Svetozar Marković's followers in Serbia eventually joined the Radical Party (Damianova 1990: 419).

leading European leftist doctrines, yet maintaining its national autonomy and taking into account the current tasks for the Bulgarian state, as they were interpreted by the party (Penev and Popivanov 2012: 538). In this sense, foreign influences were attributed a complementary rather than a decisive effect (Damianova 1990: 419).

This image of the left was to change under the pressure of the massive quakes sent by the World War I throughout the globe, Bulgaria included. For Bulgaria the end of the war meant not just a heavy military defeat. This was a defeat of the country's national ideal pursued through all four decades after the Liberation. The demographic blow, the economic catastrophe, the lack of good financial perspectives, and the widespread impoverishment created sufficient preconditions for the population's going left. Moreover, the classical bourgeois parties that had ruled the country before were completely discredited. The monarchy had lost its political authority after its decisive moves from previous years, which were perceived as mere political gambling. Three leftist options for Bulgaria emerged: that of the 'Broad Socialists' or social democrats, that of the 'Narrow Socialists', and that of BZNS.

The party led by Sakazov and his successors however quickly started losing its popularity. During hard times, when society was looking for radical solutions, and when, after the catastrophe of the national ideal, the internal divisions within the nation grew into an open antagonism, the social democracy's moderate and compromise-seeking course was not going to find many supporters. The party's behaviour also contributed to its decay, as it was seen as unprincipled, and due to its readiness to participate in all types of ruling coalitions, irrespective of their composition and the character of the participating parties. That was complemented by a perception of careerism coming from negotiations and scandals around the constitution and reorganization of cabinets in which the party participated.

BZNS was a different case. It was an authentic Bulgarian party, which, in contrast to all other parties in the country's modern history, was not created on the model of foreign organizations. The party did not bring outside ideologies to Bulgaria and instead developed its own principles and political objectives. BZNS drew its resources from Bulgaria's sizeable rural population. Among the party's reference points was the understanding that the entire modern development of the country was taking place at the expense of peasants, and that cities were exploiting villages in order to 'catch up' with their European models. The party did not identify itself in the left-right spectrum. However, it can be seen with a large degree of certainty as a part of the left—due to both its radicalism and the social structure of the Bulgarian rural areas. In contrast to, e.g., the Romanian case, the Bulgarian rural areas at that time were greatly parcelled, populated by a large number of small owners who saw their future not in the 'conservation' of certain social habits but rather in a thoroughgoing transformation of the social order. The Agrarian Union, following the ideas of its leader, Alexander Stamboliyski, argued that class divisions are a thing of the past and that actual society consists of estates based on the actual livelihood of people. Therefore, government has to prioritize that estate whose labour is of a productive nature and secures the only goods without which humanity cannot exist—i.e., the agrarian estate (Bell 1977, Popivanov 2008a).

The post-war crisis propelled the Agrarians to power. In the highly volatile situation of the early 1920s, they were the most widely supported political party in the country, followed by Blagoev's formation. How did the narrow socialist left react to the ongoing changes? It started a process of Bolshevization, taking Lenin's party in Russia as a model. In 1919, it was renamed to BCP and adopted a new Programme Declaration, in which it revised part of the tenets of the first 1892 party programme that had been effective until then. BCP went on to become a founding member of the Comintern, the international organization of communist parties, which acted and developed under Moscow's auspices. The careful evolutionary behaviour from Blagoev's earlier times was thoroughly re-evaluated. Under one form or another, featuring different types of leaders and executive structures, BCP became committed to an armed uprising against the authoritarian Bulgarian cabinet in 1923. It was involved in the worst terrorist attack in Bulgarian history, and at that moment in the entire world, the St. Nedelya Church bombing staged against representatives of Bulgarian political and cultural elite, which led to the death of 134 people. The party further organized directly or indirectly a string of other illegal actions. BCP sought out and found much broader support amongst civil servants, young people, and peasants. That was a truly unusual transition—a transition from following the achievements of Western socialism to a single-minded relationship with Russia, from political moderateness to radical activism, and from a strictly workers' organization to a broad social profile.

Shortly before the end of his life, in 1919, Blagoev made a telling reflection:

> If Marx and Engels, working in that revolutionary age when they published the *Communist Manifesto*, saw the communist revolution as conditional on the common action of the proletariat in all civilized countries; if, on his part, Lenin, who in Russia had a large proletariat to operate with, a multitude concentrated by capitalist industry in huge industrial centres and cities, and at the same time many millions proletarized or half-proletarized peasants, if in this situation Lenin also saw the communist revolution as conditional on the support of the European proletariat—then is it not clear that in Bulgaria, where conditions *are entirely unlike* those in Russia or those in the civilized countries, the communist revolution should be conditional *three fourths* on the situation abroad and *one fourth* on the situation at home? (Blagoev 2010: 515, author's emphasis).

And indeed, World War I ended with a revolutionary upsurge in many European countries: riots in Germany, a Hungarian Soviet Republic, a soldiers' uprising in Bulgaria itself. The most significant factor was the Bolshevik coup in Russia, which became known in history as the October Revolution. The resources of the Second International were exhausted, and the organization was compromised. The extreme left, in contrast, for the first time had good opportunities to seize power. At that time the full actualization of that potential was perceived by the communists themselves as conditional on a global revolutionary process. Bolshevik power in Russia did not suffice. It had to encompass many other countries. Stalin's thesis that socialism has to be built 'in one country' was to be articulated at a later point in time. At that point, the Russian Bolsheviks, Stalin included, entertained different views. According to Stalin himself in *The Foundations of Leninism* (1924), to take away power from the bourgeoisie and establish the rule of the proletariat in one country did not yet mean to guarantee a full victory to socialism. For the final triumph of socialism, the efforts of one country were not sufficient, especially the efforts of an agrarian country like Russia, argued Stalin. The efforts of proletarians from a number of developed countries were needed.

The Bulgarian 'Narrow socialists' accepted the Bolshevik interpretation of the left and took Russia as a model. It was motivated by reasons that were easy to grasp. After all, at that point it seemed that what was once spoken and written about had started to actually happen in Russia, and nowhere else. But with the October Revolution, Russia's image had changed. Tsarist Russia was widely perceived in Europe to be a backward Asiatic empire. Soviet Russia strived to forge for itself the image of a flag bearer of progress and a furtherer of humanity's hopes for a more humane world.

This was not a perception shared just by the Bulgarian communists. Towering intellectual figures from around the world showed an interest to see and experience for themselves the ongoing building of the ideal for social justice on the Russian soil. From Emma Goldman on to Henri Barbusse and Lion Feuchtwanger, dozens of leading Western intellectuals admired the processes in Russia. In the early 1920s, the great Bulgarian poet Hristo Smirnenski saw in Moscow "a star of new times".

Functioning predominantly as an intellectual formation (Dimou 2009: 284), the Bulgarian 'Narrow socialists' actually made an intellectual choice in favour of Bolshevik Russia. This means a choice of a model beyond the restraints of specific already existing social group interests which were still poorly developed inside the party to play any important role in the political decision-making process.

The October Revolution put on the Bulgarian communists' agenda the question whether what they were doing should be viewed only as enlightenment, or whether it could also have its immediate practical aspects. And even though their orientation towards the Russian Bolsheviks may be logical, as we have pointed out, it could have hardly been thoroughly implemented without the domestic preconditions which included the presence of a 'left competition' from BZNS (Dimou 2009: 417–418). The communists were fully aware that the majority of poor people in Bulgaria were not workers but rather peasants. This could be viewed as just part of the peculiarities of the local environment, were it not that those same peasants came to the political stage with their own original project for society. That gave the parameters not only of a highly successful public and electoral competition with communists. BZNS offered a principled leftist alternative to the communist views that was to a much greater degree adapted to the level of development of Bulgarian society; the Union also gave an answer, more convincing at that time, to the question as to how the poor in the country could prosper. BZNS was a challenge to the bourgeois parties, which in the inter-war period did not manage to recover from the blow they suffered and to restore their influence; but the Union was also a challenge to the communists. The Agrarians' rule and their messages put to trial the communists' self-esteem and worldview. Roughly said, the communists had to learn that peasants, too, had their own social project, and the working class could be made to serve that project. Notwithstanding BCP's early propaganda statements that BZNS and other parties exemplified two parts of the bourgeoisie—one rural and one urban—it became clear that something radically new and different was happening in Bulgaria that was undermining the until then unshakeable vision of the capitalist stage of history as a clash between bourgeois and proletarians. BCP had to acknowledge that rural Bulgaria is a political factor and to seek ways to minimize that factor. In the communists' view, the rural areas' struggle for social progress had to take place under the leadership of the working class, just like it was abroad, in Europe. That is why communism in Bulgaria could no longer remain just an educational project—it had to grow into an idea subject to actualization, the chief dimensions of which had been laid down by the Russian Bolsheviks.

In Russia, like in Bulgaria, the majority of the population were peasants, not workers. The Bolsheviks who proclaimed having crated 'the first state of workers and peasants in the world' and chose for its symbol the sickle and the hammer as an expression of the union between workers and peasants, however presupposed a subordinate role for the peasants in the building of socialism. The Bolshevik revolution was a revolution that was aiming to build a new social formation not evolutionally but rather using political will and governance from above. On its part, the weakness of the working class itself presupposed the need for a political avant-garde called to instil revolutionary consciousness into the masses and to guide their actions—i.e., it presupposed an organized avant-garde party, a party that was not an exponent of interests but rather a leader of the people. It was due to those circumstances that the Russian case was felt to be a good model for the Bulgarian communists. They viewed their relationship with the peasant movement and with its supporters in similar terms. Bulgarian peasants had to be co-opted for the fight for progress under the leadership of workers while workers on their part had to walk the way delineated by the party. That is how the Bulgarian left's educational project was gradually transformed into a governmental one, whence arose the claim that it was the left, and none other, that could guarantee progress for the Bulgarian society and state, taking into account the specific situation of the country.

The communist left's image was changing. It was growing more flexible and featured more concrete causes of a modern and progressive twist. From the Transport Strike in 1920 to the anti-fascist resistance during World War II, BCP—legal or not, under this or another name, using its civilian or paramilitary structures, its local or foreign activists—was actively trying to attract large numbers of people under its political banners. The party was given additional prestige by the brilliant defence of one of its leading executives—Georgi Dimitrov (1882–1949)—at the 1933 Leipzig Trial, when the Nazis, who had just come to power in Germany, brought false charges against him and two of his fellow activists for having set fire to the Reichstag. BCP (and personally Dimitrov as Secretary General of the Communist International) actively participated in working out the Comintern's policy with respect to fascism. Among Dimitrov's contributions in his report for the 1935 Comintern congress was the introduction of the tactic of the so-called united fronts of all democratic forces. At the Bulgarian national level, this course was implemented in a struggle with the so-called 'left sectarians' in the party, who insisted on staging an immediate uprising and refused to recognize differences between fascism and other bourgeois political movements. BCP sought allies in various parts of the political spectrum and among various social groups. The 1940 Sobolev Action is telling of the growing support for communists throughout the country, and in particular in the rural areas. In response to the calls of the Soviet emissary Arkady Sobolev for signing a friendship and mutual assistance pact between Bulgaria and the USSR, the party organized assemblies and rallies in hundreds of towns and villages across the country and gathered hundreds of thousands of signatures in support for the proposal.

The communists had resolutely set foot in Bulgaria's rural areas. Their propaganda was starting to address the people as a whole, not only workers. The active search for ties to the traditions of the Bulgarian people is an important factor acknowledged both by the party itself and those who have studied it. This is an oft mentioned circumstance. The founders of the Bulgarian social left had already underscored their continuity with the national revolutionaries from the times of the Revival under Ottoman rule, and especially with the social ideals and the egalitarian views of leading Revival figures such as Lyuben Karavelov, Vassil Levski, and Hristo Botev. The direct legacy of the struggles for national (not yet social!) liberation in the left's ideological corpus was pointed out by the official party historians during socialist rule in Bulgaria (History 1981). This legacy has been equally emphasized by both Bulgarian (Mineva 2001) and foreign (Moore 1984, Giatzidis 2002) scholars of the Bulgarian left. Of course, the sincerity and faithfulness to classical Marxism was not put to question. On the contrary, the communists' Marxist background was a characteristic viewed as necessary by Blagoev and his successors. But it turned out that this Marxist theoretical nucleus could co-exist with a number of strongly entrenched pre-capitalist Bulgarian ideas regarding the social question (Dimou 2009: 410). Of central significance here is the ideologeme of the special merits of the poor and even of poverty as such. Many examples can be found for idealization and sympathies for the poor in the Bulgarian folklore and literature from the 19th and early 20th centuries. Hitar Petar ('Smart Peter' from the series of folk stories) or Andreshko (from Elin Pelin's famous short story) exemplify this attitude that tends to place social issues predominantly in the domain of ethics and not so much of economics.

Listeners heard stories about how Hitar Petar helped his fellow villagers to partake unpunished in the sweet pears of a miser; how he gave a lesson to a tax-collector not to tie to the pillory peasants who were not able to pay their taxes; how he taught people to get rid of an usurer by coining an insulting nickname for him and thus driving him away; how he showed a rich man (who demanded that a poor man pay him his respects) that he could not talk him down; how he succeeded in making fun of an avaricious bishop. Listeners followed the protagonist's actions and admired his inventiveness and ability to actively pursue his goals. Both Hitar Petar and the many peasants featured in those tales are poor people. They do not get rich in the stories and in that sense there is no happy end for them. But they are viewed as good precisely because of that. Justice, those stories seem to suggest, is always at the side of the poor. And the poor person does not experience their fate as a tragedy or an inevitable lot, but rather constantly finds ways to achieve their goals.

In Elin Pelin' short story, poor cart driver Andreshko is driving a bailiff to Andreshko's native village late at night. When he learns that the task of the bailiff is to seize the wheat of a poor villager who was not able to pay his taxes, Andreshko decides to prevent that and forewarn his friend and so he intentionally drives the cart into a nearby bog, leaving there his customer to call for help. The readers' sympathies are supposed to be entirely at the side of the poor people crushed by life rather than at the side of civil servants, who completely legally attempt to collect the due tax revenue. It is crystal clear which party is the good and which the bad.

Such attitudes were widely shared among Bulgarians. The Bulgarian left was gradually occupying the position of a much needed defender of the poor and thus started to express collectivist messages. Those messages were now no longer addressing only workers and exploited people (like in the classic doctrine), but also included the poor and unhappy, the humiliated and insulted, the small and the injured. We know that Marx viewed exploited workers as a means for change of the whole, as the necessary central agent of history. Their mission was viewed as a global one. They were seen as the class that must free the whole world and put an end to exploitation and class division. Their goal as a class was to abolish themselves as a class. The Bulgarian reading of those tenets was starting to stress more and more on the need for constant protection of the poor due to their significance in themselves, as a goal, not as means.[29] This widening of spectrum from workers as a global factor towards vulnerable groups as a national factor, as we have seen, transpired not by mere chance.

The Bulgarian communist left was thus gradually going beyond the initial 'intellectualist' stage of its development. In the years after the 1923 fall from power of the agrarian regime, the party's organizational life had to thrive in very unfavourable conditions. It could no longer take the form of intellectual debates and party publications, which were its main manifestations some decades before. Key party figures, especially those who did not choose to emigrate but instead stayed 'on the ground' in Bulgaria, were much more involved in the national traditions and everyday life than Blagoev or Sakazov were. Their initiatives in those years showed their ability to work with different social and professional groups in both extremist and moderate undertakings. The obvious goal sought to be attained by creating youth and women's leftist structures was the growth of the party's public influence. This all-embracing approach can be perhaps best described by the slogan of the Bulgarian All-People's Student Union, a leftist youth structure founded in 1930: "People's way is our way!" The people as a whole—not just one class—was viewed as the left's ally. The geopolitical dimension of that change is also familiar. BCP further broadened its impact, using the Russophile attitudes then widespread among the Bulgarians. This was to help them later, after taking power, in transforming the lo-

---

29 Of course, this did not happen at one stroke. As early as the times around its creation, the Social Democratic Party made a point of distancing itself from Spyridon Gulabchev's so-called *siromahomilstvo*, a movement teaching the need to relieve the suffering of Bulgaria's poor. Blagoev and his associates thought that this movement was not founded on a scientifically sound analysis of the social situation and the level of society's development, and thus could have only limited and unproductive effects.

cal Russophile tradition into pro-Soviet and pro-communist beliefs. We cannot go as far as to claim that during this period BCP turned into a people's party or a rural party, but still it came out of its former narrow shell and became an important part of the social and political processes in Bulgaria. In spite of (or perhaps because of?) the heavy anti-communist provisions of the 1924 Law on the Protection of the State, the spy system and the persecution, the bloody sentences and executions during the time of anti-fascist resistance, to be a communist in Bulgaria had become something prestigious, modern, and progressive—one could be tempted to say even 'fashionable.'

On September 9, 1944, when the Soviet Army had already entered Bulgaria, power was taken by a coup by anti-fascist forces, united in the so-called Fatherland Front. BCP got its first four ministers in the new cabinet. The rural question once again came on the agenda. BCP's views regarding the future government as a regime of 'popular democracy' presupposed integrating peasants and their political spokespersons into the structures of power. Such was the view of Bulgaria's first communist Prime Minister, Georgi Dimitrov. In the course of those tense post-war years, however, Stalin's thesis prevailed that 'popular democracy' could be nothing else than a form of dictatorship of the proletariat. The Communist Party had to assume the role of an avant-garde, following the Soviet model. This led, among other things, to the restructuring of the Bulgarian political left. In 1948 the Social Democratic Party was disbanded and merged into BCP. After strong pressure and persecution of its key executives (culminating in the execution of the leader Nikola Petkov), BZNS abandoned their programme and went on to continue their existence as partners to the Communists in government, without the right to their own voice on the main political and economic issues facing the country. It is, however, an important fact that the Agrarian Union was not disbanded. The Communists were still aware that 70 years after Liberation, Bulgarian society was rural, and an efficient rule was not possible that did not take that into account.

BCP stepped forward with its avant-garde government project. Its goal was clear—to modernize Bulgaria with Soviet help and using the Soviet model, with little regard for the social and human price that Bulgarian society had to pay for that.

2.2 BCP in its Attempt to be Party of the Entire People

Around 1948, BCP assumed full power in Bulgaria. The party in effect immediately started to implement its plans to modernize the country. That was a fully rationalistic project based on the understanding that everything can be estimated, calculated, and forecasted, and that planning in all areas of public and economic life can achieve all goals that have been set in advance.

The period of communist rule in Bulgaria, which continued up to 1990, was far from homogeneous or monolithic. It had its sub-periods, its peculiarities, and internal dynamics, which should not be underestimated. But the modernization strategy covered the entire period. It was an important part of the communist regime's overall performance and public legitimation (Daskalov 2011: 292–297) and was to find expression in several directions, in all of which the results achieved—no matter how we may be inclined to judge them—thoroughly changed the Bulgarians' way of life (Kalinova and Baeva 2001; Genov and Krasteva 2001: 1–32).

Bulgaria experienced a process of swift industrialization (Feiwel 1982) that transformed industry into a leading factor in the country's economy that came to make a contribution to the country's GDP twice larger than that of agriculture. The country urbanized at a similar great speed, with the size of its urban population in the 1970s becoming twice bigger than that of the rural population (Giatzidis 2002: 26). On their part, sectors such as education, health care and agriculture also underwent great progress. Illiteracy was eradicated, child mortality dropped several times, diseases such as tuberculosis and malaria disappeared from Bulgaria. Land consolidation—a problem that had long lingered in Bulgarian rural areas—was finally effected in the process of so-called collectivization, albeit at the price of heavy violence against small rural landowners. Around the end of the communist regime, Bulgaria could compete with leading East European countries in indexes such as standard of living and purchasing power, average life expectancy, share of urban population, degree of electrification, density of railway networks and transport infrastructure. In a comparative international perspective this was reflected in the noted UN Index of Human Development.[30] The life environment of the Bulgarian citizens was

---

[30] In 1990, Bulgaria ranked 26th in the world according to that index (from the Eastern Bloc, GDR, Czechoslovakia and the USSR were ranked better) while in 2014 the

transformed. They became accustomed to living in their own apartments equipped with adequate appliances and facilities, driving their personal cars, talking on home phones, going to the seaside for summer holidays and to mountain resorts in the winter, receiving pensions after retiring from work, using international practices such as banking, and so on. The people's 'way of life', as clearly demonstrated by profound researchers such as Brunnbauer (2007), changed dramatically.

All those things were the result of the Bulgarian Communists' policies and were part of a general drive for modernization, or, simply said, a drive for adopting key achievements of Western modernity. In this respect, BCP played a role unusual for a communist party—the role of a national bourgeoisie. For the modernization efforts in Bulgaria implemented at the design and under the leadership of BCP were the work of national bourgeoisies in the classical West European cases. In the Bulgarian case, there was a paradoxical divergence of ideological postulates and political tasks. According to Marx and Engels, communism is a 'way out' of the modern age—a process that is to cancel the previously existing class divisions (the tensions between wage labour and capital) and to create a classless society of free individuals, thus going beyond modernity's 'conditions for possibility'. On the other hand, communism in Eastern Europe, and especially in Bulgaria, under the pressure of immediate tasks facing society, turned into an ensemble of modernization programmes. It thus turned into a 'way into' the modern age. In contrast with Czechoslovakia and Eastern Germany, and to some degree also Hungary, which all have a rich record of both close ties with the West and industrial and urban development, Bulgaria carried out a principal part of its process of modernization under socialist rule. It is well known that during its socialist period Czechoslovakia even made some steps back from economic levels achieved before World War II. For countries like Bulgaria the reverse can be said—they moved forward.

BCP's course while in power does not fit the canons of classical Marxism due to another important circumstance, which was, by the way, shared among all Eastern Bloc countries. A central part of Marx's teaching was the

---

country was 58th (from the former Eastern Bloc, Russia, Romania, Latvia, Hungary, Slovakia, Poland, Lithuania, Estonia, the Czech Republic, and, of course, unified Germany were ranked better, i.e., all ex-Eastern Bloc countries except most former Soviet Republics).

problem of the emancipation and freedom of humans from the powers that alienate and subjugate them (Mitev 2013). This problem was however dropped from the theory and practice in the socialist countries, including Bulgaria. BCP's modernization strategy presupposed a development steered by the party (and none other) and implemented by the state (and none other). The initiative of the separate individual was rejected. The freedom of the individual could not lie at the foundation of the model create. To the contrary, violence became a lasting characteristic of that model. This does not apply only to the period immediately after taking power, when violence could be explained (which does not mean—justified) with the party's resoluteness to crush its political opponents and the representatives of the tsarist regime's political and financial circles. Even though its intensity was different at different points of time, and as a rule it was decreasing, violence remained an organic part of the way in which BCP viewed the meaning of its rule. From the first stage of communist rule, commonly called 'Stalinism', violence encouraged or directly approved by the party took many shapes. Those included repressive actions without fair trial and sentencing (against social or political foes in the first weeks after September 9, 1944, during the collectivization of land in the early 1950s, and so on), the creation of forced 're-educational' labour camps, the dismissal from work and displacement of representatives of the bourgeoisie and their families from major cities, the limiting of access of those people to education, the introduction of mandatory character descriptions by the Fatherland Front for admission to universities, the adoption of political provisions in the Criminal Code, and so on (see, e.g., Baeva 2010: 10–15). With time, the communist regime was to soften violence against different strata of society or society as a whole—labour camps were for instance closed down in 1962. But, in a modified and lighter shape that decreased physical violence and broadened symbolic violence, violence was to abide with the regime until its very end. Here I also mean administrative punishments for those who disagreed with the party line, hindrances for career development, and, of course, censorship and spying.

The forceful channelling of the Bulgarian society's road of development in a specific direction was balanced by BCP's aspiration, especially in the late 1960s and the following two decades, to steer a political course to unify the nation. In fulfilling this function of a national bourgeoisie, which it had assumed for the sake of the modern transformation of the country, BCP made in effect an attempt to acquire the status of a party of the entire people. The ambition to be not just a class but rather a mass party—a party of all—found a partial expression in the tenets of the party's 1971 programme. But the main means of implementation remained practical rather than programme ones.

The dynamics of the party's membership is telling (see Table 2.2.1.).

Table 2.2.1.
Social composition of BCP's members (by year)

Year	BCP Membership	Workers (in %)	Peasants (in %)	White-collar (in %)	Others (in %)
1948	463,682	26.5	44.7	16.3	12.5
1966	611,179	38.4	29.2	26.1	6.2
1976	788,211	41.4	23.0	30.2	5.4
1981	825,876	42.7	n/a	n/a	n/a

Source: adapted from Staar 1982: 42 and Bell 1986: 131. The available 1981 figures refer just to workers and non-workers among party members.

The share of workers among Bulgaria's population grew through the years. This is natural, given that, in the period considered, the number of people working in the industry grew many times. And still, much more remarkable is the stable growth in the number of people employed in services, among whom a significant place was occupied by representatives of the administration and intelligentsia. It must be pointed out that BCP membership was not only a result of the personal will of the individual citizen. A complex procedure was involved. The balances among different groups of the Bulgarian society in the composition of the body of party members did not obtain so much spontaneously as in part from a certain design allotting approximate 'quotas' for each of the groups. This gives us a good opportunity to track the evolution of the party's rule. BCP started its sojourn in government with an at least partially completed workers' profile (the relative share of workers among party members was much higher than that among the general population). But in the 1970s, the share of workers among party members reached levels that do not warrant the label of a pure proletarian party. And that was a consciously intended policy of the party leaders.

BCP's broader social approach was prepared by the inter-war period, when the Bulgarian communists sought partnerships with a rich palette of social and professional groups. In the course of the communist regime, the trend towards more encompassing national representation became stronger. We should not forget that BCP assumed the responsibility for the existence of the state and people, for national borders and security. More and more, internationalism was balanced by a nationally motivated policy line legitimized by the defence and glorification of the Bulgarians' 'socialist fatherland'. This was reflected by scholars in different ways. Todorova speaks about a Communist nationalism. She is a little radical by plainly stating that "[t]he so-called communist nationalism was nothing but a transvestite, ordinary nationalism" (1995: 91). Things are more complex than initially seem to be, and claiming that Marxism for BCP was a classic example of ideological nominalism to be used just for legitimation is a pure exaggeration. Such line of interpretation was followed by others also insisting on the nationalistic nature of the Bulgarian communists (Vachudová and Snyder 1997). However, Todorova is to be credited with putting an important point on the scientific agenda. This nationalistic angle was to be further analyzed. One of the most penetrating foreign scholars of the Bulgarian left has on this occasion proposed the concept of a *Marxist nationalism*. According to Sykgelos (2011), this concept grasps a key characteristic of BCP's post-World War II political behaviour. He argued that even though in the first stages of its development the party had opposed irredentist nationalism and had more or less stayed away from the spirit of the times, still, at a later stage it resorted to consciously welding together nationalist and socialist images and to identifying with the Bulgarian people's heroic past. The author also recalls the Comintern's national course under Georgi Dimitrov, expressed in the 'popular fronts' tactics,[31] as well as the broad national platform of Bulgarian communists during the anti-fascist resistance, which combined anti-imperialism with social patriotism. The Fatherland Front, according to Sykgelos, was intentionally presented as a union of all patriotic forces in the nation, while the nation itself was presented as a unified entity that quickly overcame its internal divisions after van-

---

31 In his 1933 Leipzig Trial defense, which I referred to above, Dimitrov resorted to nationalist arguments in order to demonstrate the advantages of Bulgarian over German civilization. In an excerpt from his speech that was to later acquire great fame, he pointed out that in the times when German Emperor Karl V talked in German "only to his horses," and the German aristocrats and intellectual elite were ashamed of their native tongue and accepted only Latin, Bulgaria was already enjoying exceptional spiritual achievements, an alphabet of its own, and a culture in its own language (Sykgelos 2011: 32). As is plain for everyone to see, no doctrinal Marxism whatsoever is involved here.

quishing the bourgeoisie and the fascists, and was now ready to rally together against a common enemy. The study's main thesis is that in the course of its time in rule, BCP succeeded in learning to talk the 'native language' of the masses—which was a nationalist one. Here is a very important conclusion the author makes regarding BCP's trans-internationalist transformation: "[T]he Bulgarian communists, going beyond the Leninist tradition, had implied that it is the narod which imposed a series of restrictions on the oppressors and the parasite capitalists. Whereas, then, the proletariat exists independently in Lenin's view, proletariat, people, and nation are completely merged in the discourse of the BCP. The proletariat was no longer seen as a class within a stratified society; it had become in essence the people and notably included the Party, which, at the same time, was the soul of the state. The Party-state then merged with the body as a whole, at the same time as being its head" (Sykgelos 2011: 242). This confirms the interpretation given here of the framework the Bulgarian communists developed before World War II, in part borrowing from the Russian experience: society must follow the working class, but the working class's independence is in fact quite limited because it is to be guided by the party acting as an avant-garde.

Bulgarian Stalinism indeed does not fit well in the idea of a social whole to be defended from united national positions. However, at a later point of time and in contrast with that initial period of BCP's rule, national unity was to become something upheld more and more strongly. Here are three examples.

The Macedonian question has always been a delicate topic in Bulgarian politics and a hindrance for smooth relations between the country and Serbia (and later Yugoslavia) and, to some extent, Greece. The Two Balkan Wars in 1912–13 and Bulgaria's participation in the World War I were greatly influenced by the ambition for joining Macedonian lands to the country. Bulgaria had tirelessly maintained the thesis that there is no separate Macedonian nation and that the population there is of Bulgarian ethnic origin. This view was revised with the implementation of the Comintern's tenets that recognized the existence of a Macedonian nation into the BCP position on the issue as early as the 1930s, but even more strongly after 1944. Under BCP's pressure, the Bulgarian state presented the majority of inhabitants of Pirin Macedonia (a part of Bulgaria's territory) as ethnic Macedonians. After Stalin's breach with the Yugoslav leader Tito and especially after Stalin's death, this idea was thoroughly revised, and Bulgaria resolutely denied the existence of any Macedonian minority on its territory and, what is more, insisted for Yugoslavia to respect the rights of ethnic Bulgarians in Macedonia. Around the end of the 1960s, this line was already completed and was to be unflinchingly followed until the advent of democratic change. After that, it became an official point of view of post-socialist governments, too. Multiple times BCP put the Macedonian question on the agenda of bilateral talks with Yugoslav representatives (including Tito and Macedonian leader Krste Crvenkovski) and actively sought Moscow's support in the disputes between Sofia and Belgrade.

The 1970s were a decade of concerted efforts for national reconciliation on the part of BCP, chiefly expressed in a degree of reconciliation with national history. The books of authors who had been stigmatized and persecuted due to their supposedly bourgeois nationalist positions (e.g., Simeon Radev, Dimitar Talev) came back in print. There was a restoration of some elements of state protocol rituals from the times of tsarist Bulgaria that had to do with the commemoration of historic anniversaries and official holidays. One of the symbols of Sofia was built—the Unknown Warrior Monument, where Bulgarian and international statesmen laid wreaths, and which featured the sculpted figure of a lion created by the long-time dead 'bourgeois' artist Andrey Nikolov; a statue that had been intended for that site, but had not been placed earlier due to ideological considerations. The Tsarevets Fortress in Veliko Tarnovo—the capital of late Medieval Bulgarian rulers—was restored. National historiography started a process of reassessment of figures such as Stefan Stambolov, whose rule at the end of the 19th had been until then completely stigmatized by the communist propaganda. Efforts at national reconciliation were crowned with the grand celebrations of the 1300th anniversary of Bulgarian statehood in 1981, which encompassed all spheres of cultural life and reached dozens of countries around the world through various initiatives (exhibitions, shows, concerts, translations) designed to demonstrate the greatness of Bulgarian culture and history.

One of the most lamentable instances of the Bulgarian communist regime's actions in flagrant breach of human rights was the so-called Revival Process in 1984–89 that launched a campaign of changing the names of ethnic Turks in Bulgaria with Slavic ones and 'proving' the thesis that their origin is Bulgarian. With its propaganda call for building a 'unified socialist nation', BCP reached quite radically nationalist positions that led to social tensions inside the country, many criticisms from abroad, and the emigration of hundreds of thousands of Bulgarian Turks to neighbouring Turkey. After an initial period in which the Communists had encouraged the priority development of so-called 'mixed regions' with sizeable ethnic Turkish population (fostering local rituals and traditions, publishing newspapers and magazines, stimulating cultural life, giving privileges to those who wanted to enrol in university studies, etc.), the party went to the other extreme and directed the repressive apparatus of the state against those who were not ready to accept this encroachment on their identity. Notwithstanding what the real motives for starting the Revival Process were, and how they should be assessed, it is without doubt that BCP resorted to fanning patriotic attitudes and mistrust for Bulgaria's long-time ruler, Turkey, in the Bulgarian society in order to consolidate people around its policies.

As I have pointed out, the national tendency in BCP's development is not a chance phenomenon, but it is to be even better understood if one takes into account the process of change of party generations. After all, political dynamics is determined by the dynamics of political elites. In the first years of communist rule, the leading political posts in the party and country were occupied by former emigrants in the USSR who had spent there a significant part of the period during which the party was banned and persecuted in Bulgaria. That was the case with three successive party and state leaders—Georgi Dimitrov, Vassil Kolarov, and Valko Chervenkov—but also with dozens of figures in the senior power echelon. They all returned from emigration with the inclination to follow, above all things, the Soviet example on most political issues, including the views regarding Bulgaria's national tradition. On the one hand, they were not well acquainted with the situation in Bulgaria, they had remained for a long time outside of national public life, and thus they were not able to fully adequately orient themselves in the options given by the local situation. On the other hand, survival in the purges visited by Stalin upon communist immigrants in the USSR had to make them learn to submit. But in the course of de-Stalinization, party power was gradually seized by representatives of 'national communists', who had experienced the organization's outlaw period and the anti-fascist resistance inside the country. Notwithstanding the degree and type of merits in their resistance activities, it was the peculiarities of the national situation that their political reference points stemmed from.

Those leaders often had an origin from the lowest social strata, and their views regarding politics were more closely related to the environment in which they operated than with others' experience or ideas. Todor Zhivkov's generation was an illustration for that change. Its representatives dominated senior party executive positions for three decades, or until the communist regime's collapse. In the 1970s, however, a process developed that consisted in attracting 'technocrat' cadres into top governmental positions. Those were people of pragmatic attitudes to politics and the economy, who were growing more distant in their thinking from the dogmatic Marxism-Leninism characteristic of the inner life of ruling Eastern Bloc parties. The technocrats in power included sons and daughters of party dignitaries or persons of immaculate proletarian origin who had the opportunity to broaden their skills and knowledge. But they also included heirs to famous bourgeois families—like mathematician Blagovest Sendov or historian Alexander Fol—who had won for themselves high political or research positions. The class and party criterion considered to be central for socialist systems of a Soviet type was broadened to include not only peasants from the poorest Bulgarian regions but also elements from enemy classes. This too is telling about BCP's attempt to evolve into a 'party of the entire people'.

One could object that a party with such claims could hardly have existed under the powerful hegemony of the Soviet Union. Bulgaria was in fact the most loyal among Russian satellites, a country which not even once in the entire socialist period openly disputed Moscow's position, including what is remembered in history as the Brezhnev Doctrine: the stipulation that the socialist choice of each country from the Eastern Bloc was guaranteed by the USSR, including by means of force. No dramatic protest events occurred during Bulgaria's socialist period, at least since Stalin's death. In 1953, the Berlin Uprising erupted in an inherently internally unstable GDR, which had to constantly measure itself against its West German counterpart. In 1956 the Hungarian Revolution threw hundreds of thousands of Hungarians in desperate resistance against the merciless dictatorship of rulers imposed by Moscow. In 1968 the Prague Spring gave Czechoslovak citizens the hope for 'socialism with a human face', socialism that did not come with Soviet directives. In the 1970s and 1980s, strikes in Poland and the ascent of Solidarity contested not only inefficient state policies but also the domination of Russia, which had four times participated in partitioning of Polish lands. No counterparts of those events were to be seen in Bulgaria. The country did not either experience problems analogous to the ones in Russia and Romania raised by the identities of the border Moldavian and Bukovinian regions. Bulgaria was the most pro-Soviet country and BCP was without doubt the most pro-Soviet among communist parties in the Eastern Bloc.

A significant part of the Bulgarian society during the regime, however, did not view Soviet hegemony as something incompatible with furthering the country's national tradition. This view was backed, first and most obviously, by the cultural, linguistic and family closeness between the Russian and Bulgarian peoples. To this we can add what appeared to many as the fact of the coincidence of Soviet intentions and Bulgarian national goals. BCP strived to fulfil its modernization project with the USSR's help. And in the eyes of many Bulgarians, society's principal objective—getting rid of poverty—was to be achieved only with Russian help. Having been made the subject of mass propaganda, the 'Russian link' was a working one in the minds of the public. There was an expectation that resources and opportunities for Bulgarian national development would come from Russia. True, in too many instances the veneration for the Russians took on an unpleasant or humiliating garb, which the majority of independently thinking Bulgarians were justified in rejecting. Yet, attitudes towards Bulgaria's 'big brother' were not to be reduced to that.

The thesis that positive change in Bulgarian national development was to be expected from Russia was provided with further arguments in the years of the Perestroika. The messages for glasnost and democracy coming from Moscow inspired strong hopes in Bulgaria, especially among the intelligentsia, who saw one of the chief problems of the long lived socialist model in the barriers for the freedom of speech. In the USSR, the taboo was lifted from many topics from the past and present that for decades could not be publicly discussed. The periodicals heralding the Perestroika—*Argumenty i fakty, Moskovskie novosti, Ogonek*—were widely read in Bulgaria. Intellectual circles in Bulgaria acquired newly issued Soviet original and translated works of fiction which before that had been banned or had no chance to see print. Magazines such as *Novy mir, Nash sovremennik*, and *Inostrannaya literatura* played a major role in changing—and refreshing—the intellectual climate in Bulgaria. Against the backdrop of the Bulgarian regime's manifest reluctance to open doors to glasnost,

Gorbachev's course met with wide support in the country. Zhivkov and Gorbachev came to be seen as incarnations of, respectively, the status quo and change. So in contrast to many other CEE countries, the impulse for democratization in Bulgaria was pro- rather than anti-Russian. What is more, the USSR inspired hopes for change in 'our' status quo. BCP and its rule were not yet seen as Moscow's 'fifth column', as proxies for a foreign political will, or as a comprador bourgeoisie. Those views were to arise after the fall of the communist regime, in the course of the political clash between communists and anti-communists. Before that, they were not widely held in Bulgaria.

The national tendency, or the attempt to become 'party of the entire people', turned out to be more important for BCP's political legitimacy than the formal stages into which party ideologues partitioned the history of the regime in an attempt to present it as an 'constant ascent' from the dark past into the bright future—the stages variously called 'real socialism', 'developed socialism', 'new model of socialism', etc. Those stages were part of the party's programme development and had their importance. But in the eyes of the Bulgarian society, that programme development, marked as it was by solemn declarations for transitions to new and higher phases of the communist idea's implementation, could be reduced to a series of ideologemes. As a whole, they were accepted by the people, but they did not bring them fundamental meaning and possessed vitality only as long as the regime satisfied certain criteria for justice, equality and successful fight against poverty.

BCP's great achievement that was to exert a palpable influence on the party's political presence in post-socialist times is the circumstance that during the last two decades of the regime it came to be accepted as part of the Bulgarian society (Kassayie 1998)—even by people of provenance and thinking diverging from the party's course, and even by those who in various ways suffered from its rule. Saying that it was accepted does not mean to say the party was approved or acclaimed. Yet, even for people with an anti-communist past, the party did not appear as a 'foreign formation'—as an alien and artificially transplanted entity—but rather as something natural in their lives. The party may have held for such people entirely negative connotations (to do with the social climbing, unprincipled adaptability, incompetence, voluntarism, suppression of others' opinions, and rejection of outside people that all characterized many of the party's organs and cadres in all areas of public life)—but it was not, so to speak, a metaphysical enemy. Many manifestations of adaptability and cooperation were to be witnessed among the 'class' enemies of the communists. Even a desire for membership in the party arose in some, so that they may become part of the system and progress in their lives and careers. It was purely pragmatic, and not ideological motives that led those people to such a course of action.

Thanks to its political behaviour, around the end of the regime BCP could claim to be a representative 'sample' of Bulgarian society. The party's close to one million members (each of every nine Bulgarians) reflected the social and professional divisions in the population. The same also applies for the first years of democratic transformation when the party had to reassess its public and political role in competition with newly created political forces, under the name of BSP (see Table 2.2.2.).

Table 2.2.2.
Structure of the party electorate and the Bulgarian population (by status, in %)

	BSP	Bulgarian population (age 18+)
Workers in state enterprises	42.2	43.1
Workers in private sector	1.6	1.6
Civil servants	11.3	11.2
Defence and police officers	3.3	1.9
Liberal professions	9.4	9.7
University students	1.4	2.3
Retirees	3.4	5.1
Unemployed	23.7	19.9
Teachers, doctors, etc.	2.4	2.5
Others	1.3	2.0

Source: Center for the Study of Democracy, May 1991

We can see that, initially, the structure of BSP's electorate almost reproduced the structure of the Bulgarian electorate as a whole. Security agencies officers (the old regime's repressive apparatus!) were more strongly represented among BSP voters; conversely, there was a weaker representation of the student community (which preferred change). But seen as a general 'sample' of society after a long time in rule, the party had pronouncedly started to turn into a conservative formation—not 'conservative' in the Western sense having to do with rightist value interpretations of order, religion, family, and economic life but rather in the sense of preserving and developing an already established tradition and expressing a leftist social conservatism.

Because of this, BSP began to increasingly strongly exemplify a number of stereotypes that came to be entrenched in public consciousness (with a positive or negative colouring) and came to constitute an important ingredient of the party's subsequent public image as a democratic socialist party (see, e.g., Karasimeonov 2010: 23–26). Among those stereotypes was statism, the expectation that BSP would be looking for solutions of most of the issues facing society and the economy via state intervention above all, and that it would presuppose that the state is the principal actor in the nation's strategic development. Closely connected with statism were the expectations that the party would play a leading modernizing role in the country, that it would delineate the country's future chiefly by way of industry and technologies, and that it would be prioritizing their development. A tendency towards nationalism was another clearly expressed peculiarity that was to direct for a long time some voters of nationalist tendencies towards supporting the former Communists, and that would make them treat the party as a patriotic force counteracting the anti-communists perceived to be under strong foreign, i.e., Western, influence. As part of BSP's image, Russophilia did not conflict with nationalism but rather found expression in an understanding that the party would support the Russian vector in Bulgarian politics and would serve as the political expression of some enduring attitudes in Bulgarian society. Egalitarian beliefs are traditionally popular in Bulgaria and in effect there has been no party, apart from BCP, which has officially committed itself to transforming them into a steady characteristic of the social order, and which has thus retained the position of their proponent after the end of the regime. Traditionalist views regarding culture and everyday life complete this party image, which was further developed using the practice of rejecting and fighting against modern (of course, predominantly Western) influences. It in effect turned into a defence of the patrimonial worldview of many Bulgarians.

For Bulgaria, the end of the communist regime set in 'with decisive help from abroad' and to a large degree not under the pressure of internal resistance and discontent. At the same time, one must stress that the legitimacy of BCP's rule around its end was facing challenges that can easily be recognized as constituting a crisis. In the 1980s, the modernization strategy that had opened the doors to an impressive industrial and infrastructure development could not find answers to the creeping stagnation. Expectations that BCP would continue to lead the country to progress, be it at a high price, started to appear poorly grounded. The energy crisis, the dwindling Soviet subsidies, and a string of other problems broadened the space for public distrust. If before people thought that the party knew what it was doing, even though many viewed those things as bad, from a certain point on, the sense of direction was lost and replaced with the impression of chaotic improvisation. Equality, in the name of which the party had generated a solid social support for itself, especially among poor social strata, was put to doubt. The privileges enjoyed by the communist elite, the so-called nomenklatura, were slowly but perceptibly growing with time and the 'opening up' of the regime. It became apparent to society that a "new class" (using Đilas and Voslensky's terminology) was indeed forming—a new class living in luxury and sporting serious corruption opportunities as well as a tendency to form aristocratic dynasties. It turned out that BCP did not manage to find solutions to the expectations of younger generations, either[32]. In contrast with their parents, the majority of whom had experienced social and material progress during the socialist period, the new youth of Bulgaria took for granted their social status and opportunities, and thought they deserved more. They viewed the private residences they owned as mere panel building flats—not as lodgings furnished with the facilities of civilization, which could have as well been absent. The Lada was not seen as a car of one's own but rather as a vehicle that is no par to a Peugeot or Mercedes. The different types of garments did not represent progress from the misery of the past but rather symbolized greyness and simplicity compared to the diversity in foreign fashion magazines. And so on. Of course, consumer discontent was not the only factor. The regime had generated conditions for broader information and knowledge, which on their turn demonstrated the limitations of this very regime and fed the perception of inadequate field for personal fulfilment of the young.

BCP's rule had in effect created a large working class, which had been absent from the country before that. As a matter of fact, this working class—

---

32 Regular surveys registered an increasing alienation of the Bulgarian youth from the regime and its policies, even reaching the extent of transforming the young people into a 'collective dissident" (Mitev 1987).

which was supposed to be viewed as ruling and as the foundation of support for the communists—was far from exhibiting the expected 'class' consciousness in some critical moments. Industrialization and urbanization in effect deprived people of the property they owned before that in their villages, and this was hard to deal with, notwithstanding the pettiness of that property.

Every long stay in power, even when its fruits are viewed as positive, gives rise to inclinations towards change. BCP's more than four decades' rule is no exception. A significant part of Bulgarians were already tired of the practices and rituals used by the party in the exercise of power. They were also tired of seeing for 30 consecutive years the same person on TV—Todor Zhivkov. That is why it is not surprising that the end of the regime was met with hopes for a better future. This is even more so, given that the party's conservative image sooner or later had to produce radicalism as response. As we saw, BCP had succeeded in achieving its sustainable and stable entrenchment in Bulgarian public life. Party ranks included representatives of the diverse strata and professional group of the Bulgarian society, and BCP entered the new period of free democratic political competition with much better social resources and self-esteem than many of its 'fraternal' parties. But even at that point of time, it became apparent where support for the party was growing thinner—among the youth and workers, i.e., precisely in those circles where leftist parties should as a rule be dominant. BCP had to find its road ahead given that heritage and given that image in the minds of the public.

2.3 The Party in the Transition and the Transition in the Party

The November 10, 1989, fall from power of the long-time Bulgarian party and state leader Todor Zhivkov formally amounted to a 'change of guard'. It took place at a party plenum, in the absence of street pressure. The word was given to procedure, not revolution. The decisions taken were validated in a timely manner by the requisite state institutions. During the following few weeks, it appeared as if one team was going to replace another along the way of implementing a Perestroika of the socialist regime in the country. Of course, the change was in practice much more fundamental, and its adequate context were the processes going on in the entire—already crumbling—Eastern Bloc. By virtue of its geopolitical commitments and by virtue of events taking place 'outside' the country, Bulgaria could not remain untouched even if there were no apparent signs of regime collapse similar to those in most other CEE countries.

The transition that has been called 'a transition to democracy' encompassed all areas of politics, economy, and public life. One of the first dimensions of that change involved putting into question of the hegemony of ruling parties. Bozoki and Ishiyama (2002) have placed a special focus on the so-called adaptation strategies of CSPs. In most cases those practically amounted to *survival* strategies and, what is more, strategies that initially seemed to bear no fruits giving hopes for such survival. It is a plain fact that in less than 2 months, from mid-November to the end of 1989, all CEE communist regimes collapsed. With one notable exception: the Bulgarian one.

BCP indeed is a special case. It "survived the debacle that swept away Communist reformers after the fall of the Berlin Wall. This was largely because civil society was not yet so developed [...], nor were opposition forces so powerful" (Lévesque 2010: 331). In the weeks and months after November 10, 1989, party leaders were talking about reforms and changes, but did not see reasons for a radical transformation of their identity. To the contrary, they seemed to be convinced that they were following the right way and that under the new conditions the party had to serve the function of a reformist force just like before (Raichev and Stoychev 2008). BCP entered the democratic transition with the self-esteem of a party with no serious opposition that was enjoying the clear support of a conservative electorate and that did not see real stimuli for change (Spirova 2008). On the contrary, warnings existed that "[t]he superficial, and in the eyes of the majority of members, purely tactical remodelling of the party, was to prove a perennial Achilles heel for the BSP" (Dimitrov 2001: 42). We can imagine how absurd it would have seemed to the Polish or Hungarian society if at the same point of time the PZPR or MSzMP had declared their ambitions to be the leading force in the democratic transformation. Under one form or another, the former CEE communist parties had to admit that their rule had been unsuccessful. BCP, on its part, distanced itself not from the results of the socialist regime but only from the 'deformations' caused by Zhivkov and his entourage. In any case, its strategy was a strategy of adaptation, not survival.³³

The differences with former 'fraternal' Eastern Bloc countries now come sharply into relief. The postponed question regarding the identity of the Bulgarian communists, the heterogeneity and controversies of their party life, their diverse social base—all of that, combined with high electoral results, easily became one of the central subjects of research in Bulgarian political science after 1989 (Karasimeonov 1997a). The majority of authors working on the issue have pointed out the BCP's deep roots in the Bulgarian society. The modernization strategy that the party put to effect in the course of its single-handed rule and the lack of competing visions for the country's development until the very end of the regime turned into the fundament of the party's unquestionable domination in Bulgarian post-Zhivkov politics: "In the aftermath of 10 November 1989 the Communist Party retained all the resources needed to decide the course of events and control the process of change... [I]t was left practically on its own, without a real opposition to give legitimacy to the changes" (Karasimeonov 1996: 255). The opposition was indeed weak (Elster *et al.* 1998: 261–264). One could find all the prerequisites for an 'elite-driven transition' led by the former communists (Dimitrova 2002: 207).

The modernization strategy turned out to be of greatest significance. With the collapse of the socialist regime, BCP did not consider its role in Bulgarian society as terminated. The party did not think that the end had come to the official objectives in the name of which it had been exercising state power for more than four decades. Therefore, the party did not also think that it must step down from the stage or look for completely new causes. In the other Eastern Bloc countries (except Romania), the policies of communist parties had led to some degree of nationalization ('socialization') of production and distribution. From then on, the conclusion matured that efficiency in governance now depended on opening the door to the market. It

---

33 The change indeed appeared to be of a "Down with Zhivkov!" type rather than of a "Down with Zhivkov's model for socialism!" type. It is a symptomatic fact that at the 14th extraordinary BCP congress in January and February 1990, invited delegates included not only figures who had been expelled from the party due to dissident activities but also ones who had been expelled due to their Stalinism. They represented completely opposing tendencies of political thinking. The only thing in common among them was that the degree to which they rejected Zhivkov's leadership (Mitev 2011: 31).

is telling that all economic reforms in CEE launched in the de-Stalinization process and later were aiming at broadening the market's influence, at reassessing the planned economy, and at implementing an economic liberalization (Baeva 2010: 47). Those reforms, however, clashed with factual limitations imposed by the rules of functioning of the European socialist community and the parties' ideology. That is why pro-market reforms could only be half-hearted and their consequences could only be far from optimal. The changes in the late 1980s and early 1990s took a course in which former communist parties had not proven their skills, and the initiative had to be transferred to other hands.

BCP, on their part, also sought forms in which to introduce market elements in the economic policy of Bulgaria already in the 1960s (Crampton 2005: 193–194). With varying intensity, those efforts continued in the following decades and were especially sped up during the late years of Zhivkov's rule (Giatzidis 2002: 34–38). At a first glance, the trend was like those in the 'fraternal' countries. But there were important differences. Feigned or actual, superficial or thorough, the reforms implemented by the Bulgarian communists were only one side of the coin. The other side reflected their conviction that in, its broad parameters, the modernization course of the country was correct but unfinished. According to the BCP elite, the country had still much to achieve on the road of modernization in order to 'catch up' with the European models of a developed country, independently from the market transformation of economic mechanisms. That is why the task that the party set for itself after November 10, 1989, was to find a continuation of its ('reformist') political role in the new waters in which the Bulgarian ship had set sail (BSPa 2008: 16).

As quickly became clear, the roughness of those waters depended to a large degree on the manifestations of political pluralism indispensible for democracy. No matter how one is to assess the readiness of the Bulgarian communist elites for the market economy, we must admit that they had practically no readiness for political pluralism. The last 70 years of the party's existence had passed either in a situation of a de facto existence of a single party, or in a struggle for domination that rejected any pluralist view of political life, or in an outlaw status. In the Perestroika years Todor Zhivkov introduced the concept of 'socialist pluralism' to refer to the richness of opinions and interests of people in society—within the confines of the old regime and system, and not as could be formulated in the presence of multiple parties (Kandilarov 2010: 138–139). Zhivkov's thesis that in Bulgaria there is no soil for parties other than BCP was based on his overall policy of turning BCP into a 'party of the entire people'. We could accept to some degree that it corresponded to the relative homogenization of Bulgarian society about the end of the regime; a society that was marked by the lack of a clearly expressed cleavage structure back then and also during the democratic transition—notwithstanding the multitude of active situational factors (Karasimeonov and Lyubenov 2013). Political parties can however spring up not only on the basis of strong and deep social rifts. And the citizens' right to refer their expectations to different parties could not be denied if BCP did not want to isolate the country from global processes and to make a step back not only from November 10, but also from Zhivkov's policies; in other words, if it did not want to turn the page of change.

In that sense, in Bulgaria, in contrast to other CEE countries, the initial steps of liberal democratization depended on the behaviour and initiative of the Communist Party, which was renamed to Socialist. It was hardly possible for a pluralist democratic system to take hold without including some place allotted to that party: "In fact, it is probably BSP's integration into a competitive party system, and their adoption of the rules of the democratic game, that will do the most to legitimize and stabilize the new democracy in Bulgaria" (Kanev 1996: 186).

During the socialist period, Bulgaria had not given birth to a powerful dissident movement or to non-communist civic organizations of significant public weight (Spirova 2008: 484). Some informal structures nevertheless arose around 1988–89. And already during the first weeks after November 10, 1989, former representatives of old political organizations that had been banned or dissolved by BCP in the course of taking hold of state power during the 1940s started to organize themselves in order to restore the participation of their formations in political life. Other groups chose to start building completely new parties. On December 7, 1989, SDS was founded as a coalition of 15 structures of differing views and ideas united by their ambition for political participation outside of the Communist Party. However, before the end of that year, they could hardly be said to have had any significant public influence or recognizable image, either separately or together in the coalition. BCP faced a choice in which it could not refer to national or international precedents and so had to decide on its own. One option was to adopt a passive behaviour of waiting during which it was highly probable that the party would start falling apart and that parts of it would migrate to other niches of the political spectrum, the power of the new formations growing in the meantime. The alternative meant for BCP to define its political adversary and look for public support in competition with that adversary. The dilemma was: disintegration or designation of an opposition (Karasimeonov 1996: 255).

Events showed that the second option was chosen. BCP could have taken advantage of its comfortable position of being able to make a choice at all. Other communist parties did not have such a choice, for their opposition was already structured (Poland, Hungary, Czechoslovakia). In Romania, communists went one step ahead of their Bulgarian counterparts—some PCR circles decided, instead of designating an outside opposition, to designate themselves as a ruling power in opposition not to other parties but rather to an overthrown regime and an already dead leader. The option chosen by BCP presupposed two things: preservation of party unity and a leading role in building political pluralism in Bulgaria.

BCP (later BSP)[34] turned out to be the only one among significant Bulgarian parties after 1989 to allow internal factions and ideological groups (Todorov 2013a). As we have seen, this option given by the party's statute was quickly put to practice, and the following few weeks saw the founding of dozens such structures with different goals, platforms, messages, and weight among party members. We are justified in thinking that this was the way for the party to stay unified and not split at the crossroads of post-socialist development. Political life and the debate among different points of view stayed inside the party. Those points of view received an opportunity for expression (not only an organizational one but also through media) and did not have to pay the price of splitting in order to defend positions alternative to the official party line. There can be no doubts that the initial result was positive. BSP remained strong and did not experience a collapse, in contrast with its counterparts in Poland, Hungary or GDR, but at the same time relatively quickly started functioning in a real democratic situation, in contrast with its counterparts in Yugoslavia, Albania the USSR and even Romania (Penev 1992: 63–64).

---

34 Let us recall that on April 3, 1990, the Bulgarian Communist Party changed its name to Bulgarian Socialist Party, keeping full organizational and programmatic continuity.

This achievement can be viewed from two sides. It is true that an abundance of ideological visions (Stalinist, neo-communist, social democratic, nationalist, etc.) found some form of coexistence within a single political organization. At the same time, however, the poor compatibility among some of those visions as well as the desire of party leader Alexander Lilov's team to manoeuvre among them and balance opposing poles naturally lead to a long-term ideological indeterminateness for BSP, and to a lack of strategically minded programme orientation and of a clear road (social democratic, neo-communist, or other) that could lead the party to the ideological hallmarks of the then current West European political life. A way out of that situation was attempted in the lasting efforts towards formulating the party's programme image in nationally specific political categories, using labels such as 'modern left party' that provoked not only objections among social democrats within BSP but also misgivings among the party's potential international partners.

BCP entered a dialogue with the just forming Bulgarian opposition. In itself this action should be viewed as positive. From then on, the party was to invariably insist on constructive political behaviour, on conducting the political process according to rules, norms, and institutions rather than under the pressure of the street or of leadership voluntarism, as well as on a peaceful transition that leaves no place for violence against political adversaries. However, there was sometimes a great distance between words and deeds. Conflict, rather than dialogue, often shaped BCP's (later BSP's) political course. Nevertheless, the party proved in practice that it did not view power as power at any price, and that it was not ready to defend it using all means (Kanev 2002). In the domain of pluralism, the party demonstrated a consistent parliamentary behaviour in the spirit of the constitutional provisions for democracy and rule of law (Pirgova 2011).

The dialogue with the opposition took place as a Round Table in January-May 1990, at which representatives of the former Communist Party and representatives of SDS discussed the foundations of democratic process, civic rights and freedoms, election and media laws. The format was familiar from the recent experience in Poland, Hungary and Czechoslovakia for dismantling the single-party socialist state and moving on to a liberal democracy. The Bulgarian case is, however, once again striking with its peculiarity. In Poland and Hungary, the until then ruling communist elites negotiated with an already organized opposition that sported an immense public support. In Czechoslovakia, the opposition stepped only recently onto the political stage, but in the course of the brief Velvet Revolution it managed to win the position as the key spokesperson for mass hopes for change. In Bulgaria, it was not the opposition that made the Round Table important, but the other way around. State radio and TV, at that time the only electronic media in the country, covered on a daily basis the sittings of this untraditional institution and in effect served to acquaint Bulgarian society with key opposition figures. One can hardly believe that BCP, which was still in full control of state media, allowed that by pure good will. In the first place, for BCP the Round Table served the function of 'legitimizing through antagonism'. In Poland, Hungary, and Czechoslovakia, political adversaries (communists and anti-communists) had been legitimized by their roles in the historical process, and the Round Table just reaffirmed an already present proportion of powers, in order to be able at that basis to work out decisions for the future that were at least partially acceptable for the two sides. In Bulgaria, the Round Table itself was a legitimizing mechanism and in fact created a proportion of powers, instead of reaffirming an already existent one. The Round Table fixated the opposition to BCP's rule and gave it the opportunity to gather public popularity and trust with its actions. But at the same time, it also fixated the still ruling party as an irreplaceable participant in the democratic process and as an adequate alternative to the opposition. In respect of state power, the mutual alternative of the two sides of the Table was formed. It became clear, that if not the former communists, then it would be the opposition who were going to rule the country. But, what is not less important: if not the opposition, then it would be the former communists who were going to rule—not one faction of that opposition against another (Raichev and Stoychev 2008). In the second place, the Round Table also served as a mechanism for sharing responsibility on the part of the ruling elite with an opposition that was still too weak and inexperienced to be clear about what kind of responsibility it could assume and regarding what. Here stands a conclusion in that direction: "Bulgarian RT [Roundtable Talks] were preemptive measure by the BCP. The preemptive activity was possible and successful because of a lack of a dissident and opposition tradition in Bulgaria" (Kolarova and Dimitrov 1996: 181). Therefore, the ground was laid for the formation of a communist-dominated two-party system (Drezov 2000: 200–201).

To note that BCP had a role in the institutionalization of an opposition against itself does not mean to assert some conspiracy theory or to presuppose some ubiquitous powers of the party. The new party formations, in particular SDS, did not possess organizational experience compared to the communist party. Part of that experience was externally obtained by those organizations. BCP (later BSP) helped the opposition with material resources, granting it the use of buildings and vehicles as well as the opportunity to have its own print editions, etc. The Communists also 'helped' the opposition with respect to cadres. A large part of opposition functionaries did not have anti-communist biographies and, to the contrary, were BCP cadres that had changed camp. Their motives were diverse, including an earnest exasperation with the condition and behaviour of the old party and a true desire for change. Moral assessments of those actions were also diverse. For some, that was treason, while others saw it as pragmatism. But it is a fact that such people remained an important element of the opposition's image. In this case BCP demonstrated not only perspicuity (in seeing it must work for democracy) but also short-sightedness (in thinking that the opposition was going to be constructive). The party elite initially thought of SDS as a partner with which it could share responsibility. It saw an anti-nomenklatura force in the opposition, not an anti-communist one. During the first weeks, the new organization indeed turned against Zhivkov and his entourage, and its main messages gave a concentrated expression of the mass discontent with the privileges of the high party echelon. There were no strong voices raised against socialism, and BCP's governance was not subject to wholesale rejection[35]. The opposition however quickly started to take more radical positions (not without influence from West European countries and the US) that challenged both the ex-Communist Party and the entire period of its rule. The free elections for Grand National Assembly, negotiated at the Round Table for June 1990, were preceded by a campaign in which SDS was already decisively acting as an anti-communist organization. The central slogan of the campaign was *45 Years Are Enough*, which referred to the socialist period as a whole—a negatively painted whole. And among SDS's campaign symbols that came to be most prominent in the public's eye was the so-called 'map

---

35 It is symptomatic that at the Round Table's first sittings, SDS representatives were using the Communist Party form of address, 'comrade'.

of skulls', in which Bulgaria's territory was marked with the sites of the communist labour camps from the past.

The orientation towards political pluralism implied that BSP had to give up its convenient status of a party-state and to find its place in the political spectrum. It had to give up being the Party with capital 'P' and become one of the parties. This was an issue that can easily be constitutionally solved, but in practice required an appropriate strategy, especially in the context of the already mentioned lack of experience in a democratic environment. The emerging pluralist system in Bulgaria, just like those in other countries from the collapsing Eastern Bloc, was looking to foreign reference points. Those points could no longer be Soviet or Russian. The standard scale of the West European democratic political process—left-centre-right— naturally turned into a model for the ideological space in the 'new democracies'. I must stress that I mean the left-centre-right scale in the guise it had acquired in the course of its European historical development until the end of the 1980s. But the CEE countries had been cut off from the context and logic of that development.

The distribution of political forces on that scale (moving from left to right) involves the articulation of a far neo-communist left, socialist and social democrats, liberal centrists, Christian democrats and conservatives, nationalists, and formations gravitating towards the radical extreme right (e.g., Smith 1990: 122–123). Organizationally, that distribution has found an expression in international structures (such as the Socialist International, Liberal International, etc.) and in the distribution of political groups in the European Parliament (e.g. the European People's Party, the Federation of Liberal and Democrat Parties in Europe, etc.).

The road taken by Bulgarian 'Narrow Socialists' after World War I and especially after winning control over the country in the late 1940s put them among extreme left political forces, officially subscribing to the Stalinist and post-Stalinist versions of the left. The ideology of so-called Marxist-Leninist parties further solidified that identity. At the same time, as we have noted, the objectives and results of their long rule had been increasingly imparting social conservative elements to their Marxist-Leninist image, something that was to acquire even greater significance during the democratic transition. In the beginning of the transition, BSP in fact played a conservative political role that was a guarantee for stability against the radicalism and extreme tendencies among anti-communist forces (Todorov 2013*a*). This conservatism was noted and analyzed parallel to its articulation in Bulgaria's new democratic situation. It was expressed in a fear of abrupt revolutionary change, a desire to maintain the organic wholeness of society, an overall negative attitude towards extremism, and a belief that reforms need to be implemented by an elite and to take place gradually (Penev 1991).

The European conservative tradition, however, is of rightist rather than leftist nature. This fact has made scholars admit that classifying BSP in the democratic political spectrum is a complex problem. One of the approaches suggests distinguishing between socio-economic and political identities of leading parties. In this way we can see that BSP was leftist in the socio-economic respect and rightist in the political respect, while its main opponent, SDS, was a new, urban, leftist political formation in the political respect and rightist in the socio-economic. BSP could be admitted to be leftist in so far as the socio-economic dimension is of chief significance both for mass perceptions and the party's self-identification (Kanev 1996). Another author, drawing a broader historical contest, has directly used the concept of 'right-left ambivalence' to describe the Bulgarian political reality. According to him, this ambivalence was already manifest during the communist regime. The forces that were established in power in the Eastern Bloc were leftist in an economic sense (since being directed against former owners), but they were politically actualized as rightist because from a certain moment on they were working most of all towards their own preservation (and found a vivid expression in the tendency towards gerontocracy of political elites). This ambivalence was also characteristic of democratization, albeit in a different way. From the point of view of political revolution the left formation was SDS, while the right one was BSP. But, on the contrary, with respect to economic transformations SDS were rightist and BSP leftist (Mitev 1992). There are authors who reject the appropriateness of the concept of political left and right for the Bulgarian situation. According to this view, the democratic changes in the Eastern Bloc were a revolutionary process similar to the upheavals in Western Europe and the US in 1968. In both 1968 and 1989 it came to the same pressure against the superrationality of the modern social system in the name of the dignity and rights of the separate independent person. But even though those two processes largely shared direction, we are talking by force of mere habit about the 'leftist' 1968 and 'rightist' 1989. That is why we should give up the instruments of left and right in analyzing what happened in Bulgaria and Europe and to accept its common contra-cultural identity. That is, on this model BSP was seen as a bearer of dominating culture, against which the forces of free individuals stood up, as politically represented by SDS (Dainov 1995).

The difficulties to determine a clearly distinguished left in Bulgaria's new democratic history have another objective foundation in the lack of a distinct cleavage structure in the late socialist Bulgarian society, something that Karasimeonov (1996, 2010) has discussed in his works. On the basis of those considerations, it is easier to explain the character of the dominant political conflict of the early 1990s, which was expressed in the opposition between communism and anti-communism. BSP and SDS did not come to antagonize each other as leftist and rightist political forces; instead, they turned into 'pseudo ethnic communities' (Mitev 1992) that were in practice striving to build parallel political spaces for themselves: one communist, which would proclaim itself reformist, and one anti-communist, which would proclaim itself democrat (Pirgova 2002).

For long years, SDS was a loose coalition of parties and organizations that could hardly be put under a common rightist denominator. The greatest influence within the Union right after its founding was exercised by the historical parties of the Social Democrats and Agrarians. They coexisted with trade union structures, environmentalist unions, monarchist and religious formations, student and rights activist societies, conservatives and liberals, and even successors of neo-fascists from the years of World War II. This diverse political space was united under the banner of anti-communism (Malinov 2010: 3–5). BSP appeared to be more homogeneous, but also organized its own political space. Here I mean not only the different ideological currents in the left from Stalinism to social liberalism which had their own formal factions, but also the party's political messages which were addressing the entire political spectrum. "There is almost no ideology that has not been in one way or another represented or approved by BSP" (Penev 1991:7)[36]. The impression was created that two spaces were in existence,

---

[36] During the stormy 1990, senior party functionaries spoke about the benefits of the monarchy; the party elite *en masse* took part in Christian Orthodox church services; the one-party socialist cabinet launched liberal economic reforms; in regions with ethnically diverse population, the party was in an open partnership with nationalist committees.

each independent of the other and each claiming to represent the entire people.
The 'legitimizing through antagonism' tactic chosen by BSP did good service to SDS's more radical wings. This gave rise to a strongly confrontational two-bloc "barricade" (Mitev 1996) political model of the democratic transition in Bulgaria, which gradually took over other possible models for development of the political process (Pirgova 1992). Each of the two poles united its supporters by way of antagonism against their common foe. If we accept with some qualifications Kitschelt's thesis about the peculiarities of communist regimes similar to the Bulgarian one, the conclusion is certainly justified that after the democratic changes the market-liberal and democratic forces were a "mirror-image of the unreconstructed postcommunist parties" with unclear programmes and aims, and bellicose messages (1995: 465).
At first sight, it appears that the conflict between communism and anti-communism had supplanted the left-right opposition. However, in practice it turned out that it was in the context of that radical two-bloc confrontation that the two big opponents would orient themselves towards the left or right political spectrum. The establishing of the classical typology did not draw resources only from the past or from mass attitudes but also from the different solutions for the problems with the democratic transformation of the country offered by the parties. For BSP, the question of its own place in a pluralist democratic environment increasingly took the shape of a question regarding the monopoly on the left spectrum. Party unity, which had been an issue of prime importance for BSP since its 14th congress in January and February 1990, would be much harder to achieve given a real competition within the left. Roughly said, it was much more probable for the different factions within BSP to remain part of the party if they knew that they had nowhere to go if they left. By entering into a sharp confrontation with SDS, BSP decided the issue of its 'leftist' monopoly and forewarned left-leaning people in Bulgaria that, without the party, they would be left defenceless against the powerful 'rightist' adversary.
Because of this, the potential leftist political space in Bulgaria—such as it existed after the fall from power of the communist regime—became BSP's space. The left and BSP came to be perceived as being almost identical. This result, far from being the product of necessity, stemmed from a consciously chosen political course. After 1989 in Bulgaria, due to ideological

and historical factors, agrarian parties, social democrats, environmentalists, and communists could all, in addition to BSP, claim their own place in the leftist spectrum. But for a long period of time no one was able to secure such a place. What is more, in the larger framework of the political process that thus emerged, it seemed that there was almost no one to make such a claim.

Bulgarian environmentalist structures had originated from the resistance against the industrial policies of the communist regime and the damage they inflicted upon the environment. It was environmentalist rallies that made a great share of dissident activities in the late 1980s (Krastanova 2012: 6–11). So for Bulgarian environmentalists, the former Communist Party was an original chief adversary. The same applies for the 'old' social democrats, who had a history of close to a century of conflict with BSP's predecessors, and who had been persecuted and banned by them. Part of Bulgaria's agrarians also had a similar unhappy fate. Another part, who ruled together with BCP during the socialist period using the communists' program and under their dictate, had lost much of their hold in the Bulgarian rural areas, where they were being successfully displaced by their 'senior' partner. After 1989, those agrarians, too, ostensibly distanced themselves so as to not be considered part and parcel of BCP. Social democrats, agrarians, and environmentalists entered into the anti-communist SDS coalition, or else formulated political views similar to those of the coalition. And even though some of them were to subsequently split and modify their rhetoric, they have remained adversaries to the left in people's minds, thanks to the logic of confrontation.

The case of the communist left is special. A possible early turn towards social democracy on the part of BSP could have perhaps opened space for more radical leftist formations. But, as we know, such a turn was not made. And even though the former communist party predominantly relied on its supporters from the socialist period and invariably insinuated, explicitly or covertly, that it remains 'their own', there were certainly those who were disappointed by the fact that BSP had abandoned the Marxist-Leninist interpretation of society and embraced the market economy. At the party referendum that changed BCP's name to BSP, almost a hundred thousand party members voted for retaining the old name of the party. Those people were a natural resource for extreme left formations. Such formations actually sprung up even before June 1990 elections, but did not succeed in making a convincing start. After that time, their political presence came to be marginalized even more (Karasimeonov 1997b). The reason for that is not that there were several of them. Even hard-line supporters of the former social order knew well that changes had come that required an update of strategy and tactics, while 'new' communist parties put their bets entirely on the clumsy party propaganda jargon from the past, which everyone had grown weary of. Here too, the confrontation model of the political role played its role in favour of BSP. If the 'new communists' viewed SDS as their veritable dangerous foe, then their reasons to oppose of the 'bourgeois' changes within BSP were losing some of their social legitimacy. Moreover, there was another factor which was actually playing in favour of the development of democracy on the Bulgarian soil. An authentic democratic drive in Bulgaria since 1989 would be impossible through the preservation of the radical left identity of the former communists. PDS in Germany and KSČM in the Czech Republic were able to remain loyal to radical left principles, but they acted in the context of existing powerful moderate left formations which served as guarantees of a truly democratic political change. In Bulgaria one could not find analogues of either SPD or the Czech Social Democratic Party. BSP was to play the democratizing role usually reserved for social democrats in CEE.

All of the factors discussed above allowed BSP to strengthen its 'left' monopoly. But the question remained open as to what to do with it. The Bulgarian society's inheritance from the old regime was a dominating state with powerful levers and resources for control as well as a predomination of state ownership in all areas. The main political parties were expected to formulate answers to the question as to what type of development this state would be employed in (Karasimeonov and Lyubenov 2013). The changes in the collapsing Eastern Bloc in 1989–90 were aiming for the liberalization of the economy, culture, and welfare systems. In West European political terminology this is viewed as a rightist political course. The failure of the socialist system—even though it directly involved the government projects of the communist party—was a blow on the political vitality of the left as a whole. For the left to have a chance for revival, it had to offer a socially acceptable leftist answer to processes to which rightist parties could much more naturally respond. It is highly debatable whether we should interpret electoral successes by leftist parties as revival of the left, in cases where they did not formulate such an answer. The following three questions are much in order here: "Is it not true that electoral success is ephemeral unless it is supported by a "left project" for the development of a society in a state of unpredictable transition? Does such a project exist, and if so, what are the chances for its realization? Are the left parties capable of accomplishing it?" (Kanev 1996: 184–185).

In contrast with the classic West European case, in which capitalism developed to a large degree spontaneously, unevenly, during many centuries, and in many forms, which in most cases were only subsequently sanctioned by states, after 1989 in CEE and especially in Bulgaria, it was the task of the state (and the parties that had taken hold of state power) to build capitalism and to turn it into a process governable 'from above' (Mitev 1996). What can be the role of a leftist party in the political delineation of the process of capitalist accumulation? In 1991–92 the dilemma looked roughly as follows: shock therapy or a smooth transition. The first alternative consisted of swift, radical reforms for withdrawing the state from all public area on the model developed and put to practice by Polish neoliberal financier Leszek Balcerowicz. The other alternative involved gradual steps that included elements of half-protectionism on the part of the state and longer periods of adaptation to change for the population. In Bulgaria, one could suppose that SDS would stand for the first alternative, while BSP would defend the second. And, formally seen, this was indeed the case. Yet, there were many qualifications hiding behind those broad generalizations. With a string of steps it took, BSP committed to swift liberalization and did not come to fill in with sufficient content its intentions for 'adaptation'. In 1994, the party, chaired by young economist Zhan Videnov, won absolute majority at general elections. The situation looked very similar to those of the former communist parties in Poland or Hungary. The societies' disappointments with slow reforms, declassation, sharpening of social inequality, and drop of living standard materialized in a decisive electoral support for the left. But there were also differences. The left came to power in Poland and Hungary in a completely different guise from the one it had built during the communist years. MSzP claimed that the rightists' reforms were slow and half-hearted, and offered radical liberal changes to society; what is more, using a political cooperation with liberals. SdRP even avoided calling itself 'leftist' and made a special point of advertising its pragmatism, in order to contrast it with the perceived Catholic dogmatism and intransigence of the right. BSP appeared to have changed much less, and in many respects it called not for trust in its 'new' image but rather for support in all that people associated the party with in the past—stability, social policy, care for rural areas, prioritization of industry—in counterbalance to the perceived radical and chaotic reformism of SDS.

The BSP government however did not succeed to formulate and defend its own 'leftist project' for rule. The internal pluralism of views within the party this time over turned out to be a shortcoming hindering the resolute upholding of a unified position. Some of the objective limitations of the environment—including the international environment—were opposing the implementation of many of the party's intentions. The impression arose that the party in power was acting ad hoc, without coordination and vision. There were many factors that led to Bulgaria's economic and financial collapse in the late 1996 and early 1997. Even without discussing them, I must mention that BSP definitely failed in erecting a 'leftist' alternative to the 'rightist' transition. It is controversial whether we can call BSP's rule a 'leftist government'. But it is certain that it did not bring Bulgaria a positive leftist experience. In 1997 Bulgarian capitalism was not more social than it had been in 1994.

Some authors have argued that the crisis within BSP and the heavy defeat at the early elections in 1997 were a stimulus for starting long postponed processes of renewal in the party (e.g. Spirova 2008). The situation in BSP was rendered even more complex by two further interrelated challenges. The first was the transformation of the main adversary SDS from a coalition to a unified party with categorically rightist self-identification and rightist programme for governance. SDS sent two very clear messages: that the successful road of development for the country passes through a government policy of thoroughgoing privatization, and that SDS and none other is the true modernizing force in the country. BSP was conclusively placed in the left party space—saddled with the popular perception that the left is a retrograde force unable to produce progress. In this sense, occupying an 'isolated' seat in politics, the party was lacking a 'European' identity and a competitive modernizing image to effectively counterbalance the 'European-path reforms' pretender, the SDS (Cholova 2008: 196–197). The second challenge was the first major split of the party. In the past, individual persons or groups had left the party and tried separate political paths of their own. But this time around, many leading party functionaries split, and what is more, the social democrat formation they created—the

Bulgarian Euroleft—entered the new Bulgarian Parliament. BSP's monopoly on the left was put under question. If the thesis prevailed that BSP was the retrograde left and the Euroleft was the modern left, then that potential risk could at some point become irrevocable reality.

BSP faced a choice of two roads: to try to defend the left from attempts for it to be rejected as part of the 'shady past' of the country, or to try to defend its monopoly on the left spectrum. The first road was harder, most of all because after Videnov's failure the party did not know what left programme alternative to rightist rule it should formulate. The second road was more akin to the party elite's mode of thinking. Thus the stance towards social democracy emerged for the party as its framework of development and political presence.

There were three main roads for the restoration of social democracy in Bulgarian political life after 1989 (Todorov 2013a). Those were: a refounding of the 'historic' social democratic party; divisions in the former Communist Party, such as those that led to the creation of the Euroleft; and strong social democratic currents within the former Communist Party, such as were favoured by party leaders after 1997. The logic of the Bulgarian political process marginalized the first option. The second and third options were interestingly interrelated. BSP's new leadership team, with historian Georgi Parvanov at the helm, considered that entering in direct public competition with the Euroleft could affect it negatively. The situation could easily be presented dichotomously—as a clash of 'new' against 'old'—and it could heap on BSP the negatives of being 'retrograde', 'non-reformed', and 'stuck in the past', while giving the Euroleft's image the positive resources of the country's European perspective and the then much discussed Third Way of the British Labour Party. That is why Parvanov's course in effect amounted to gradual and systematic efforts towards BSP's social democratization. If the party could take over the terrain of alternative social democratic structures, that would render them pointless. The radical anti-communist rhetoric of the 1997–2001 SDS cabinet created objective conditions favouring those intentions. The feeling that all that was 'left' was under the threat of lustration, expulsion from work, or other unfavourable measures on the part of the new rulers disposed the Euroleft and other smaller social democratic parties to be co-operative. They knew their voters would not be pleased by a categorical reluctance for dialogue and rapprochement with BSP, notwithstanding the distrust they harboured for the old party. At BSP's initiative, meetings of leftist organizations' leaders were held in the Bulgarian mountain village of Lesidren in 1997 and in the Greek city of Thessaloniki in 1998. Gradually, an agreement for common activities was reached, to be performed under the 'New Left' format. And even though the Euroleft decided to withdraw from the initiative and to run on their own in the following general election in 2001, Parvanov's tactic gave all indications to be a working one.

What were Parvanov's achievements? The turn in BSP's orientation in the field of foreign policy was of prime importance. Since the start of the democratic transition in Bulgaria, the party had been supportive of EU membership for the country, but at the same time it had been harbouring strong reservations against NATO and maintaining the perception of close ties with Russia, which it in fact did not have. The left received Moscow's support neither in the dramatic events of 1990–91, nor during its cabinet term in office in 1994–97. The turn took place almost unexpectedly. In spring 1999, BSP decisively stood out against NATO bombings in neighbouring Yugoslavia and organized protest rallies. Just one year later, party leaders succeeded in winning the internal party debate and to support with an express declaration Bulgaria's membership bid for the Euro-Atlantic structures.

Parvanov was also successful in preserving BSP unity so that the 1996–97 splits were to prove to be the last ones for a long period of time onwards. The party's social democratic turn was far from smooth. But no old or just emerging hard-line leftist factions gained ascendancy within the party[37]. The party leader was apt in manoeuvring among differing and often irreconcilable party circles. The preservation of the confrontational model in Bulgarian politics also worked towards the preservation of BSP's image as an alternative. And this was an image to be donned by BSP in its entirety, not by any separate party wing. The Euroleft's ambition to follow a constructive "nationally responsible" course and to support "reasonable" and "working" governance ideas, no matter whether they came from the rightists or BSP, turned out to be a failure. In the eyes of public opinion this appeared to betray inconsistency, a lack of ideas, and tendency towards un-

---

37 Although new factions indeed sprung up, such as the so-called 'generals wing', chiefly composed of figures related to the former secret services of the communist regime, or the Open Forum that initially united part of the hard-line supporters of the Videnov course.

principled compromise. And this behaviour was heavily punished at the 2001 election. It was very important for Parvanov to show that BSP was not isolated—that it was not, so to speak, sitting at the defendant's seat—but, to the contrary, it was a welcome partner for co-operation. In that sense, the construction of an election coalition of smaller parties around BSP, under the moniker Coalition for Bulgaria, was an important success. The coalition included neo-communist, social democratic, nationalist, and even ethnic organizations, which in that way were all integrated into BSP's orbit in the eyes of the public. Voters entertaining such views could vote for BSP and believe that their ballot was cast to further, say, nationalist or agrarian policies. And at the same time the BSP leaders received more freedom to develop policies that they viewed as correct, at the same time maintaining the perception of being active in other ideological directions.

BSP went on to lose for another general election in 2001, when the vote was won by the formation of just returned Bulgarian Tsar Simeon Saxe-Coburg-Gotha. But only five months later the BSP leader, on his turn, won the presidential elections, becoming the first Bulgarian socialist to be elected head of state by the people. Almost all analysts were extremely surprised. But in addition to the crucial role of specific situations during the campaign, Parvanov's tactics also turned out to have contributed to his victory. It was Parvanov who is to be credited for building the party's image not as an image of the left but rather as an image of change. This was something that received the sympathies and partial support of the Bulgarian society, which was looking for change after years of rightist rule. Even the competitors for the left-wing political field and the traditionally hostile trade-unions were not able to avoid declaring their full support for Parvanov (Kanev 2002: 96–98). Authors have described the results of Parvanov's as the finalization of BSP's transformation into "a European social democratic party" (Spirova 2008: 491), "part of the global and European social democratic community" (Kanev 2011: 246), "a modern and democratic party organization" (Karasimeonov and Lyubenov 2013: 417), "a decentralized and democratic social democratic party" (Todorov 2013a: 403). During his term in office as Bulgaria's President, Parvanov took part in the process of Bulgaria's achieving full membership in NATO in 2004 and EU in 2007. Parvanov had nominated BSP's young international relations secretary Sergei Stanishev for the party's next leader. Following more or less the direction given by his predecessor, Stanishev was to attain BSP's membership in the Socialist International in 2003 and the Party of European Socialists in 2005 and was to personally become the Bulgarian to achieve the highest position in the European party hierarchy yet by becoming the President of the Party of European Socialists in 2011.

It appears as if BSP has belatedly walked the road delineated by CSPs in Central Europe, in particular in Poland and Hungary—the road to social democratization and liberalization of policy views, including the due doses of adaptability and flexibility. The party's 2008 programme and statute reflected those tendencies, and even though they were extremely careful to avoid the words 'social democracy', they presented a party organization that was now different from that of the early 1990s. The party leaders were aware that a big part of party members and supporters did not support the social democratic turn, and so they did not officially refer to it. On the one hand, this minimized internal party upheavals. On the other, it created 'time-bombs' that could start to go off at some future more critical moment.

After more than a decade of democracy, the development in Bulgaria on its turn illustrates the above mentioned thesis that the debate on the post-communist left has been structured as a debate regarding the fate of CSPs. Around the time of Parvanov's election for president the following conclusion was completely valid: "The present and future of the left both still depend most of all on what is happening with BSP" (Kanev 2001: 16). Two of the central goals that had been facing BSP since 1990 had been achieved: to maintain party unity and to preserve the monopoly over the left space.

BSP's strong political position at the beginning of the 21st century stemmed from certain actions of the party's leader teams in complex situations but to a much greater degree from the country's pre-democratic tradition. The strength of that tradition was expressively attested throughout the transition. BSP as a party was part of the Bulgarian society and even its adversaries had to take account of that fact. We were able to see that a dramatic programme and political post-communist re-orientation was not a necessary condition for winning democratic elections. But we also saw an (apparent) paradox: in order to preserve its monopoly on the left, BSP in practice decided to give up on the idea to formulate a leftist project for the transition and for a full-scale strategy of its own against the dominant liberal vision. This is something admitted by party leaders. In his report for BSP's 45th Congress in June 2002, the new leader Stanishev stated that the transition had been 'rightist' and had not given a chance for the welfare state and social justice (Stanishev 2002). After defeat at the 2009 general elections, at a sitting of the 47th Congress in October, Stanishev formulated a similar conclusion: "We have remained being the same projection of a model inherited by the transition—a model that did not bring a feeling of justice and retribution in the public." (Stanishev 2009)

What was the chance that BSP was able to give?; and What was the exit from the model of the transition?—Those remained open questions.

3 Leftist Elite and Leftist Supporters: An Emerging Divide

3.1 Has the Socialist Leadership been Sliding 'Right'?

In the years after 1997, the Bulgarian Socialist Party's leaders committed to reforms that can be placed under the general label of a 'course towards social democracy' in spite of the concept's not being openly used in the party's vocabulary. A major political consequence of that change was the party giving up its bid to formulate an alternative to the rightist liberal model of the transition in Bulgaria. BSP accepted for a fact that it was not able to put forward a viable notion of a 'leftist transition' against the dominating ideas of a 'rightist transition'. The failure of the socialist Zhan Videnov cabinet came to be identified with a failure of the very possibility of an alternative 'leftist project' in government.

At first glance, this thesis is contradicted by official party documents. BSP leaders have kept on speaking about a 'leftist project' of their own during the period after 1997. The party's programme declaration from the May 2000 44th congress pointed out that the new challenges for the country, Europe and the world had stimulated the formulation of a "new leftist project for Bulgaria" (BSP 2008a: 228), based on a "new balance between market freedom and social security" (ibid.: 232–233). According to that plan, BSP was to always remain "a party of labour—a party of hired and free, of physical, intellectual, and managerial labour, a party of initiative and creativity" (ibid.: 231). A decade later, in October 2010, the party's 47th congress adopted a document called *Bulgaria 2020—a European Welfare State*, with the suggestive subtitle 'Chief Parameters of the Leftist Project'. According to that document, the left had to pursue "goals relating to the country's catching-up, in order to guarantee medium European levels of quality of life, competitive businesses, and prioritized economy sectors, under a guaranteed programmed fiscal stability." The welfare alternative offered was interpreted as "an organic unity of the welfare state, competitive economy and programmed budgeting." (BSP 2010)

The careful reading of those texts however calls for criticism against the use of the word 'project', if it was meant to refer to an all-encompassing vision for society's development. What we find are two other elements that distinguish the left from the right—as a position, not as a project. Those are, on one hand, the values and principles lying at the basis of a party's messages, and, on the other, the policies specifying and expressing those values and principles at the political level. The very idea of a project presupposes a systematically formulated disagreement with the legacies, actions and intentions of other political actors as well as a systematic and opposing view of one's own.

The rightist liberal project for the Bulgarian transition received its most completed and distinctly expressed guise during the term in office of the 1997–2001 SDS cabinet. I am calling it a 'project' because it envisioned a change of Bulgaria's model of development in practically all areas of social and economic life—and that was something that its political bearer, SDS, to a significant degree put into practice. It was that cabinet that implemented the decisive part of the privatization of state enterprises that had retained the structure of their ownership from the times of the communist regime. The withdrawal of the state took place chiefly using the technique of so-called cash privatization, which in most cases gives decision making freedom to the private investor and minimizes the roles of employees and society as a whole. The state's fiscal and budgeting affairs were put under strict discipline following the guidelines of international financial institutions (the International Monetary Fund and the World Bank). Their support for Bulgaria, including their financial support, was given in return for specific and measureable reforms mostly involving spending cuts seen as a road to stabilization. New models for reform were developed and adopted in healthcare, social security, the retirement system, and partially in education, under which the principle of solidarity was strongly limited in favour of market regulation. A regulation of economic actors was introduced that allowed administrative control but not direct participation in the market on the part of the state. On its turn, the currency board, created after the 1996–97 crisis, deprived the state of an independent monetary and credit policy (see Detrez 2006: lxii-lxii).

BSP mounted strong criticisms against SDS's governance project with its very start. Later, when its first results came to show, those criticisms were to grow into a rejection of all of the project's aspects, except Bulgaria's bid for EU membership. I would like to refer to another strategic document of the Socialist Party, the political platform called *BSP—A Party of Change, a*

Party of the Future from the 45th party congress in June 2002. In that document, the diagnoses of the current situation in the country were more than pessimistic. The outcome of the transition, argued BSP, was the establishing of "capitalism at its most deformed," which led to "a social, economic and spiritual decay". In a social and spiritual perspective those results were allegedly expressed in a "dismantling of the welfare state", a demoralization of society due to the "strong stratification and marginalization of many Bulgarians", an "explosion of crime", an "explosion of poverty and unemployment", an "abdication" of the state from education, research, and healthcare. The governance of the economy, argued the Socialists, came to be based "exclusively on the demands of the market". Agriculture experienced a "grave devastation". Privatization allegedly turned into a "process of plundering and destroying state property". The administration came to be "criminalized" due to the perceived "symbiosis of business and criminal groups". Huge national resource capitals—including human capital—came to be squandered. For all of that, according to BSP, there was a clear ideological and political culprit. The ideological guilt was to be carried by the "shock monetary rightist economic model". And the SDS was "the principal exponent and factor for the implementation of this rapacious, antinational, and anti-constitutional politics" (BSP 2008a: 243–249).

Since the Socialists argued that the democratic transition took place according to a rightist model and inflicted heavy damages on industry, agriculture, the social systems, and people, the question as to the way out of this situation was only natural. It was obvious that solutions had to be sought within the confines of market economy. BSP leaders described the priority of state ownership, the negative views on capital and business, and the limited nature of economic reforms as "dogmas of the past" from which the party was now free (BSP 2008a: 249). Therefore, it was not the mechanisms of the market economy but the role of the state that was to be reassessed. And the state was found to have significantly withdrawn from its positions in welfare regulation.

It was thus that the question regarding the welfare state came to the foreground for BSP (Pirgova 2013). Already in its definitional characteristics, the welfare state presupposes some degrees of inclusion of individuals in societal and economic life through the policies of the state; i.e., it presupposes some proportion between the regulative roles of the market and of political redistribution. The classical reason for the emergence of the welfare state is rooted in the need for the state to serve an integrative function regarding society. After European modernity introduced the market into the role of a leading social regulator, risks for the efficiency of the emerging representative system started to arise. Large groups of people started to 'drop out' of the market system. Without producing, they were also not in a position to consume and therefore—to participate in the reproduction of market relations. And in order for the state to not give up its claim to be granting civil rights to those persons, it had to take up an additional commitment towards them, preparing the ground for a legal balance between the opposing interests of those 'up' and those 'down' (Wahl 2011: 20–28; Kaufmann 2012: 202, 217). On this general basis, different types of welfare state shaped up, depending on the history, tradition, experience, and specific situation in different countries. The story briefly sketched above was revived and received an update in post-socialist CEE where the restructuring of economies along market lines provoked similar results and similar motives for 'emergency' reassessment (Inglot 2008: 214–219; Offe 2009: 237–241).

What type of protection BSP was ready to offer for vulnerable groups is not just a theoretical question. It also asks about the heart of the party's interpretation of the welfare state and the content that interpretation was to be given. The favouring of a limited and supplementary role for the state is a rightist policy course incarnated in practice by the SDS's social model. Classical social democracy to a much greater extent stands behind the idea of equal opportunities as a principle of organization of the welfare state (Collignon 2012: 45). But it was just in that time period that the West European social democratic forces themselves started to significantly revise their views. Having adopted West European reference points for building its strategy of development after the communist regime, Bulgaria was naturally under the influence of economic notions dominating in the West, including regarding the role of the state and of economy in society. This is valid to at least an equal degree for BSP after 1997 when the party was intensively trying to find its way to the European social democratic family and to accept the framework in which that family envisioned the future of the leftist idea.

What was the context of the welfare state concept that came from the West? During the 1990s, there was a process of re-thinking of the welfare state's functioning, in part stimulated by globalization and the rise of neo-liberalism. Opinions spread that, in its Cold War form, the European welfare state is unwieldy and inefficient, that it stifles growth and impedes entrepreneurship. A distinct political expression of those views was given by two European leftist leaders, the 1997–2005 British Prime Minister Tony Blair and the 1998–2005 German Chancellor Gerhard Schröder. In June 1999 they published a joint document of key significance for the turn taken by the European social democratic movement. In that paper, Blair and Schröder (1999) declared that most people had long abandoned the worldview offered by the dogmas of left and right, and that a new pragmatic approach had to be found. According to the two leaders, the task of the left was to create opportunities for creativity and innovations, and to foster the economic dynamics of societies. That is why they rejected or corrected some important 20th century leftist postulates. In a nutshell, Blair and Schröder's conclusions go as follows. Striving for social justice does not mean striving to equalize incomes. The means to achieving social justice are not greater levels of public spending. It is not always the task of the state to mend the errors and failures of the market. Rights are not always superior to responsibilities because else responsibility would be foremost a burden for the state and not for the separate individual. National governments do not possess the capacity of managing the economy in a way to ensure growth and jobs.

These intentions were qualified as pushing forward neoliberal ideas about the role of the state in economy (Lavelle 2008: 20). A little later Schröder launched a large-scale 'paradigmatic' reform of the German welfare state in such a depth as had not been undertaken since World War II (Fleckenstein 2011: 1–2), and, moreover, strikingly similar to that implemented by right-wing governments in France (Palier 2010: 372). Schröder's plan of reforms, which came to be known as Agenda 2010 (Schröder 2003), was aiming for market liberalization and involved a reduction of taxes, smaller subsidies for medical treatment, shrinking of retirement rights, and a decrease of unemployment benefits. In the UK, Blair initiated changes that were to be sharply criticized by leftist circles in the Labour Party, who described them as continuation of Thatcherism in a new guise (Heffernan 2011).

BSP did not sympathize with those ideas, and they were not automatically transplanted to Bulgaria. But the message issued was too clear to be disregarded. After all, SPD was considered the most influential European 'exporter' of hegemonic left ideas to CEE (Sloam 2005). During a period in which the Bulgarian socialists wanted to come out of isolation and to find a new field of activity, it was important that Western Europe was not offering active support for leftist policies of a classical type.[38] To the contrary, what Western Europe was showing was a sliding of the left towards the centre and an upgrade of political liberalism with economic liberalism. Undergoing a process of social democratization, BSP apparently decided that it was not up to the party to play the role of an entity opposing the tendencies dominating in the social democratic left, all the more after having once in the early 1990s attempted and then given up interpreting the modern European left in its own independent way. The turn of the century was however a different point of time for the country, and this has to be taken into account. After more than a decade of transition, the Bulgarian society was much more drastically polarized into rich and poor than the German or the British society and was also enjoying much weaker protection of social rights. Political parties were also different. BSP was the successor to a party whose legacy was much more to the left in the political spectrum than was the case with German Social Democrats, not to speak of British Labour.

BSP tacitly assumed that in Bulgaria there is a hegemonic social and economic philosophy of a rightist nature and destructive consequences, which nonetheless is hard to reverse and, in the short term, is only susceptible of partial limiting. Notwithstanding that BSP ruled by itself or as part of a coalition during the first and most decisive phase of the transition (1990–91), then gave parliamentary support to another cabinet (1992–94), and was to later again directly participate in the executive (1995–97, 2005–09, 2013–14), the party claimed that the transition was not 'its own' but rather 'belonged to others'. In other words, it was the party's stated view that others

---

38 The question however remains open as to why the Bulgarian left followed so closely the actions of Blair and Schröder while almost neglecting those of the Socialist Party, which was ruling in France during that 1997–2002 period. Possible explanations include: the traditionally stronger influence of German social democracy in Bulgaria (compared to French socialism), the much greater resonance of Blair and Schröder's initiatives in Europe, the influence of German foundations working in Bulgaria (in particular the Friedrich Ebert Stiftung that had established lasting contacts with BSP), as well as the circumstance that in the said period France oriented its foreign policy with priority towards the Mediterranean and North Africa and to a much lesser degree towards CEE and Bulgaria.

had carried out the transition, while its own culpability consisted not in the character of the transition itself but rather in not having been successful in reducing some of the transition's negative consequences. For instance, in 2000 the party officially stated: "During the transition, BSP did not succeed in responding to the hopes of the working people for protection of their social interests" (BSP 2008a: 231). In December 2005, when already in power, BSP warned, again in an official document: "Part of our social priorities is not going to be fulfilled during the first year of our term in power" (ibid.: 540).

The refusal to assume responsibility for the lack of efficient counteraction against the 'shock monetary rightist' model had its own objective reasons. In the end, as we have mentioned, the same also applied to a greater or lesser degree for other socialist or social democratic parties in Europe. In a Bulgarian national perspective, a role was played by the peculiarities of the current political situation and the limitations imposed by partner interactions.

It is true that during the term in office of the SDS cabinet, BSP had been isolated and had functioned in a considerably hostile public, political, and media environment. Almost any initiative on the part of the Socialist Party was tainted by its rivals' propaganda with associations with the recent 'Videnov catastrophe'. The struggle against BSP's moral legitimacy had its parliamentary front, too, after the Bulgarian National Assembly passed a law declaring the communist regime criminal. But it remained true that the party did not sufficiently resolutely oppose policies intended to limit the social protection of labour, or the marketization of sectors that, according to the party's own programme documents, should work for the public benefit. The same situation repeated itself during the term in office of the 2009–13 centre-right GERB cabinet, which implemented an effective freezing of incomes and put forward ideas for cancellation of a string of social protections (such as lifting the minimum wage limit, a revision of collective bargaining, etc.). The Socialists' protestations retained a predominantly declarative tone. What is more, the cabinets in which BSP participated did not make serious efforts to correct the rightist liberal reform models inherited from SDS or GERB. Party leaders chose to excuse lack of palpable movement in that direction on their part with the compromises stemming from governing in coalition with liberal partners. The coalition formulas were presented not so much as an opportunity to implement some of the party's ideas while the party is in power but rather as a lack of opportunity to implement other ideas. Coalition partners were described as hindrances for leftist policies. If we are to judge from public statements of Socialist Party executives, the best that society could hope for was that the consequences of rightist governance become more bearable. It appeared that Socialists viewed the welfare state as a mere social wheel damper to soften the bumps on the country's rightist political course.

The 2005–09 term in office of the so-called Three-Way Coalition (composed of BSP, the liberal party of former Tsar Simeon Saxe-Coburg-Gotha, and DPS, supported largely by part of Bulgaria's ethnic Turks) marked a critical moment in the change of image of Bulgaria's post-communist left. After two full 4-year cabinet terms that BSP had spent in opposition, the time came in which the party had to demonstrate the positive aspects of its new social democratic image and to impose changes in the hard-line liberal economic policies of the preceding two cabinets.

The fact that BSP was a (senior) cabinet partner to parties of rightist liberal economic persuasion did not hinder the Socialists to clearly declare their priorities. With a special congress decision in December 2005, the party adopted 11 official goals for its policies in government. It is striking that the first 5 (!) of them can hardly be called specifically leftist: accession to the EU, a radical reform of the judiciary, limiting crime and corruption, social and economic catching up, and boosted economic growth (BSP 2008a: 540). As a matter of fact, BSP accepted some general modernization tasks that were of prime importance for the process of Bulgaria's European integration. The Socialists justified the development of defence capacities as a priority by referring not only to 'national priorities', but also to the full integration of the country within the Euro-Atlantic structures. Even 'social' goals such as the furthering of education were subordinated to meeting European standards. Boosting employment was motivated with the requirements of the EU's Lisbon Strategy. The increase of employment rates is of course something that can and must be a goal not only for leftist but also for rightist parties. It was only in the areas of healthcare and regional development that one could feel a leftist approach that would not be entirely supported by a rightist party. Notwithstanding the general directions laid down for those areas, the congress did not formulate as a goal the formulation of alternatives to existing models of functioning for welfare systems. The Socialist Party's intentions were far from being maximalist.

But if in that initial stage BSP seemed to be facing difficulties in putting into sharp and convincing relief its 'leftist' role in the 'centre-left' cabinet, those difficulties became drastic when during the course of its term in office the cabinet implemented a string of policies suggesting strong arguments in support of the thesis that the Socialist Party leaders had actually 'slid right'. All of those policies were approved and publicly defended by the BSP elite, with some of them initiated and implemented by the Socialists themselves. The most prominent example was the exchange of the previously existing progressive taxation scale for proportional taxation—in other words, the introduction of a so-called flat tax in 2008. The Bulgarian citizens, no matter their incomes, now had to pay 10% of those incomes, with no non-taxable minimum for the lowest strata. In the traditions of the West European welfare state, this is seen as a socially unjust policy of leftist and rightist governments alike because decisively benefiting the rich and putting the burden of tax revenue for the budget on the poor and vulnerable parts of the population.

Together with the flat tax, the Three-Way Coalition introduced the lowest corporate tax rate in Europe (again 10%). The cabinet strictly followed its predecessors' policies of strict fiscal discipline, maintaining sustainable budget deficits by purely monetary measures. Delegated budgets were instituted for education and regional policies as part of a strategy for financial decentralization and relieving of the central government from direct commitments in those areas. There are other examples that appear to show a discrepancy between the Socialist Party's actions and the messages it was sending out to its supporters.

During the time in office of the Saxe-Coburg-Gotha (2001–09) and the Three-Way Coalition (2005–09) cabinets, banks gradually acquired a new role in Bulgaria public life. The significance of consumer lending grew, something that can in part explain the higher standard of living of broad portions of the population. In parallel with processes in North America and Western Europe, Bulgarians started to more often live at the expense of the future, with all risks involved—risks with which borrowers were quickly becoming acquainted. High expectations towards this model brought quite immediate disappointments that served BSP badly at the 2009 elections. Around that time, in Western Europe the meaning of leftist policies started to change anew. The left was beginning to speak up more resolutely against banks and the financial capital, and to oppose their growing presence in people's everyday lives (Dullien et al. 2012: 63–66). BSP appeared to be staying away from those issues. The party was not trying to capitalize on them, acting instead as more of an advocate than a critic of the banks' behaviour and courses of action.

In the areas of foreign policy, steps were also taken that were exposed to the disapproval of the traditional left electorate. Those included Bulgaria's decision to accept the creation of joint Bulgarian-US military bases in the country, and the government decision with which the country recognized the independence of Kosovo, which had seceded from neighbouring Serbia. Russophile attitudes that BSP had explicitly or tacitly fostered during the transition had to face the fact of close military cooperation with the country that had for decades been presented as a foe by the former Communist Party propaganda. This circumstance acquired additional weight given the fact that, although Bulgaria passed for USSR's most loyal satellite during the Cold War, there were never any Soviet bases, armed forces, or military equipment on the country's territory. This was something completely different from the situation in countries such as GDR, Poland, or Czechoslovakia, where impressive Soviet military contingents were stationed whose very presence gave additional strength to local anti-Soviet attitudes. In 2008, when Bulgaria recognized Kosovo, the memory was still fresh of NATO bombings in the then still existing Yugoslavia—an intervention that had its immediate consequence in the de facto separation of the Kosovo province, predominantly populated with ethnic Albanians, from the Belgrade government. BSP's resolute opposition against those bombings had enjoyed the support of a considerable part of the Bulgarian society that saw Serbians as close in their culture, Slavic roots, and Christian Orthodox tradition. This applies especially for BSP supporters. That is why the recognition of Kosovo was the culmination of a course that the party and many of its supporters had opposed in the very recent past.

In itself, partnership with the US is not an expression of leftist or rightist political thinking. But seen in the network of factors constituting the political identity of a great part of leftist people in Bulgaria, it acquires rightist dimensions and becomes a part of what 'the left' has traditionally stood against. And this stands in contrast with the view of a large part of the party elite that the rapprochement with the US was a success. During the rule of the Saxe-Coburg-Gotha (2001–05) and especially of the Three-Way Coalition (2005–09) cabinet, American state leaders were palpably starting to view BSP as a 'normal' party and not just as a post-communist formation. The long-desired (and called for by Washington) legislation on revealing collaboration with the secret services of the communist regime, initiated by BSP; the party's and PM Stanishev's approval of a reform of Bulgarian special services using American expertise and a subsequent creation of a new national security agency; the 2008 Sofia visit of US President George W. Bush, when he expressed serious praise for the anti-corruption and pro-democratic policies of Stanishev—all of those events were seen by the party elite as an extremely important component of its international legitimacy. For them, it was important to be clear that the Americans, too, saw the Socialist Party as the sole democratic left in Bulgaria.

At the same time, the BSP elite considered the cabinet's moves not as a 'going right' but rather as pragmatic politics in a situation in which some 75% of the economy was already in private hands, and the country needed economic growth. The argument that economic growth in the end results in higher incomes does not fit classical leftist thinking, but it was precisely this position that BSP leaders were supporting, something clearly evidenced by then party leader and Bulgarian PM Sergei Stanishev.

At the end of his term in office Stanishev published the book *Because We Are Socialists*, which attempted to offer answers to many pressing questions that faced him as a leader, the Socialist Party, and those in power as a whole. Economic growth in a market economy with predominantly private property, argued Stanishev, is to be achieved with measures for improving the business climate (Stanishev 2008: 67), which have to constitute the focus of a cabinet's policies. The BSP leader rejected the traditional distinction according to which leftist economic decisions are 'just', while rightist measures are 'efficient'. Stanishev argued that the introduction of the flat tax was an instance of combining efficiency and justice. First, because it leaves many additional resources in the hands of businesses for them to reproduce and invest. And second, because it increases the collection of real state revenue and so increases the opportunities for redistribution. The flat tax, according to Stanishev, shows how a maximal number of people can get maximally high incomes. His arguments regarding the 'justness' of the instrument used were based on its social effects—jobs, pensions, maternity and childcare payments, unemployment compensations. The conclusion in a nutshell: "Our tax policy gave the state the opportunity to carry out a freer and more efficient social policy targeting precisely the 'injured' strata of society. Each year, we have been increasing retirement pensions on two steps, something that has not happened for the last 15 years. Only for 2007 this has amounted to 21%! Thanks to this 'hateful' tax policy and the improving business climate, within 4 years, the average pension will have increased with 100%. We have much better opportunities to grant targeted aid for heating, childcare support for families, as well as healthcare support." (Stanishev 2008: 60).

In his book, Stanishev demonstrated that he identifies left policies with social policies. When he tried to substantiate the 'leftist' nature of implemented measures, he was foremost stressing their effect upon people's incomes, avoiding the broader context of quality of life, social protection, and equal opportunity. According to this interpretation, if a certain policy brings an increase of incomes, then it is by definition leftist. Stanishev ignored the fact that social policies are in principle the key instrument of any type of welfare state, no matter whether it is organized around liberal or conservative values. The thesis that if something is social, then it is also leftist, ignores the essentially social nature of all ideologies claiming to provide some sort of social integration. However, the 'supra-ideological' claim of the book's argument is only apparent. Deng Xiaoping's popular saying "It doesn't matter if a cat is black or white so long as it catches mice" does not explain what will happen to our cat after we have sent the neighbour's cat for mice. Both Stanishev and BSP's broader executive had many motives to defend their new stance. The party was not in a position to ground its actions on a preceding positive experience in carrying out a left democratic alternative, or to borrow current European models of successful theoretical and practical opposition to neo-liberalism; yet it still had to defend its modern and pro-European image against lingering accusations in backwardness and crypto-Bolshevism.

On all accounts, no matter whether this is to be judged as something positive or negative, as part of the Three-Way Coalition cabinet BSP directly participated in the bolstering of existing private wealth. The Socialists were trying to counter the perception that 'the Socialist Party is working for the rich' with the assertion: 'yes, but it is *also* working for the poor'. However, BSP's historical tradition has always been oriented towards an idealization of the poor and a rhetoric in their service. Former party leader Zhan Videnov was a continuator of that legacy, in one of his public addresses as Bulgaria's PM famously describing the nouveau riches who had emerged in the first years of the transition to market economy as "blood-sucking *chorbadzhis*."[39] Videnov wanted to stress that the majority of businessmen who had gone rich during the transition had no sense of solidarity with and responsibility to society. BSP's negative attitude towards business and capital was described in party documents as "a dogma from the past", yet was still widespread among party supporters and activists. The perception that BSP was losing its sensitivity for the growing social separations was sharply and succinctly expressed in 1996 by party daily *Duma*'s editor-in-chief Stefan Prodev, who at one plenum said that the party is divided between 'red grannies' and 'red mobile phones'. On the one pole was the elderly and poor electorate living on the verge of survival. On the other were party cadres with big bank accounts leading lavish lives[40].

The left's image as working for the rich is part of the picture. Additional moral damage accrued from the widespread perception that the left was working for the rich in its own ranks. In the course of the term in office of the Stanishev cabinet, corruption scandals erupted in which suspicions were directed at senior party cadres in power[41]. Periodically, the public was made acquainted with the personal and corporate fortunes of members of the senior party apparatus, with schemes for siphoning of public and EU funds, with procedures for acquisition or swapping of sizeable properties, with ongoing illegal construction, and so on. In the conditions of a growing social polarization in Bulgaria, such information—true or exaggerated—was making an impact on the general social and psychological climate in the country and was eroding BSP's claims to be on the side of the transition's losers. According to one study, a leading explanation for the increase of patronage practices under the Three-Way Coalition was BSP's desire, after two cabinet terms in opposition, to maximally benefit from its time in power and to guarantee a party patronage in the largest

---

39 This expression from Bulgaria's 19th c. National Revival denotes rich Bulgarians perceived to be mercilessly exploiting their poor servants and townsfolk.
40 In 1996 it had already become apparent that BSP supporters were concentrated in high the senior age groups, and the level of penetration of wireless communication in Bulgaria was still so weak that mobile phones were owned by a few, who almost always were people of high income.
41 Two key Socialist Party executives had to resign from their positions—Minister of Economy Roumen Ovcharov, accused of covering up major abuse of funds in public companies, and Minister of Interior Roumen Petkov, implicated in dubious contacts with organized crime.

possible extent (Spirova 2012). The label 'corruption' stuck firmly upon the practices with which BSP and the Socialist-dominated cabinet implemented Bulgaria's EU membership (Andreev 2009).

By giving up the ambition to formulate a Bulgarian 'leftist project', under the influence of European social democracy, and with its strong preferences for political pragmatism around the end of the Three-Way Coalition's term in office, BSP was building an image that could only with difficulty attract new people with leftist attitudes in addition to those who had traditionally been supporting the Socialist Party. The party was able to draw in professionals or pragmatists who would nevertheless be disposed to work with different governments or parties without developing loyalty to the messages or ideologemes of any one of them. As a matter of fact, with its 'rightist sliding' BSP was left to rely to an exceptionally large degree on those groups of people that would stand behind it on the basis of historically formed expectations—statism, a modernizational role, a tendency for nationalism, Russophilia, egalitarian attitudes, and traditionalist views on culture and everyday life.

Yet, those expectations were on their turn put to a serious test. While in power, BSP played its part in the process of decentralization, even though it was speaking up for more state influence in social regulation. The party's leading role in the country's modernization was exchanged for claims that economic growth is created by businesses and foreign investors, with a prioritization of the services sector rather than the previously favoured industry. Nationalism was left behind in the party's resolute strategy for European integration, opening the door to national populist parties such as Ataka, which took advantage of the disappointment experienced by leftist voters with nationalist attitudes. Russophilia was directly weakened by military base agreements with the US. Egalitarian perceptions came to be contradicted by the Socialist Party's stance towards the rich and towards wealth in general. Traditionalist views came to be confronted with efforts aiming at a more modern identity, in which the party leader was freely cohabiting with his girlfriend, and the party's candidate for mayor of Bulgaria's capital Sofia officially supported the local Gay Pride.

BSP executives were certainly convinced that their actions involved increased realism and pragmatism. At the same time, we should not forget that, as a historical tradition, the left is something that claims to seek new horizons and offer new visions—simply put, a movement that offers a dream to believe in.

So here we have the objective preconditions for a crisis of the Bulgarian Socialist Party—a crisis not only of identity but also of support. After a successful term in office (according to all financial and economic indexes), in July 2009 the Socialists suffered a heavy defeat at the parliamentary election. In the whole history of Bulgaria's transition until then, the party had not received so few votes (absolutely counted) and so few MP seats. What happened to the Socialists' electorate?

3.2 Has the Socialist Electorate been Sliding 'Left'?

A huge array of information, both empirical and analytic, has been accumulated regarding electoral processes in contemporary democratic Bulgaria. Elections that have been held after 1989 have provided a significant amount of statistical data on the geographical and demographic dimensions of voting. Demoscopic studies have regularly been making available data on the electorates of the different political forces in play. We are in a condition to make cross-sections of voters' attitudes with respect to various political, economic, social, as well as value or worldview questions. A still greater precision is given by so-called exit-poll studies registering citizens' attitudes immediately after expressing their political will.

For the needs of this study, demoscopic methods can be extremely useful in the electoral analysis of the left. Of primary concern in this section will be not so much the overall picture of BSP's electoral body but rather the dynamics and tendencies it has manifested.

As I have pointed out, in the very beginning of the democratic period, BSP's electorate was relatively evenly distributed among different social and professional groups in the Bulgarian society. Studies have shown that the same applied for the electorates of the other leading political formations, with some variations (Todorov 2010: 216–217). At least initially, socio-economic motives appeared to play no major role in electoral behaviour. The situation was not one in which certain social groups tend to vote for specific parties.

Given this, what was it that was leading voters to cast BSP's ballot rather than that of some other party? The tradition of the communist regime was certainly a key factor. During its long time in power, BCP had crafted for itself an image consisting of features that were valued positively by parts of the Bulgarian society. The socialist period acquired a positive connotation for many, which in its turn became a reason for them to direct their political choices to the successor of the main driving force during that period. And vice versa, negative attitudes to the past have tended to strongly reduce chances for a vote in favour of the 'culprit' for that past. Generally speaking, this is the public expression of the opposition between communism and anti-communism, which has served as a central axis of the Bulgarian political process for the first decade of transition, and partially after that (Todorov 2004; Karasimeonov 2010: 82). Those for whom communism was of value turned to BSP. Those who considered anti-communism to be important turned to SDS or some of the smaller new formations. Anti-communism played a major role in the democratic process in all former Eastern Bloc countries. And still, it seems that in Bulgaria this conflict was markedly standing in the foreground (Cotta 1996: 95; Bozoki 2005: 93). Comparative studies have confirmed this observation. A telling piece of evidence is that, as late as 2001, the attitudes to the communist past in Bulgaria were the factor ranked highest as an explanation of differences between parties in the minds of their own voters. Division on the issue 'communism *vs.* anti-communism' was placed first among other possible options that respondents in the country pointed out, well ahead of other divisions such as 'urban *vs.* rural areas', 'market *vs.* State', 'nation *vs.* Europe', etc. An average of 30% of respondents from the former Eastern bloc stated that the communism/anti-communism opposition has a big importance for differences between parties. In Bulgaria this share was 45% (Berglund and Ekman 2010: 103).

That is why the distinction communism/anti-communism does not account only for parties' positioning or occupying different niches in political space. It has also acted as a demarcation line between voters in their differing valuation of the past. According to some assessments, there has been none more important demarcation line in Bulgaria. The political process in the country developed as a battle regarding the past rather than as a competition of strategies for the future. Therefore, it was easier for parties and their supporters to reach agreement on issues of current or longer-term policy, than on issues regarding the positive and negative characteristics of the Zhivkov regime (Raichev and Stoychev 2008). Such a point of view however did not remain value-indifferent with respect to the behaviour of parties. The natural advantage was reserved for those that considered the past to be bad because they had a much greater motive to change things, that is, to be an energetic actor in politics—in contrast with those that considered the past to be good because the latter tended to remain closed in that past, and their electoral choice tended to look backward.

From the dawn of democracy, BSP voters were accused of only looking into the past. Both rightwing forces and analysts have often stressed that the Socialist Party is doomed to a natural extinction and a slow disappearance because its supporters are gradually but eventually going to vanish 'due to purely biological reasons'. Similar forecasts have been formulated for all other CSPs in CEE, but they have been voiced especially frequently with respect to BSP. In this case, the party's long history turned into a minus. BSP was ironically called a 'centenarian' to hint that the old party is a party of the elderly incapable of rejuvenation. SDS was fond of saying that BSP is on the decline.[42] The failure of the 1996–97 Socialist cabinet made the feeling of an imminent collapse spread among parts of the party elite. One of its representatives even left BSP with the statement that it was a "dying party".[43] The 'red granny' became ubiquitous as a generalized image of the party's 'traditional' voter.

Was the leftist electorate truly just a nostalgia electorate? There are indeed good arguments in support of this hypothesis. A study from as early as the first half of the 1990s has noted that there is a one-way trend in the age distribution of BSP voters. In other words, the number of its voters was uniformly growing from the lowest to the highest age groups, being smallest among the youngest and largest among retirees (Kitschelt et al. 1995: 148–149).

This observation can lead to generalizations about the dynamics of the Bulgarian transition. If the direction of progressive change be posited as rightist and liberal, BSP supporters are those who react to it in a retrograde way and attempt to stop it or at least delay it. In that context, they seem to support a lived out status quo and to oppose change, calling this position

---

42 The lyrics of one of the most popular songs from the first election campaigns of the emerging anti-communist pole in the early 1990s treated the issue of BSP's impossible efforts to change itself; the song carried the suggestive title "Posleden vals" ("Last waltz").
43 Nikolay Kamov, who at that point was a member of the party's highest executive organ, the Executive Bureau.

'left' by virtue of the tradition connecting BSP with the extreme left part of the ideological spectrum. This type of thinking allows making a conditional parallel. For a long time, CEE communist regimes had fostered a vulgarly determinist view of communism. According to this view, objective social processes are leading with iron necessity forward to the building of communism, and hardships along that road stem from the not entirely lived out legacy of the bourgeois age, or what Marx called the "birthmarks" of the new society. With time, the residue from the past is liable to be overcome. Such a scheme of thinking can be applied to the post-socialist situation. Some supposed that it leads to the triumph of the rightist liberal trend, but turns and zigzags, even delays and slight steps back, are still possible. Those are due to hindrances coming from the influence of the past and the incapacity of all citizens of new democracies to be 'in step' with the new time and its requirements.

Seen from this perspective, the Bulgarian post-communist left (more so than that in other former Eastern Bloc countries) truly appears to be a barrier to progress. Its insufficient transformation seems to bring it further away and even oppose it to West European models. It is as if we are seeing an inverted image. The post-war development of the left in Western Europe solidified the impression that the usual leftwing voters are younger, more educated, residing in larger cities, forward thinking, and atheistically minded. This was still visible even in recent times (e.g., Muxel 2011: 45–47). In Bulgaria data show something completely different. BSP was becoming more and more attractive to voters who were older, less educated, residing in smaller settlements, traditionally minded, and even in many cases religious. An outside European observer would probably have a hard time believing that an electorate with such social and demographic characteristics can be called 'leftist'. Therefore, it is easy to make the conclusion that what we have here is not an authentic democratic left but rather a legacy from another regime with which the democratic political system will have to co-exist for a long time.

Under one form or another, this conclusion has been frequently present in interpretations. Starting with Kitschelt and his associates (1995) on to Lyubenov (2011), the available empirical material has been used to reject the hypothesis that socio-economic or, so to speak, class factors have exerted a statistically significant influence on the vote for BSP.

Kitschelt and his team have defended the position that the chief factor determining preferences for parties in the early 1990s were the positions and opportunities of people for adaptation to changes. The authors have argued that, in the situation of a confrontational political model, the more adaptive one is to the mechanisms of democracy and market economy, the more probable it is for one to vote for SDS (seen as a bearer of change), and, vice versa, the less adaptive one is, the more probable it is for one to choose BSP. The authors put the social and professional groups in the Bulgarian society along an axis according to their presumed degree of adaptability. The beginning of the axis includes the least adaptive (pensioners, agricultural and industrial workers, low-level white collar workers), the end being the position of the most adaptive (those working in the service sector, experts, students, businesspeople). The hypothesis was checked that BSP's electoral range would be strongest in the first group and would gradually decrease along the axis, and, conversely, SDS will be strongest among businessmen and weakest among retirees. Data from the study have confirmed this hypothesis, with some qualifications. It turned out that BSP has marked a drop in the category of industrial workers and a growth among experts. When socio-demographic characteristics are viewed, BSP's electoral influence decreases from low to high education, but marks a sudden increase among those with university-level education. The same also applies to electoral geography. BSP is strongest in villages, weaker in small towns, still weaker in regional centres, but grows in Bulgaria's capital. The team has provided explanations to the deviations it registered. BSP was less convincing among the working class because workers have for a long time been suppressed by the communist apparatus and state supported trade unions, and thus they do not see themselves as represented by the communists' successor. Relatively better results in the capital, among those with university education and among experts are seen as due to the presence of a certain stratum of communist nomenklatura that built itself professionally and was socially integrated during the years of the old regime, and which is ready to take advantage of its strong initial positions in seeking fulfilment in the new social configuration. However, all of those peculiarities have a situational character. The authors of the study are convinced that the deviations would gradually resolve into the more general trend. And this trend stipulates that the Bulgarian left has a conservative electorate whose main motivation is fear of the future (Kitschelt et al. 1995: 152–159).

Many years later, another important study of party preferences in the Bulgarian society, which covers a much longer historical period and works on a much richer empirical basis, also took the division between bearers and opponents of positive change as leading in the analysis of electoral attitudes. In his analysis of electoral dynamics during the 1990s, Lyubenov (2011) addressed the sphere of the economy, drawing a demarcation line in voting motivation between liberal economic change and social economic populism. The very term 'populism' as a rule often carries negative connotations and insinuates the author's stance on those two types of voters' political thinking.[44] Data on electorate attitudes allow BSP supporters to be separated from those of all other political parties on the question of economic development. The reason given for leftist supporters to be called 'social populists' involves their resolutely expressed agreement to the use of regulatory measures in the economy. The ideological homogeneity of BSP voters, which has been additionally checked using other questions, placed them in the position of defenders of the indefensible. The author comments on the fact that some hard support for the leftists for more state involvement in the economy was declared in late 1997, just months after the failure of the Socialist Party's government, which on its part also attempted to boost the role of the state. In this way, the expectations of the BSP electorate for something that had already demonstrated its futility, has placed them outside of realistic thinking about the goals facing the country (Lyubenov 2011: 68–76).

The available data, however, allow for other hypotheses about the character and motivation of the Socialist Party's voters in the times around the beginning of the 21st century. The nostalgic tinge in the orientation of many of them is not to be doubted. But it can hardly be seen as exhausting the reasons for their self-identification 'in red'. We have reasons to believe that this identification rested not only on nostalgia, but also on the hope that BSP was a bearer of a strategy for the future of Bulgarian society. Let us consider the conflict between communism and anti-communism. Scholars

---

44 Another possible terrain for criticism has to do with the issue of whether the term 'populism' has been correctly used. As a rule, this term presupposes a political use of the division between elite and people (see e.g. Mudde 2004), while data do not show the presence of anti-elitist attitudes among BSP voters.

are unanimous that this conflict has exerted a significant influence on the course of the Bulgarian political process during the 1990s. But what they have left less thoroughly discussed is the explanation for the generation of this conflict. It is true that the conflict was fostered by BSP and SDS leaders, who had obviously estimated that the two-bloc confrontation services the internal cohesion of the two 'large' electorates, decreasing the chances of less radical formations. Those influences 'from above' have their important significance. However, self-determination 'from below' should not be underestimated. Whether the separate individual will count themselves as one of the 'communists' or 'anti-communists' was not only a question of a different assessment of the past because such assessment should in its turn have its own foundation. In the absence of a powerful dissident movement during the years of the old regime, we cannot consider that the anti-communist camp was built by staunch adversaries of communism from the past. A not inconsiderable part of leading figures in the anti-communist SDS turned out to be former BCP members and even people who had enjoyed privileges in the hierarchy of the old regime.[45] And conversely, albeit on a smaller scale, people who had not been BCP members or supporters earlier, started to support the 'communist' BSP in the new democratic situation. The factor of biography is not everything. Figures with biographies in the 'old' BCP continued them in anti-communist circles, and conversely, part of people persecuted and suppressed for their dissident activities around the end of the 1980s returned to the 'new' BSP. That is why party identification cannot be reduced to the elementary division: "those who lived well under the communist regime and regret its end tend to vote for the Socialists, while those who back then lived badly and now welcome change, tend to vote for their opponents." Voters were able to see a chance for change and a better future not only in SDS but also in BSP.

In the light of the above considerations, the available empirical material can receive a different interpretation. The growth of the relative share of supporters of the Socialist Party among Sofia residents and people with higher education registered in the early 1990s is not based only on the preserved symbolic, political, and economic assets of the communist no-

---

45 This includes the first SDS chair and later first democratically elected Bulgarian President, Zhelyu Zhelev (1935–2015), who had been a BCP member, later expelled from the party.

menklatura, although they have also played their significant role. During the last two decades of the socialist period, in the conditions of a partial liberalization of the regime and a partial opening up of the economy, a generation of cadres had sprung in different areas of the economy and public life, which was no longer looking at the world through dogmatically ideological glasses, but was instead pragmatically and technocratically disposed. Their belonging (in most cases) to circles of the former Communist Party oriented such people foremost to its successor in their search for the best project for the country's future as voters but sometimes also as experts ready to participate in that project. This is the 'anomaly' in educated or 'elite' groups. The problem with the weaker degree of support for the Socialist Party in one of the key 'non-elite' groups, that of industrial workers, looks paradoxical and brings to mind a possible 'irony of history'. The Bulgarian proletarian party had been built in the absence of a proletariat, and when with its decisive efforts a proletariat came to be created, that proletariat turned against the party.[46] Explanations with recourse to oppression by communist apparatchiks and officially sponsored trade unions should not be exaggerated. Such control and arbitrary rule was exercised in all professional areas, but by far not all of them have reacted in this way, either during the regime, or in the subsequent period.

Another hypothesis is possible that we could with some qualifications call a 'class-related hypothesis'. If we return to the historical retrospective, the group of industrial workers in Bulgaria was formed relatively late in the context of European modernity. It was a result of the accelerated state-driven industrialization of the country between the 1950s and the 1970s, during which significant numbers of people left villages and small towns to start work in new industrial enterprises. In this situation, the state was the owner of the industry. As a rule, the standard of living of those people rose palpably. From another point of view, however, the majority of them passed from the group of owners (be it only that of small land owners) to the group of hired workers whose property was expropriated (transferred to co-operatives or nationalized). Such people were integrated in the system of industrial production without being able to determine the conditions for

---

46 And that is not a first. One of the heaviest blows against the legitimacy of communist regimes in CEE resounded in Poland with the ascent of the Solidarity trade union in the early 1980s, when it became clear that workers en masse were not supporting the 'United Workers' party.

their role in it. The accumulation of significant social benefits notwithstanding, such individuals found themselves in a situation of de facto exploitation in which they were selling only their labour. The coercion was political. In Western Europe it was again coercion, but that time around economic one, which had initiated a similar process of proletariat formation during the period from the 17th to the 19th century. Nowhere had this proletariat harboured sympathies for the entrepreneur who was exploiting it. Discontent with entrepreneurs gave rise to class conflict, summoned the ghost of social revolution, and gave a powerful impulse for the creation of the emerging leftist political parties. In CEE and in Bulgaria in particular, we can also suppose that the workers viewed negatively the entrepreneur-exploiter, which in those cases was the state. An insofar as the Communist Party in Bulgaria played the role of a national bourgeoisie in its modernization strategy, it was natural for workers' discontent to be directed against communists as representatives of that exploiter. In that case, in contrast with West European examples, the political impulse for rejection of the 'bourgeoisie' would not drive 'the left' but rather 'the right', giving fuel to the 'anti-communist' instead of the 'communist' camp. As studies have documented, during the 1990s, BSP's electorate was strongly supportive of state interference in the economy. At the same time, at least until the carrying out of privatization, industrial workers were sceptical of state interference, which had constituted them not as a hegemonic class but as a performing class—again, independent of the official slogans of Marxist-Leninist propaganda and independent of considerations having to do with the living standards and the dynamics of income.

The collapse of the BSP cabinet in 1997 is correctly considered to be a pivotal moment. A heavy blow was dealt not only to the party, but also to the very idea that it was capable of leading the country into the 'appropriate' direction, one way or another. Around the end of that year, data were showing a high degree of homogenization of the Socialists' electorate. 57.9% of it identified themselves as 'extreme leftists', 40.2% as 'leftists' or 'centre-leftists', only 1.8% as 'centrists', and no one at all as 'rightist conservative' or 'extreme rightist' (Lyubenov 2011: 79). We have reasons to believe that there was a withdrawal of conformist voters from BSP, i.e., of those disposed to support the party just because of its power or significance. With SDS's resolute taking hold of power and implementation of a clear cut programme of transformation in the country, there was a decrease in the number of people who saw in SDS just an ad hoc formation created along foreign models and using foreign prescriptions for action. Part of what might be termed as the 'nationalist' vote was redirected after 1997 from BSP—until then potentially seen as 'the Bulgarian party'—to SDS, which had already demonstrated its stable presence in Bulgarian politics. BSP was also left by those voters who saw in the party an agent of a project for the future. It is not surprising that the people who remained to support BSP were those of a leftist identity, who were motivated to vote for the party because it was a leftwing force drawing its legitimacy from its own historically leftist identity.

It was here that the seeds were planted for the crisis of the two-bloc confrontational model of the Bulgarian transition. The 2001 return of former Bulgarian Tsar Simeon Saxe-Coburg-Gotha to the country and his stunning victory at general elections that year were a follow-up to changes that had set in 4 year earlier. Voters were seeing the BSP-SDS clash less and less as a fight between two competing projects for Bulgaria's future that was giving reasons for the existence of two parallel political spaces, one communist and one anti-communist. In the context of the two-bloc model, BSP appeared to be *the* alternative to SDS, the natural counterbalance to anti-communist forces. The Socialist Party however was gradually giving up effectively maintaining this image. Adherence to BSP was distinctly becoming adherence to a leftwing party, i.e., to a party for which one votes if one identifies with the left. In other words, it was now just adherence to one of the entities in Bulgaria's party system. In the period when BSP leaders effectively gave up formulating a convincing leftist project, supporters were starting to expect a demonstration from the party that it is leftist.

SDS's 1997–2001 term in power created immense transformations in the socio-economic status of in effect all Bulgarian citizens. Bulgarian society underwent a very significant social differentiation. Its effects strengthened already articulated trends in BSP's electoral development. Scholars have argued that during that period in Bulgaria, a new social conflict between centre and periphery emerged (Todorov 2010; Lyubenov 2011). Its character stemmed from the public assessment of an already completed process of economic development, which had established lasting social distinctions. Broadly put, this was a conflict between the winners and losers of the transition, between those who considered that reforms undertaken in the context of the rightist liberal course had improved their situation, and those according to whom those reforms had pushed them down the social ladder. This conflict found its political expression. BSP started to be seen as the political representative of the losers of the transition. This was so, first, due to situational factors. The former Tsar's party swiftly imposed a liberal agenda, putting at the centre of its messages initiative, innovation, desire for success, and new opportunities for professionals. Discredited due to some negative perceptions about its term in power, SDS underwent a crisis and came to be lastingly associated with the rightist reforms it had carried out. People who did not believe that the new perspectives painted by the former Tsar were realistic, against the backdrop of poverty and de-classation in which they were residing, as well as those who were blaming SDS for lost jobs and slashed hopes for a better life, comprised a very large part of the Bulgarian citizens. Part of them chose BSP not only on traditional motives but also on the basis of a new type of reasoning. They were not seeing BSP as a driving force of changes that were working in favour for the rich. What had happened was not being interpreted as the result of policies of the Socialist Party. This reasoning also featured classical leftist views regarding the care for the poor and the support for vulnerable groups, with which the Socialists were at least partially identified in the minds of the public.

The circumstance that voting for BSP has been for the large part a choice of those who lost from the transition can be considered as a process of 'sliding left' of the party's electorate. Of course, here I am not claiming that those trends are absolutely definitive or run along only one track. Nevertheless, many components to this process can be found in the dynamics of the Bulgarian society to stimulate voting for the Socialist Party. Among them is the impoverishment of large groups, both absolute and relative, as purchasing power and as position in social stratification. Imbalances in regional development had led to heavy disproportions between some parts of the country generating economic activity, investments and growth, and others, in which unemployment had become a structural problem and social opportunities were geographically plugged. Sharp social polarization is a factor of potential instability. De-industrialization, apart from being a source of unemployment, had made many Bulgarians stop seeing Bulgaria as a modern country. Excessive regulation of small business, often supplemented by political and administrative arbitrariness, came to be perceived as an intentionally imposed brake for all efforts to achieve anything outside the shadow of big corporations and big capital. The feeling that the transition was 'unjust' was spreading widely. The idea that the state was working in the favour of those with great wealth, crushing the common individual, was resonating strongly.

Attitudes of this kind tend to be poor in potential for creating an alternative vision. In this sense, BSP was no longer envisioned by voters as providing a hope or 'open window' to the future. The attitudes of the 'losers of the transition' were indeed in many cases pointing to BSP, but that was more by virtue of traditional associations and traditional voting. BSP's public image at the start of the new century was attracting with ever increasing difficulty committed new voters outside of those who, due to old associations, were expecting from the party to more actively help the poor and to limit the influence of Western economic and cultural fashions on Bulgarian public life. The curve of electoral dynamics could be presented as counter-evidence to this argument. Indeed, at the 2005 general elections BSP received 1,129,196 votes, or 345,824 more than in 2001, while in 2013 its result was 942,541 votes, or 194,427 more than in 2009. However, behind those amplitudes we can find the palpable influence of specific situational factors. For instance, in 2005 the anti-communist rightists SDS were in collapse and were falling apart while the party of the former Tsar had provoked many disappointments in the course of its term in power. Apart from BSP, there was practically none other who could seriously pretend for the future rule of the country. And we should not forget that the vote for the former Tsar in 2001 was significantly influenced by social populist expectations which his party was not able to answer while in power. If we turn to 2013, elections that year took place after the GERB rule, remembered by many people with heavy social restrictions, austerity measures, and a systematic pressure on businesses and opponents. Studies have shown that those who voted for BSP at the 2013 elections included many rightwing supporters who decided to vote for their former foe only so as to not allow a continuation of GERB policies.

Data speak about an increasing support for BSP (in terms of share) in social groups that tend to least frequently tend to produce historic change and that in the highest degree tend to need some sort of social protection. We can trace this trend using the figures of exit-poll studies revealing the social and demographic profile of voters at parliamentary elections in 2001 and 2014 (see Tables 3.2.1 and 3.2.2).[47]

Table 3.2.1.
Dynamics of the structure of the BSP electorate over time (in %): 2001

		National Movement for Simeon II (centre)	Union of the Democratic Forces (right)	Bulgarian Socialist Party (left)
Age	18–30	21,5	28,1	7,5
	31–40	20,7	21,5	9,8
	41–50	21,5	17,8	15,8
	51–60	17,7	16,1	22,1
	60+	18,5	16,5	44,8
Location	Capital	14,3	22,2	13,5
	Regional city	38,6	33,4	28,9
	Town	21,9	16,2	21,3
	Village	25,1	28,2	36,3
Education	Higher	15,5	27,6	21,4
	Secondary	60,5	55,5	50,1
	Primary	19,9	14,4	23,3
	Lower than primary	4,1	2,5	5,2

Source: Gallup International, exit-poll after Parliamentary elections 2001.

Table 3.2.2.
Dynamics of the structure of the BSP electorate over time (in %): 2014

		Citizens for European Development of Bulgaria (right)	Bulgarian Socialist Party (left)	Movement of Rights and Freedoms (centre)
Age	18–25	9,5	5,7	14,3
	26–35	18,3	8,2	17,5
	36–45	21,2	9,9	21,5
	46–55	20,3	15,3	20,2
	56–65	17,1	21,5	14,6
	65+	13,6	39,5	11,9

---

47 The two tables show the structure of electorates in relative shares. For the correctness of analysis, I must recall that they are based on quantitatively different electoral pools. Compared to 2001, the BSP electorate in 2014 was smaller, in absolute values, with more than one-third (from 783,372 votes in 2001 to 505,527 votes in 2014).

Location	Capital	14,5	12,3	0,9
	Regional city	48,1	33,9	13,3
	Town	19,0	24,4	15,7
	Village	18,4	29,4	70,1
Education	Higher	44,3	37,8	10,6
	Secondary	49,5	46,6	50,6
	Primary	5,7	14,2	31,9
	Lower than primary	0,5	1,3	6,9

Source: Gallup International, exit-poll after Parliamentary elections 2014

A national representative survey by Gallup International conducted in July 2014 allows us to trace the profile of BSP voters with respect to additional indicators. The relatively recent time when the survey was conducted makes its results highly up to date. According to data obtained, around July 2014, some 19% of Bulgarians with a right to vote were disposed to choose the BSP ballot. They included 25% of 'poor' voters, 20% of those 'below the medium level' of income, 13% of those with medium incomes, and 18% of those with over medium incomes. With respect to educational status, 15% of voters with higher education declared that they would vote for BSP, in addition to 18% of those with secondary and 25% of those with primary or lower. With respect to professional status, 8% of workers in private companies were oriented to BSP, 20% of those employed in state firms, 11% of self-employed (having their own businesses), 44% of retirees, 12% of unemployed, and 4% of non-working (predominantly young people). 48% of BSP's potential voters stated that they have no bank savings, an indicator much higher than in the voters' pool of most other formations. BSP voters were also the electorate with the highest degree of lack of knowledge of foreign language. 8% of socialist supporters declared that they know English (against 24% average for adult Bulgarian population), with 74% stating they do not know any other language except Bulgarian (against 59% average among Bulgarians). A similar situation is present with respect to work with computers. 25% of BSP voters said they use a computer at home (53% average for the country), and 14% said that they use computers at their work place (26% average for the country). BSP supporters were also found to be the electorate of the lowest degree of mobility. 70% of them had not been at a holiday or business trip in the country or abroad during the past year (52% average for Bulgaria).

Close to two-thirds of BSP voters belong to senior age groups predominantly composed of pensioners and unemployed, i.e., people who have the greatest difficulties in finding a job at their age. Those are the people most of all relying on protection by the state. In the vast majority of cases, they are biographically connected with the former communist party, and their electoral behaviour manifests tradition rather than specific political or economic interests. The party has continued to win voters among the youngest only with the greatest difficulty. In a situation of a low birth rate and a demographic crisis, this symptom is more than alarming. The in-depth analysis of data shows that very few of those young people have chosen BSP because they liked its messages, ideas, or policies. Most of them have acted on a family choice.

If the 'anomalies' in social-demographic profiles noted by Kitschelt et al. (1995) were characteristic of the early 1990s, in the new century they have taken a course towards 'cleaning themselves out' and a straightening up of trends. BSP has been losing positions in Bulgaria's capital and major cities, where the most active population is concentrated, and has maintained a still relatively strong support in smaller towns and villages, where incomes are lower and unemployment has been a lasting and chronic phenomenon.[48] The stratum known as leftist intelligentsia is 'melting'. BSP has managed to preserve more significant support among those with lower education and professional qualification. Generally speaking, its electoral area encompasses people of the worst-off economic situation, or those most negatively affected by the processes of democratic and market transformation. The geographical distribution of the vote provides further arguments for this observation. The Socialist Party has been making its best showing in the country's poorest regions and municipalities. It was a tradition during the years of transition that has lately become even more distinct that the party's highest election results come from North-western Bulgaria (the country's poorest region), from smaller towns and regional cities in the south-western part, and from remote mountainous areas. Rightwing forces (especially GERB) have been uncontested winners in Bulgaria's six biggest cities, including the capital, where economic life is at its most inten-

---

48 It is important to note that, in rural areas during the second decade of the 21st century, BSP has been facing increasingly strong competition by DPS, a party traditionally supported by members of Bulgaria's Turkish minority, even in locations where there is no ethnic Turkish population present.

sive. Of course, situational factors have played their role at many places. Notwithstanding that fact, BSP has been receiving the support of an electorate which is leftist in terms of social status and expectations from the state—and which is so in a higher degree than during the 1990s.

The tendency of a 'sliding left' on the part of Socialist Party voters coincided with and was confronted by a tendency of a 'sliding right' on the part of party leaders, which was discussed in the previous section. The possibility opened for a distancing between the attitudes of the party's supporters and the policies offered by the party's elite. According to some assessments, this discrepancy has been reflected in the gradually decreasing intensity of internal party life. Factional activity, which was so intensive and pivotal during the 1990s, has been on a decline. Most alternative ideological currents within BSP disappeared formally or in practice. The Socialists have continued to function as a mass party in which issues in public and political life stand for discussion and proposals from different levels of the party's organizational structure, but the participation of ordinary members in decision making has remained relatively limited (Todorov 2013a).

We have sufficient data for the divergence between supporters and elites, but it is also certainly true that this divergence has for a long time not been visibly reflected in the self-identification of those supporters with BSP (see Table 3.2.3).

Table 3.2.3.
Left-Centre-Right structure of the BSP electorate (in %)

Leftists	Centrists	Rightists	N/A	Total
89	2	*	10	100

Source: Gallup International, National representative survey, July 2014

Whatever the motives for choosing BSP's ballot, they almost univocally presuppose that the one making that choice would see him- or herself as a person of leftist convictions. The policies of the Socialist Party, while in power or in opposition, might be criticized or acclaimed, but even its most pronouncedly rightist aspects have not given a valid reason for a significant number of rightist voters to choose BSP. For instance, the introduction of the flat tax rate was seen as an unambiguously rightist policy, but neither the groups in Bulgarian society who see themselves as rightists nor those who were palpably favoured by the flat tax due to their high incomes made an electoral turn in BSP's direction. To the contrary, it was the losers of the flat tax rate who stood behind the initiators for its introduction.

Data show that it was not just that people who have tended to vote for BSP are such that see themselves as leftists. People who see themselves as leftists have most often voted for BSP and no other party. With respect to the Socialists, there is a high degree of overlap between self-identification in the ideological spectrum and choice of political party (see Table 3.2.4).[49]

Table 3.2.4.
Voting for BSP in different political sectors

% of Leftists	% of Centrists	% of Rightists	% of non-affiliated
64,4 (14,8% of Leftists declare they do not vote at all)	1,8	0,3	4,8

Source: Gallup International, National representative survey, July 2014

What is the reason for this high degree of overlap between leftist self-identification and choosing the Socialist Party? Firstly, BSP supporters have been making their choices based on a spectrum of reasons much broader than their assessment of a given political course or term in power. Conservative and biographical motives have lingered and continued to play their role. Secondly, notwithstanding the pragmatic-liberal views of sections of the party elite, that elite has in fact never lost dialogue with the members and has always succeeded in finding a common language with them and maintaining the exchange of opinions inside the party. Thirdly, even when BSP supporters have been disappointed with the party's policies and even when they have accused it in 'sliding right', they have realized that that is the only party in the years of the democratic transition which has underscored the importance of their lives and their views—the only party which has never been ironic towards them, and which has never underestimated them or framed them as expendable, in contrast foremost with the political formations on the right. Fourthly, other leftwing projects outside of BSP before 2014 have never appeared convincing enough as leftist, and this holds even for the entity that performed best among them,

---

49 Those data reflect the situation that has to do with the 2014 emergence in Bulgarian political life of ABV, the formation of former socialist President Georgi Parvanov. Before that voters who identified themselves as leftists practically always chose BSP's ballot.

the Bulgarian Euroleft during the 1997–2001 SDS cabinet. In other words, there have been many reasons for leftist people in Bulgaria to support BSP, separate from their disclaimers, reserves, and disagreements with what the party has been actually doing. But then comes the natural question: Isn't this group of supporters—who are motivated much more by tradition than by current political offers—going to thin out? Party leaders have probably hoped that symptoms of distrust in BSP's leftist identity and leftist image would be minimized by the party's 'guaranteed' monopoly over left-wing political space. But perhaps the time is coming in which it cannot be taken for granted that if one is leftist and politically active in Bulgaria one has nowhere else to go but to BSP.

4 The Bulgarian Post-Communist Left in Crisis. Is a New Left on the Way?

4.1 The Challenge of New Leftist Projects

The former communist party in Bulgaria, now renamed to socialist, managed to retain its monopoly over the leftist political space in the country. This is one of the chief conclusions to follow from an analysis of the political, ideological and organizational dynamics in the country during the 1990s. The social democratic formations that had arisen as an attempt to provide an alternative to the Socialist Party went on to relatively quickly lose their public influence, thus remaining at the periphery of the political process. The various communist parties that had engaged in an outdated rhetoric did not succeed in inspiring a sense of perspective and a vision for the future. The creation of Coalition for Bulgaria around the Bulgarian Socialist Party in the beginning of the 21st century, on its part, allowed some circles with a communist, social democratic, agrarian, or nationalist orientation to place their personal bets on the old leftist party.

As we have seen, processes of splitting of new formations from BSP were part of the party's entire development in democratic conditions after 1989. The party went through several such waves. A number of party activists and executives, some of whom were enjoying considerable authority among voters, left the party and attempted to forge a political future of their own. And so the issue of the Socialists' 'monopoly' in the left did not of itself preclude a certain dynamics of splitting. Those processes were not something limited to BSP and were far from having to do only with periods of crisis or opposition. That is why the emergence of new left formations of this kind at the end of the first and the start of the second decade of the new century should not be viewed as a great surprise. But still, my hypothesis is that this is a new and important phenomenon that puts into relief some essential differences with respect to previous similar cases. This hypothesis however should be further substantiated.

I argued that the first years of the 21st century were marked by a 'sliding right' of the BSP executive's policies and messages, parallel with a 'sliding left' of the party's electorate, which consisted predominantly of people who were to a great extent negatively affected by the ongoing economic liberalization and social polarization in the country. The perception arose of a tension in the left's image—of a lack of consistency and absence, or at least crisis, of authentic leftist political representation. This problem emerged sharply during the government of the BSP-dominated Three-Way Coalition (2005–09) and led to a search for new leftist solutions.

Those decisions were of two types. The first had a genealogical relation with the tradition and practice of the Socialist Party; the second arose independently of that genealogy. The first type found an expression in the creation of new leftist projects—both within the party and in an outside competition with it. This is what I am going to discuss now. The second type, embodied in the emergence of new leftist groups, will be the subject of analysis in the next section.

The union of leftist socialists which became popular under the Left Wing moniker was founded as a faction within BSP. In August 2006, it stepped forth with a programme document entitled "Manifesto of the Left in BSP". The name of the faction and the title of the document have a somewhat paradoxical ring. The questions are plain for all to see: What could socialists be if not leftists? Even if we recognize that in the past there were communist or social democratic currents in the party, what does it mean for a socialist group to emerge within a socialist party? Why is a left to be created within a leftist party?

This strange choice arose as a consequence, answer and reaction to accusations of 'sliding right' on the part of BSP. We are talking here about a point in time less than one year after the start of the 2005–09 parliamentary term. But opinions were already clear and widespread that, within the coalition format, the leftist party was following the liberal course of its partners rather than its own platform. In the Manifesto, activists explicitly noted that reforms within BSP should continue on a leftist, not on a rightist foundation. The goals the document formulated are also important because they involved not only a definition of immediate problems, but also called for a return to the party's traditional image in Bulgarian society. The faction insisted on the "leftist political character" of the party, on overturning "the sliding right of the BSP policies and executive", on overcoming poverty in Bulgaria, and on BSP becoming the leader of a "technological and infrastructure modernization" of the country. Some expectations towards the Socialists that were familiar in the past were reactivated: the expectations for the party to first defend the poor (who in the given situation were starting to be considered as the losers of the transition) and for it to be the bearer of Bulgaria's modernization project. That is why it is natural that the critique against the new coalition government was concentrated in the social area (income policy, healthcare reform), the rule of law (organized crime and corruption), and morality (the quota distribution of appointments among coalition partners, an arrangement implicated in parcelling the state apparatus in separate party fiefs). The Left Wing thought it important for the party to widen the space of its presence in society, to open up its activity for civil society, and to establish itself as a "modern left European socialist party, a true member of the Socialist International and the Party of European Socialists." (Manifest 2006)

In the following years, the faction was quite active. It took a strong part in the discussion regarding a new BSP programme in 2008. The faction was to come out with what was perhaps the sharpest and most accurate assessment of the reasons for the heavy defeat at the parliamentary election a year after. The Left Wing argued well for the thesis that the road to reform and new mobilization in BSP must start from bottom up and to include the strengthening of the party's position and influence in Bulgaria's communities. That is why in the preparation of the 2011 municipal elections the group developed and offered a special document entitled "Leftist Policy Charter for Local Authorities." Ahead of the presidential election that same year, the faction even nominated its leader, Yanaki Stoilov, for BSP's candidate for head of state. In 2012, the group put forward resolute proposals for ideological change in the party, calling for a course to a "radical leftist reformism." According to the framework of this course, BSP had to part ways with "social liberalism and rightist social democracy" and to transform from a "capitalist" into a "socialist" left. The question was raised regarding the inconsistency of the party's political behaviour, in which the faction saw a key factor for the outflow of supporters and the loss of trust. According to the group, BSP has to overcome its "chronic ambivalence between being leftist while in opposition, and being opportunistic while in rule." And since a few years later, in May 2013, a new rule with BSP's participation started, the Left Wing maintained and developed their critique. At a conference in January 2014, the faction declared that the principal question facing the left at that moment is the issue of social justice, and without resolute steps for its solution, social policies would hardly be able to achieve any satisfactory result whatsoever.

The Left Wing invested continuous and consistent efforts to introduce into BSP a leftist image based on the traditional values of the social left in Bulgaria. The efficiency of those actions is however greatly contestable. The main sharply criticized rightist decisions of the Three-Way Coalition cabinet (2005–09) were taken not before but after the emergence of the Left Wing and its manifest. In spite of its aspirations for an ideological turn in BSP, the faction lost the battle for the new party programme, which was to a great degree based on the social democratic views of part of the executive elite rather than on those of the 'leftist socialists'. The latter had to acknowledge their defeat by stating that the 2008 47th party congress that adopted the program in effect "officialized BSP's sliding right." The Left Wing experienced further losses in terms of cadre and image, when in early 2009 many of its prominent representatives reached the conclusion that the Wing is not capable of reforming BSP and to direct the party into another, more authentically left direction, and left both faction and party to create a new leftist formation. The "Leftist Policy Charter for Local Authorities" did not come to be used in the process of nominating candidates and of preparing the campaign for the municipal election in 2011. In spite of the nomination on the part of the Left Wing, Yanaki Stoilov did not succeed in running as BSP's presidential candidate that same year. The party instead chose the figure of Ivaylo Kalfin, former Minister of Foreign Affairs, who had left BSP and was well known for his social democratic views—in other words, a figure with a political profile different from the one promoted by the Left Wing.

In early 2013, BSP appeared to be listening to the warnings and calls of the Wing. The sitting of the party congress in February that year called for "radical leftist politics"—something that echoes the Left Wing call for "radical leftist reformism." Stoilov himself was elected for party vice-chair. The ensuing new coalition rule with BSP's dominant participation in 2013–14 did not succeed in fulfilling the congress ambitions. Thus it appears only natural that when he ran for party leader in June 2014, Yanaki Stoilov secured a mere fourth place in the competition. The support he received had greatly thinned, especially compared to previous high levels of trust in him on the part of the party supporters.

The problems of the Left Wing that led to its downward motion stemmed foremost from its own political behaviour. The faction called for a return to the leftist track, for a radical left turn, but was constantly declaring its desire for that to happen within PES; i.e., it did not put into question the party's social democratic course. The adoption of a new party programme in 2008 that was considerably discrepant with the Left Wing's views did not result in efforts towards a new programme re-orientation. The Left Wing confined itself to the terms of that party document. But the heaviest blow on the faction was dealt by the short term in office of the 2013–14 coalition government. Earlier, one could argue that the insufficient influence of the Left Wing over party policies stemmed from its views not being accepted as strategic for the entire party. However, it then turned out that the Wing's ideas were implemented in the 2013 government program, without however coming to fruition in the 2013–14 cabinet rule. The problem with BSP's 'sliding right' emerged to be more complex than was recognized by the Left Wing. And the victory in the fight for ideas did not materialize into a victory in the fight for policies. Party supporters started to realize that if a change is possible in this respect, that change is yet not to take place in this fashion.

This is to a great extent due to the historical road of the party within which the Left Wing attempted to put its resolutions into practice. BSP's 'rightist sliding' was not the result of a sudden whim, an ill intent, or a temporary deviation from an otherwise one-track course. The attitudes of that formation towards privatization during the entire long history of Bulgaria's transition was far from being as critical as it was retrospectively attempted to be presented by activists both from the Left Wing and from outside of it. BSP took advantage of the privatization—and this applies to both the party as a political formation and individual party executives. At least from mid-1990 on, BSP was building capitalism in Bulgaria and its leaders were clearly realizing that fact. This was also true of the team of the 1995–97 Prime Minister Zhan Videnov, who most of everyone else endeavoured to construct—ultimately unsuccessfully—a leftist version of the transition. BSP was one of the three big parties (together with SDS and the ex-Tsar's party) to take responsibility for Bulgaria's governance in hard times during the erection of capitalist relations, and it was undoubtedly the best organized one among them. BSP participated in processes that inevitably and by definition gave rise to inequalities. During that period of the democratic transition, Left Wing leader Yanaki Stoilov was constantly part of the narrow or broader party executive. He was also the MP with the longest run in Parliament, having been a part of all compositions of the legislature from 1990 onward. That is why both he and his associates were in a position to be well aware that the problems diagnosed by them are not just rooted in the decisions of party leaders during the time in office of the Three-Way Coalition (although they solidified those problems) but rather have much deeper foundations. It was against those deeper foundations that the Left Wing had nothing to offer but verbal radicalism. The Left Wing had to face failure because it did not show resolve to impose a reassessment of BSP's role and objectives in the Bulgarian political life as a whole. The faction did not have a vision about the practical overcoming of the compromises that the party had made in its partnerships with other political formations and with representatives of business. And it thus remained in the confines of abstract leftist humanism.

The Bulgarian Left. If since its very emergence the Left Wing was seeking solutions for problems within the framework of current programme and political confines of BSP's operation, there were other politicians who were convinced that those confines had to be transcended. In spring 2009, a group of political activists from the leftist spectrum, predominantly connected with the Left Wing, left the Socialist Party, deciding to found a new formation, which came to be called 'The Bulgarian Left'. As reasons for their move, they cited the process of BSP's 'rightist sliding' during the rule of the Three-Way Coalition, the failure of the Left Wing as an 'internal opposition' within the party to defend and introduce leftist values and policies, as well as the rightist sliding of European social democracy, which, they argued, had come too close to the views of the political right, diverging only in points of nuance and not in points of principle.

The dominant figures among the new party founders were people of much more radically leftist positions than were manifested in BSP not only at that time, but also earlier. Some of them were considered close to former party leader Zhan Videnov and his unsuccessful efforts to implement a leftist rule in Bulgaria a decade earlier. But there were also people with a communist, agrarian, anarchist, or, broadly put, anti-fascist mindset. Two of the factors that differentiated the Bulgarian Left from the communist parties that emerged 'left' of BSP in the early transition period were the presence of young people with extreme left views and the search for a new, more attractive image of the extreme left, alien to the unwieldy jargon of the former communist regime propaganda.

The international context was also of significance here. Not just the European social democratic left was viewed as turning right after Blair's and Schröder's initiatives. During that period, at the European level, a grouping of the extreme left was formed, which received institutional weight with the creation of the Party of the European Left in 2004. Thus the opportunity opened for radical left formations to cooperate internationally and receive a representation that was not obliged to conform with processes within PES. The Party of the European Left accepted the Bulgarian Left as a member in 2010, and at its 4th congress in Madrid, December 2013, it elected Bulgarian Left leader Margarita Mileva for its vice-chair.

In its programme documents (Levicata 2009), the party isolated three large threats for Bulgaria: growing poverty, widespread unemployment, and deepening decay of entire regions. The solutions offered involved a ruthless fight against corruption, a reform of tax legislation to restore progressive taxation and terminate the practice of placing the main tax burden on the shoulders of the poorer and more vulnerable social strata, a special emphasis on communal services that most sharply affect people by depleting their personal budgets in the favour of rampant monopolies, a re-evaluation of the privatization, and a return of the state in the regulation of key areas of public life. The Bulgarian Left showed a love for the term 'modern'. Constantly invoking it, the party was striving to emphasize its reluctance to be associated with nostalgia for the collapsed socialism and the past as a whole. The formation insisted that it is a "contemporary anti-capitalist party" building "a modern, democratic socialism of the future" to create "a modern and future-oriented Bulgaria."

The Bulgarian Left, however, did not manage to seriously expand its influence beyond the initial circles out of which it sprung up. Some of the young people who saw in the party an opportunity for a true left, oriented towards the current European leftist issues and alien to BSP's economic dependencies and political inconsistency, gradually grew disappointed and withdrew. The party's messages were not clear enough. Two distinct lines can be identified that are hard to be accommodated with each other. On the one hand, there is the 'pro-European' tendency defending an up-to-date image of the left that is not yet traditional for Bulgaria and that focuses on the politics of identities, discrimination practices as forms of oppression, and anti-globalist ideas. On the other, there is the much more traditional rejection of BSP from the position of an earlier and more hard-line BSP, solidly grounded in the past of the Communist Party. At the three consecutive parliamentary elections (July 2009, May 2013 and October 2014), it transpired that the Bulgarian Left's results hovered around 0.1–0.2% of those who voted, with no upward trend. The founding of the party did not bring significant organizational shake-ups for BSP, which in effect did not allow an outflow of members in that direction, following the first wave. However, the Bulgarian Left is an important phenomenon in another respect. In the 1990s BSP activists left the party because they thought that it had not gone social democratic; i.e., that it had remained too leftist. The Bulgarian Left broke away with the opposite motives: that BSP is not leftist enough.

Alternative for Bulgarian Revival (ABV). Both the Left Wing and the Bulgarian Left featured popular BSP figures but still not ones from the highest peak of party hierarchy. Both the Left Wing and the Bulgarian Left were critical of BSP's path of development, but did not voice the criticism that the party had isolated itself. For a former party leader to attempt to do something broader than BSP itself is a new situation. Under the moniker 'Alternative for Bulgarian Revival', in 2010 a platform for political discussions was started by then Bulgarian President and ex-BSP leader Georgi Parvanov. In 2014, the platform was to transform into a political party that broke away from BSP and participated in May European Parliament Elections and the Bulgarian parliamentary election in October that same year.

The figure of Georgi Parvanov is central for making sense of this political project, which is up to now the most ambitious leftist venture in Bulgaria outside of BSP. Chair of the Socialist Party during a difficult period, when he led it on the process of social democratization, Parvanov won two times the direct popular vote for head of state and occupied that position for an entire decade (2002–12). This undoubtedly makes him the left's most successful politician for the whole period after the democratic transitions in Bulgaria.

Parvanov's officially stated reasons to dissent with BSP are quite different from those of the Left Wing or the Bulgarian Left. Following the Socialists' heavy defeat at the 2009 elections, Parvanov argued that the party was too attached to its role of a 'leftist' opposition, that it maintained a too confrontational relationship with then ruling rightists GERB, and thus remained closed for broad circles of civil society, expert communities, and the NGO sector. His aspiration to build for himself an image of a unifier rather than of a divisive figure had been already characteristic of his political practice in office as party leader and was clearly expressed in his policy of rapprochement with social democratic formations to the right of BSP. This aspiration had a logical continuation in Parvanov's terms in office as Bulgaria's President, when due to constitutional reasons he had to balance separate powers and to stand for the unity of the nation. Already in his programme address as a newly elected President in January 2002, Parvanov stated that ideologies were over in Bulgarian politics, and the time had come for pragmatism. This was something that he would recall in November 2010, at the foundational discussion of the ABV debate forum, organized by him. At that event, Parvanov declared that he viewed ABV as "a territory of historical compromise... between the left and right", as a bearer of a "new political culture after the confrontation of the transition", a bid to put an end to "polarized thinking and actions" and to "artificial fault lines", to give a chance to "professionalism and expertness rather than narrow party adherence". Parvanov saw reasons for such reassessment in the then raging global economic crisis, which had heavily affected Bulgaria, as well as in the decreasing trust on the part of citizens in parties and party executives, who were accused of living in their own world, different from the world of people's real problems and interests. "There is no leftist or rightist way out of the crisis", argued Parvanov, offering to seek decisions not in the coordinate system of left and right, of social policy, or stimuli for businesses but rather in the "healthy and well regulated state", working in a synchronized and efficient manner instead of burning out society's energy in conflicts and party clashes. "We don't need a new leftist or rightist party project. We need a civic project that will unite what is strongest from the left, the centre, and the right". This statement gave a continuation to the same thesis, according to which the left would revive if it is based on a position of national reconciliation that would delineate the points of concord among people (Parvanov 2010).

Parvanov maintained his critical stance towards the BSP executive in the ensuing years. In May 2012, after the end of his second (and constitutionally last) presidential term, he made an unsuccessful attempt to run again for BSP leader as a rival to his successor Sergei Stanishev, upon which he voiced similar motives: Parvanov said he was seeking to overcome the party's confrontation and self-isolation from actual society. Subsequently, ABV morphed from a 'civic' into a 'party' project. With its vehicle, Parvanov went to national elections in 2014, succeeding to pass the 4% threshold for entry into Parliament. In this way, for a second time after the Euroleft's breakthrough, BSP lost its monopoly over the leftist space in Bulgaria and entered into competition with an up-and-coming formation targeting voters of a similar social and demographic profile.

ABV's programme declaration, adopted at the party's founding conference in June 2014, expectedly did not talk much about divisions and ideologies. The dilemma it described addresses not different approaches to achieving one and the same goal (a prosperous Bulgaria) but rather different goals that we have to choose between: "Bulgaria as someone else's 'appendage', a Bulgaria divided into rich and poor, a country plundered and exploited", or a Bulgaria of "sustainable development, wide middle class, and social security". If we choose the second, alleged the programme, there cannot be divergent approaches. The approach must be founded on a compromise and consensus thinking among political forces. And since a newly emerged political party is after all obliged to identify its ideological coordinates and position itself, ABV did this in its programme, albeit in the last, fifth section of the declaration. Even though the party once more made the now traditional disclaimer that Bulgaria's political life is not so much about choosing between left and right but rather about choosing between status quo and change, ABV also added that it "identifies itself with new trends in the development of European social democracy, with the new reading of the left, with the new roads of the left as a whole, the new dimensions of leftist and social values: freedom, equality, solidarity, and justice". Immediately after stating this, the text added that this self-identification is not to be viewed as a self-limiting within the left spectrum. ABV's founders insisted that they would welcome people of differing ideas and thinking—people who might be disappointed, not represented, or having no one to vote for, irrespective whether they are leftists, rightists or centrists (ABV 2014a).

ABV's time in existence has been yet too short to formulate consistent conclusions regarding the movement's character and practical political presence, as well as regarding the image of the left offered by that organization. Another complication comes from the fact that in November 2014 ABV took the decision to participate in the newly formed centre-right ruling coalition in Bulgaria. A hypothesis can however be formed, using several reference points.

ABV built its identity foremost on the basis of a rejection of BSP—something that is to be expected given that it had to prove the need to separate from the Socialists. Parvanov's criticisms against the Socialist Party's leaders for their alleged self-isolation found a strong continuation in 2014. Already with his first public address, in which he stated his intention to separately participate in election, in January that year, the former President claimed that BSP's leaders are bound up in heavy oligarchic dependencies, that their decisions are taken in narrow circles and do not reflect the attitudes of party members, and that BSP's behaviour in the executive at that time enjoyed the comfort of a "media umbrella" over its misguided actions, the string of unfulfilled commitments, and its forgotten programme. In a resolution from the already mentioned June foundational conference, ABV gave a central place to the thesis that there is a "total moral and political crisis in BSP, an incapacity on the part of its leaders to assess the facts, and a danger that the left lose its influence as a significant factor in public and political life". That is the reason for ABV to present itself as a "clear alternative to the political impasse in the left and the failed term in office in the executive". (ABV 2014*b*)

There are international models against which Parvanov measured his political course. At the first place, this is Polish left politician Aleksander Kwaśniewski, who won two successive 5-year presidential mandates (in 1995 and 2000) using a rhetoric of national unification and attempting to demonstrate he is impartial and non-partisan by co-operating and opposing both leftist and rightist cabinets, favouring market reforms, and at the same time supporting the fight against unemployment and social exclusion. At the second place comes the experience of Greek left party PASOK which, instead of using strict levels of hierarchy, has preferred to craft for itself an image of a broad social movement uniting different ideological lines and engaging NGOs and common citizens in its internal life. The idea of the left as an 'umbrella' of a national movement with manifold manifestations is one that seems to fit the ABV mindset.

In addition, ABV is the first serious and successful attempt to create a 'presidential' party in Bulgaria. Bulgaria's democratic constitution gives comparatively limited powers to the head of state, corresponding to the president's role in a parliamentary republic—but it also provides for a direct popular election, giving the president a high degree of legitimacy. Bulgarian presidents have traditionally tried to take part in the formation of the policies of the parties that nominated them, but have often met the resistance of party leaders, who have tended to consider such interference as uncalled for. That is why the ambition to 'transfer' the presidential institution's legitimacy into a political project of one's own is easy to understand. And that is why Parvanov obviously had to rely on the thesis of a national consensus—a thesis strongly upheld by the presidential institution, thanks to the force of both constitutional provisions and the visions of the persons who have occupied it.

ABV invested efforts to develop two parallel geopolitical courses—once again in continuity with the view that politics needs 'balance'. On the one hand, Georgi Parvanov has been often associated with a pro-Russian position and has been defending joint Bulgarian-Russian investment projects, including the construction of a second nuclear power plant in Bulgaria and the building of the Bulgarian section of the South Stream natural gas pipeline. On the other hand, Ivaylo Kalfin, the second most popular ABV figure, has as a former MEP engaged in a much more distinct advocacy for Bulgaria's EU commitments. All of those factors have given a reason for ABV to be crafting, in the first months of its existence, an image in which social, conservative, and nationalist elements co-exist—but packaged as a manifestation of the 'modern' left pitted against the shortcomings of the 'traditional' left.

Movement 21. Apart from ABV, another formation emerged in Bulgarian political life taking its origin from BSP and subsequently succeeding to find some public support by distancing itself from the Socialist Party. This is the political project of noted ex-BSP MP Tatyana Doncheva, which resembles that of Georgi Parvanov in at least one respect: Both initially arose not as parties but rather as self-styled forums for discussion and policy formation, and only later, in view of a specific political moment, did they transform into full-fledged political parties. Movement 21 was created as a civic union in April 2010 on the premise that the left needs a more active dialogue and it was only in February 2014 that it was constituted as a party. Much like Parvanov, Doncheva had consistently upheld the thesis that BSP has isolated itself and that the left needs to open itself up to new public circles, something that cannot be achieved by the party itself. As a former chair of the parliamentary committee on control of security services, Doncheva used as a focus of her rhetoric the poor state of the rule of law in Buglaria, the corruption and oligarchic dependencies among the political elite, and the lack of transparency and integrity.

It is interesting to note that Movement 21's being recognized as part of the left spectrum is due above all to its leader's former affiliation with BSP. The movement's political programme and statute do not mention even once, in any form, the word 'left' (D21: 2014). The only references to the left's ideological arsenal can be found in the reference to the traditional social democratic values of freedom, justice, and solidarity, but without any deeper specification. It is true that the principal formulated goal in those documents is achieving a just society in Bulgaria, understood as giving "freedom in personal, public, and economic relations, without allowing sharp social divisions". Those social points are, however, distinctive not only for leftist but also for Christian democrat or conservative formations, e.g., those who have embraced the ideas of rightist leaders Adenauer and Erhard for a social market economy. The political course announced by Movement 21 includes general democratic goals, such as preservation and development of the democratic model, rule of law and defence of principal rights and freedoms, sophistication of citizens' legal, economic and political culture. Those vows are hard to position in one single ideological coordinate system. If they are close to a specific ideology, that would be liberalism rather than socialism.

The disapproval of BSP policies was again one of the chief lines in the party's self-identification. Movement 21 saw a reform of BSP as 'mission impossible' and envisioned the normal future of political life in Bulgaria in achieving freedom from the influence of oligarchic circles. According to the movement, change has to be driven by people of liberal professions and the small and medium enterprises. So the social basis sought by the movement can be described in social liberal categories. It can be admitted that at the present historical stage those layers of society need state support for a decrease of the pressure on them—administrative and oligarchic—and for an economic revitalization that would allow them a breath of fresh air after the heavy and lasting stagnation of previous years. Another feature not to be ignored is the pragmatism with which Movement 21 was presenting itself to the public—"we will offer the solution needed, without being held hostage to what doctrines view as left or right". We are once again witnessing the leaving behind of 'left-right' thinking announced by

ABV. But while Parvanov introduced in its stead some ideas involving nationalism and traditions, Doncheva appeared to be looking entirely forward—to the future, to the young, to a technocrat rationalism that must bring Bulgarians closer to the way of life of advanced globalized nations.

In one way or another, the newly emerged leftist projects have challenged BSP's hegemony over leftist space and over the image of the left in the Bulgarian political thinking. We must again recall that those processes are too dynamic to allow any final conclusions. I will venture some considerations but only in the form of a cautious recapitulation.

A chief motive in the emergence of new projects was the BSP-dominated rule of the Three-Way Coalition cabinet (2005–09) and its consequences. It was that rule that engendered a public and media atmosphere in which the Socialist Party was the object of systematic accusations that it has lost its left identity and political integrity. By reserving for itself the point of view of left identity or political integrity, a string of politicians decided that they could mount an opposition to the old left party. In public opinion, their motives have been often associated with economic dependencies and business interests, something that is not to be disregarded. But their own public argumentation always includes a disapproval and rejection of the politics conducted by BSP.

However, the new left projects' decisions, as different as they might be, have remained closed in BSP's coordinate system. The leaders and other public figures of those projects practically do not include people of political biographies stemming from outside of the Socialist Party. The claim of part of them to be broadening the left's territory can be seen as grounded if it refers to the lower echelon of their hierarchies but yet not to the elite. The initiators of those movements are not just associated with BSP—those are people that have enjoyed considerable weight and presence in the party. The Left Wing is chaired by the Bulgarian MP of longest service, Yanaki Stoilov, who initially received strong support from former party chair Alexander Lilov. The Bulgarian Left was initiated by Iliya Bozhinov, son of a long-time member of the communist Politburo under Todor Zhivkov. After Bozhinov's sudden death, the project came to be led by other MPs from different BSP parliamentary groups. ABV dealt the heaviest blow on the old left party's unity because for the first time an alternative formation was created and led by a former chair of the Socialists, Georgi Parvanov—who on top of that was the party's most successful and popular politician.

Movement 21's leader, Tatyana Doncheva, was for long years BSP's 'sharp blade' in Parliament and in front of media.

Personal relations within BSP have also played a role for the emergence of those new projects. The long accumulated hostility among certain figures surfaced first as a series of public distancings and later—as a series of splits from the party. The most striking example, which transformed into a key storyline in Bulgarian politics, was the hostile relations between former President Parvanov and his BSP successor Stanishev. After being elected President in November 2001, Parvanov pushed through the candidacy of Stanishev, who was hardly popular, for the leftist party chair position. Thus Stanishev to a large degree owes to his predecessor his heady political career to the top of power. But the subsequent conflict between the two, apart from being a battle for the power resources in the Socialist Party, is also a question of intellectual competition. The two leaders have two completely different biographies. Parvanov is a politician born in a relatively poor village. He rose through the party's youth structures during the communist regime without using serious protections. He graduated in history and went on to receive a PhD, but for a long time remained within the confines of party life and without stable contacts outside the country. On the contrary, Stanishev is a 'party aristocrat', son of the person in charge of foreign relations in the closest executive team of communist head of state Todor Zhivkov. With his international upbringing, Stanishev easily fitted in the European political circles and their intellectual discussions. In the Socialist Party, there was actually a similar broader line of division: between intellectual politicians, often hated for their status of party aristocrats, and others who claimed that they have made themselves and that they carry a social authenticity. Biographic trajectory is in its own fashion a source of political pride for both Parvanov and Stanishev. And their clash was prepared not just by their characters or institutional roles, but also by the very nature of the political process inside the Socialist Party.

The issue about the interpretation of the 'left' also acquired a central spot in the emerging divisions. Some of the new projects have insisted on their 'leftist' profile, while others have avoided stressing it or preferred to leave it in the background. Media and society viewed the latter as leftist most of all due to their BSP genealogy, and not so much due to their programmes or ideas. In their guise of being left 'by their own choice' or 'by definition', the different organizations diversified the nuances in the left's image: socialist views in the spirit of BSP's programme bids from the 1990s (the Left Wing); a modern neo-communism, with some important conservative disclaimers (the Bulgarian Left); quasi-nationalist social conservatism (ABV); pragmatic liberal technocratism (Movement 21). Those entities have enjoyed different opportunities to become established as sustainable actors in Bulgarian politics. In the first two cases, those opportunities have visibly decreased (in part due to a failure in coming up with attractive messages and in tying securely together ideas and politics); in the second two cases, opportunities seem to be growing (stimulated by the stronger demand for new players at the political stage and the indubitable media and business backing). However, negative aspects can have their positive sides, and vice versa. In the first two cases, the consistent leftist rhetoric could be able to resonate anew in some parts of the public, e.g., those with ever shrinking social perspectives. In the second two, the unclarity and underarticulation of their public presence could be able to provoke a fast disillusion among voters and a reorientation to the next 'new left'.

4.2 The Challenge of New Leftist Groups

In the end of the first and the beginning of the second decade of the 21st century, Bulgaria saw the emergence of groups with a radical leftist agenda oriented towards a thoroughgoing social change. Those groups were rejecting the Bulgarian Socialist Party's role in that change either explicitly, by describing the party as one of the forces of status quo, or implicitly, by refraining from mentioning it at all in their documents, initiatives and statements.

In the literature, the term 'new left' usually refers to the radical movements and the actions of progressive activists and intellectual figures in North America (most of all) and Western Europe during the 1960s and to some extent the 1970s. The concept most often includes the creation of a culture of participation of the community in all levels of public life during that period. The result is a radical view of democracy which does not always get its explicitly formulated dimensions, but still unites the diverse manifestations of the 'new left'. If we can talk about heirs to this movement in later times, scholars have suggested that we can find them in the circles of the academic left in the Western world (O'Neill 2001) or, in a broader sense, in the growing anti-globalist trends of recent times (Roussopoulos 2007).[50]

There are several reasons to choose such a name to also refer to the new social movements arising from 'bottom up' in the contemporary world including Bulgaria. First, some of them are using the term 'new left' to describe themselves. But what is not less important, their ambition in the end is to change the image of progressive anti-authoritarian thinking in an age of globalization, to discover the manifold hindrances for fulfillment of contemporary individuals and their rights, to demonstrate the need for a radical activism in the name of social change.

In Bulgaria, there is already a rich spectrum of such radical groups.[51]

Part of those groups directly identifies itself with the left. The New Left Perspectives project, for instance, makes in its manifest a distinction between 'traditional' and 'new' left. The people united around this undertaking declare that in contrast with the traditional Bulgarian left, they are calling for political and economic equality, that they consider equality, freedom and human rights to be their principal priorities, and that they want "everything for everyone." Opposing what they call "liberal hypocrisy", they consider that new left perspectives presuppose tearing down the monopoly over the left by the "traditional political tribune" and dethroning its "political and economic usurpers" by breathing a new meaning into concepts such as citizenship, society, people, community, minority—"the concepts that we ourselves are" (New Left 2012).

---

50 There have been also researchers who have used the term 'new left' in a newer context to denote the changing image of communist and neo-communist formations in Europe after the end of the Cold War—in Germany, France, Italy, but also in the post-socialist Czech Republic. The expression has also entered the language of politicians. Oskar Lafontaine, one of the major representatives of the German radical left, explicitly spoke of a 'new left' in the late 2000s when he was referring to the hopes for a reconstitution and revival of leftist parties in Europe (Hudson 2012: 96).

51 I have found extremely helpful the availability of a survey by Italian authors who have interviewed representatives of 10 Bulgarian left and anti-authoritarian formations in January 2014. Bulgarian respondents were asked to answer in writing a set of questions from a standardized survey touching on the occasion for the creation of the given group, its goals, actions, co-operation with others, attitudes to global problems, etc. The answers given present a very rich view of the situation with the 'new left' space in Bulgaria (Ferrario and Modesti 2014). In this section, I will be often referring to this study. Unless otherwise stated, quotations come from this source.

The participants in another group, Life After Capitalism, however claim that they do not "in any way" consider themselves to be leftist because although the left entirely or partially rejects capitalism it still does not oppose the state or representative democracy. Insofar as the left has been historically seeking some form of state control over capitalism, which has led him either to social democracy or to authoritarian communism, it has after all remained a defender of the status quo. The choice between free market and state is according to Life After Capitalism a false choice because it is in essence a choice between two forms of suppression.[52]

Notwithstanding that fact that some accept, while others reject the 'left' label, taken as a whole those emerging groups have usually been, objectively seen, part of the tendencies of the left, by virtue of the values that they have upheld and the goals that they have followed. In one degree or another, they have stood up against capitalism, exploitation, inequality, the encroachments against the individual person's dignity, the privileges of wealth, and the consequences of imperialist globalization, and they have defended the importance of social rights and public goods as central for the functioning of society as society.

Let me stress again that the 'new left' in Bulgaria comes in a quite broad range. The Solidary Bulgaria group has associated itself with social democracy. The main figures in the groups identify themselves as social democrats "without seeing themselves in the policies implemented in recent years by a large part of social democratic parties in the European Union, which have bowed their heads under the pressure of corporations." The Federation of Anarchists in Bulgaria, as is obvious from its very name, sees itself as a continuator of the tradition of the anarchist movement in the country (FAB 2007). The 23 September movement on its part has been named after the date of the 1923 September uprising.[53] This movement

---

52 I will use a longer quotation: „To claim that capitalism and/or the state can be good is just like claiming that the nuclear bomb can be good. Left and right are just like the two sides of the nuclear bomb—in their two-dimensional world, they might look different, but in three-dimensional reality they are in fact one, they ARE the system, they ARE the status quo. The goal of the nuclear bomb, of capitalism, and of the state/of representative democracy is one and the same—subjection, plundering and destruction of the majority in the benefit of a limited elite."

53 On 23 September 1923, Bulgarian communists started an armed rebellion against the country's authoritarian government that had taken power with a coup against the legally elected power some months before, and had after that imposed serious

has stated that it accepts Marxist-Leninist theory, and appears to be closest in its messages to the tradition of the former communist party, even though it has updated that line with the views of Che Guevara and contemporary fight against globalization (Septemvri 2006). In addition to social democrats, anarchists, and communists, among Bulgarian 'new leftists' we can witness various combinations of communist, anarchist, environmentalist, and cultural liberal theses that shape their worldview and attitudes to current reality.

The question of values takes pride of place in this quite broad perimeter of views. It is not mere chance that those new groups see their reasons for existence in the re-discovering and re-establishing of values that the political establishment in Bulgaria and throughout the world has allegedly corrupted with its practices and neglected with its actions, or else, in a more radical scenario, has attempted to marginalize and take out of societies' agendas. Solidary Bulgaria has repeatedly recalled that it was created as a discussion network of citizens upholding the social democratic trinity of freedom, justice, and solidarity. Solidarity is also a key value for practically all other such groups. Most of them to a very large degree see freedom as bound to equality, understood both as equality of rights and equality of standing. An important new aspect is contributed by the widespread reference to self-governance, not only among anarchists. The practical development of this value lies at the foundation of attitudes for rejection of exploitation and oppression for diverse entities such as the Xaspel Social Centre, the Bulgarian Social Forum, the Adelante Social Centre, where self-governance is intimately tied with self-organization and civic activism.

Some among the 'new left' developed an (almost) all-encompassing vision for the situation in Bulgaria and the world, identifying the defects of the present moment and what stands to be changed. Others have seen themselves in a much more modest position as a forum for engendering and clashing of alternative ideas, as intellectual workshops or laboratories. According to the Federation of Anarchists in Bulgaria, the modern world has reached a crossroad and the inadequate choice of development can make the entire civilization collapse. This civilization, argue the Anarchists, is

---

repressive measures. Bulgarian historiography during communist rule described the September Uprising as "the first anti-fascist uprising in the world," and the events of its eruption and suppression became part of the pantheon of communist resistance against fascism.

heavily burdened by problems such as changes in the environment, the degradation of resources, the complicated demographic picture, the contradictions between productivity of labour and distribution of goods produced. According to them, the only correct decision leads to direct democracy, solidarity-based economy, social equality, justice without compromise and the true federative structuring of all society. People from Life After Capitalism have also expressed the conviction that they are witnessing the collapse of a civilization "based on constant growth... and the subjection and exploitation of people, animals, and nature." In order to come out the self-destructing dominant model, they argue that we must leave the two-dimensional reality in which the choice of people and society is one between state and free market, and enter the three-dimensional reality, which replaces certain social models with others and leads humanity beyond the forms of hierarchy and suppression, called 'capitalism', 'central planning', 'state', and 'democracy'. Against this backdrop, the Adelante Social Centre sounds more moderate with its declaration that it sees itself as a place of discussion, maximally open and accessible for everyone, a place in which "alternative models and structures can arise." The same applies for the Xaspel Social Centre, which has formulated as its vocation to give a "working place for meetings, work, and creativity to individuals and collectives." Adelante have stood against capitalism and "vicious representative democracy," while Xaspel—against neo-liberalism and austerity, but they do not leave the impression of possessing a unified picture of global problems and the roads for their solution. Adelante have spoken about "a new mode of politics, a politics without taking power," while Xaspel have referred to their resolve to "win true social change," but it is clear that their 'meta-narrative' theoretical layers are much more weakly developed. The 'new left' also include groups which, even though they take active positions regarding many questions of public life, are concentrated around one leading issue and strive to entrench their values and views regarding that issue's development.[54]

Some among the groups have viewed politics as a principal field of change. The Adelante Social Centre believe that the true achievement of

---

54 An example here is the Civic Initiative for Public and Rail Transportation. It was founded on occasion of the strike of railway workers against the attempt at privatization of part of Bulgarian State Railways in 2011 and has maintained a string of initiatives in the name of a transport system efficiently working for society.

new groups is to show that outside of the traditional world of power, new horizontal movements are growing, as well as new ways of doing politics that will displace the hierarchies that have been dominating until now. According to them, autonomous structures and initiatives have to replace the model that reduces renewal to the party system and creates new political projects only to feed new illusions—a project that, they argue, is spiraling down into greater and greater crisis. A key point questioned by most new leftist groups is the liberal democratic matrix of political action, which according to them tends to marginalize the participation of citizens in the political process and to serve non-representative interests. That is why in their eyes the decision is to part ways with the practice of representation known up to now and to think politics not vertically, as the exercise of power and dominion, but rather horizontally, as inclusion and participation. There are however alternative positions. Solidary Bulgaria holds the view that Bulgaria needs changes not so much in its political as in its economic model of development, which has been subjected to big capital, monopolies, and oligarchy. According to this view, representative rule retains its advantages and has to be freed from the residue of economic distortions that have turned it against the people's interests.

There is also the issue about the means used. Even though in some of the cases groups have warned that the distinction between revolutionary and reformist means is not absolute, the distinction still exists in practice. The No Logo movement has explicitly formulated as its goal "the abolition of contemporary society by revolutionary means and the building of a global, free, non-hierarchical, and socially just society". The Federation of Anarchists in Bulgaria believes that the cyclical crises typical of capitalism will at some moment lead to a revolutionary situation for which masses have to be ready. The strategic goal that they have formulated is simple: "social revolution and the start of building a communist society". 23 September activists are convinced that they have to lead a "fight for freedom," together with freedom fighters in the entire world, with the task for them as a structure being the creation of "a revolutionary group—the first step towards the creation of a revolutionary organization". On their part, social centres are noticeably more reformist in their messages. Adelante have questioned the idea that a decision of global and Bulgarian problems can be given using the vehicle of power, arguing that this would be the result of a long process of transformation of our understanding of politics and using the word "dream" when talking about "a society without exploitation, without oppressors and oppressed". Xaspel envision their vocation to some degree in the spirit of Gramsci, not as a political clash, but rather as a "contra-hegemony struggle for the creation of a new language in media and public discourse". A new language can be perhaps created using force, but it is manifest that their intention is far from that.

However we might analyze the views of new left groups in Bulgaria, the diversity of viewpoints is impressive. It becomes clear that under the common denominator of 'new left' we have to put together positions that are far apart and sometimes mutually exclusive. They contradict each other on many questions regarding the present and future but also regarding the past. 23 September call on their supporters to become familiar as much as they can with their ideology, in which a leading place is occupied by the figure of Stalin. They have praised the regimes of Real Socialism, in which, they argue, public services became accessible to all, the economies experienced an upsurge, and young people had opportunities for holistic development. All that was quenched with the restoration of capitalism and thus progressive people have as their cause the new removal of this capitalism and the return to common ownership over the means of production, a planned regulation of production, a distribution of means in accordance with the labour provided by everyone, and the building of a classless society. I have already pointed out that according to other groups contemporary liberal democracy and communist authoritarianism are the two sides of the one coin of oppression. The New Left Perspectives manifesto categorically rejects the traditional left, which apart from the oligarchic dependencies of BSP leaders consists of "a handful of people ridden with nostalgia and unable to step in the present and to look into the future", whose leftist thinking is reduced to "aggressive talking, old-fashioned slogans and waving of empty symbols". It can sometimes appear as if some of those groups are describing others. But if 23 September paints with bright lively colours the life of socialist society as "a first attempt for transition to a society without oppressed people", New Left Perspectives seem to remember completely different things—"prison camps, repressions, secret services, snooping, monuments, and mausoleums" as well as "the most terrible crime", the so-called Revival Process of changing the names of Bulgarian Turks during the late part of the Zhivkov rule.

The opposition among the groups' views regarding the past is not something stemming from situational circumstances, from personal sympathies or antipathies, or from biographical trajectories or policies of memory. It stems from their completely different methodological presuppositions. The Bulgarian 'new left' is a meeting spot for partially updated versions of classical anarchist and communist visions, on the one hand, and new post-materialist tendencies, on the other. One of the cups of the scales holds the logic and even the conceptual apparatus of a Bolshevik or anarchist left, which talks about the contemporary transnational monopolistic capitalism as a "highest stage" of capitalist accumulation, about the "predatory interests" and "imperial plans" of capital, about the need for an "vanguard" in the fight for freedom (23 September in their *Principles*), about "terminating once and for all of all institutions for oppression and plunder", about "deceit and mockery with the people's aspirations and dreams", and about "peoples as our brothers" (Federation of Anarchists in Bulgaria in their *Declaration of Principles, Ends, and Means*). The other cup of the scales holds views placing human identities at the basis of the left and defending vulnerable and pressured minorities of all kinds—from ethnic to sexual ones. Here come into play the discursive construction of reality, the power relationships entrenched in language, the experiences that have been subjected or pushed in the periphery, Foucault and Žižek. Those topics are present more or less strongly in the documents of the social centres, New Left Perspectives, and others. This does not mean that those two broad types of groups do not share common points on a number of issues, including ones of worldview. But it comes to show that the so-called 'new left' groups feature a huge spectrum of trends—from Stalinist to post-modern, from Western to Eastern, from academic to trade-unionist, from class- to identity-based.

Even though they may sometimes be very different, separate groups have quickly demonstrated that they are able to co-operate on specific public causes and to work together very efficiently. I will mention several such examples of simultaneous initiative or partnership among diverse representatives of the 'new left'. Those have to do most of all with protest actions, insofar as they addressed extremely pressing problems that provoked progressive groups of different views to unite around common causes and to go out in the street.

An important share among those is taken by anti-fascist initiatives, petitions, and protests. The impression was created that no matter the ideological colour of those in power, Bulgarian public authorities tend to tolerate or not treat with the needed severity acts reminiscing fascism. The new leftists have stood firmly against the so-called Lukov March held yearly in Sofia.[55] They have expressed, among other things with official letters to institutions, their resolute denunciation of the founding of a political formation expressing explicitly Nazi views.[56] They have been consistent in seeking responsibility from neo-Nazi gangs in Bulgaria, who have many times staged acts of violence against immigrants or representatives of minorities. Another entry is made by mass actions against uncontrolled attempts on the part of major countries or transnational corporations to impose their interests in Bulgaria, given well-founded doubts that this is at the expense of the health, security, or other interests of Bulgarian citizens and businesses. Protests were repeatedly held against allowing major companies to raise or import products involving genetically modified organisms. Warnings for a possible environmental disaster motivated actions against the ambitions of US companies to explore for and produce shale gas in the country. In both cases, under the pressure of those initiatives Bulgarian institutions had to step back and impose regulatory bans. The ACTA agreement on the protection of intellectual property adopted by the EU was in the end rejected after massive protests in most European countries including Bulgaria, which were organized by groups that saw in ACTA an attempt for control over internet space and its users. Among the latest rallies with active participation of radical left groups are to mention protests against the creation of a zone of free trade between the EU and USA, the so-called Transatlantic Trade and Investment Partnership, accused of taking away a number of powers from nation-states and their citizens to the benefit of corporations and big capital.

---

55 This is a march staged by nationalist groups in honour of the memory of a senior Bulgarian army officer, Gen. Hristo Lukov. Well-known with his public support for Nazism and Hitler's regime during World War II, he was assassinated in 1943 by communist conspirers.

56 I mean the so-called Nationalist Party of Bulgaria, which attempted to be formally incorporated in 2013 with extremely xenophobic and violent views of political action. The date for the party's founding was symbolically chosen to be November 9, the 75th anniversary of the anti-Jewish pogroms during the Kristallnacht in Germany.

Rights advocacy is another major area of co-operation among the 'new left' and with other groups of Bulgarian civil society. This includes resolute and public manifestations of dissent with different types of discrimination in the exercise of labour and the enjoyment of individual freedoms, focusing on drastic instances of workplace exploitation (e.g. in the light industry throughout Bulgaria) or on negative attitudes towards sexual identities. Environmentalist events, too, have had their part in the new leftists' ambition to defend the common person and their rights against the arbitrary rule of capital. A string of protests were staged against construction on pristine beaches at the Bulgarian Black Sea coast and the cutting down of mountain forests to develop the tourist business. Part of those rallies were crowned with success and made the institutions revise their initial good-will for those intended business ventures.

The new left groups are a relatively recent phenomenon in Bulgarian. They sprung up and articulated their profiles, with some small exceptions, two decades after the end of the communist regime. One of the probable reasons for this is the dynamics of social and economic processes in the country, which in the early 21st century started to produce a sharp social polarization, to widen the gap between poor and rich, between developed and prosperous regions, between successful and stagnant businesses, between prospering major capitalists and personal and family companies struggling for survival; i.e., a dynamics that brought up anew questions regarding the meaning of the left and its tasks in such social situation. What is more, allegations came to be widespread that Bulgarian governments are serving similar agendas differing only in details, which presented political life as static and fed the desire for a 'radical' future in contrast with the 'stagnant' present and for 'change' as a reaction to the 'status quo'.

For some segments of society such change is not to be recognized in the political offers of parties, which have come to be seen more and more as different faces of one and the same dominant model of governance. Preconditions were created not for alienation from one party or another but rather from politics in its present guise—and this stimulated the conviction that a better perspective for society is possible outside of the confines of the traditional party system, in a radically new type of politics with radically new rules and organization. This alienation is especially characteristic of younger generations, among which mistrust in institutions, parties, and politicians has reached critically high levels (Mitev and Kovacheva 2014: 143–

146). A peculiar political crossroad was opened in front of the Bulgarian youth. In looking for solutions some of them have taken the road to nationalism and radical rightist explanations of existing problems. Others, a smaller part, have taken the left road.[57] But what does 'left' mean here? We must also underscore the growing mistrust that in Bulgaria there is an authentic political exponent of leftist ideas. For many people, the humanist ideal of social relations working in the benefit of the common person does not have significant points of intersection with the messages of any political force, including those that call themselves 'leftist'. According to such views, the contact with power (parliamentary, executive, or municipal) has placed all parties on the other side of the barricade, among the exploiters and not the exploited. 10 or 15 years earlier, it was not even theoretically possible for a movement to emerge that would seek the 'third way' between neo-liberal mainstream and the traditional left, stepping at the same time on the liberal doctrine of the priority of human rights and dignity, and on the leftist idea of solidarity and social sensibility. A 'new left' came to be possible (again: theoretically possible) only in the new century, on the basis of the already walked historical miles.[58]

The peculiar national crossroad has its supra-national dimensions. The stimuli for the creation of new leftist movements should not be isolated from the global context. The emergence of new social movements in Western Europe, the radicalization of the extreme left, the strengthening of informal co-operation and of the network approach in the construction of communities have had their effect on Bulgaria. Practices such as the

---

57 The comparatively more limited attractive force of the 'left' road compared to the 'nationalistic' one has been long noted in studies of the structure of ideological attitudes of the youth. In Bulgaria, similar to Macedonia, the share of young people with rightist views in 2014 was almost two times higher than that of leftist young people—in contrast with the relative parity that existed for instance in other Balkan countries. Explanations might be sought in the hegemony of rightist discourse regarding the transition but also in the domination of right populist formations in the political process (again Mitev and Kovacheva 2014: 147).

58 "[T]he left of the generation that now judges democracy using its own criteria, instead of confining itself to the opposition to communism that has become a cultural norm. This is a generation that is not afraid that communism will come back. It is afraid for democracy and thinks that it urgently needs a leftist perspective". This is the assessment of the Bulgarian new left's generation potential by one prominent Bulgarian political scientist, who goes on to add his understanding of the characteristics of this leftist perspective: socially sensitive, culturally liberal, anti-nationalist, secular, solidary, anti-corporate, civic, anti-racist (Todorov 2013*b*).

World Social Forum also found their supporters in the country. Many of the new groups have analogues in other European countries, draw from their experience, and import some of their causes, modes of organization, and methods of dissemination. The 2011 mass anti-austerity protests in Greece clearly exerted their influence, both with their radically leftist pathos and with their forms of mobilization. The Greek protests' cause and readiness for change make a greater impression than their insecure party or political backing. In the light of the Greek experience, leftist masses appear to be politically more mature than leftist parties (Kouvelakis 2011). A motivating role was also played by left movements in Poland that engaged in vibrant public activity in the context of the crisis in the Polish post-communist left—such as Krytyka Polityczna and Praktyka Teoretyczna. We could also mention the effect of the 'Subversive Festival' in Croatia that united different groups, or the initiative for "democratic socialism" in Slovenia, which achieved parliamentary representation. From a financial and organizational point of view, the role of the German foundation Rosa Luxemburg is not to be underestimated, not only with its register of partner leftist groups in CEE but also with its continuous support of their different endeavours and the ties among them. In the course of those processes in Bulgaria key thinkers of the contemporary left, such as Slavoj Žižek and Alex Callinicos, have become popular. Not least, one of the most important reasons for the development of the 'new left' has to do with the communication revolution. The rise of the internet and social networks, as is well known, has made grouping according to interests and values much easier. It has also made possible the self-organization of such groups without great expense and the need for generous sponsorship, creating preconditions for them to become 'visible', at least in the all too high waters of information in today's world.

The authors of the January 2014 survey of the Bulgarian 'new left' have formulated some important and precise observations that deserve to be mentioned and commented, if we are to assess the specifics of the phenomenon under question. The researchers have noted that in the great majority of cases, the new groups are composed of young people. That can be a minus because it might suggest a lack of connection with preceding generations and their experience, but it can also be a plus because it could concentrate energy for the future. In fact, for several Bulgarian generations, the left self-identification tends to lead almost directly to the communist and later the socialist left. In this case, it is an advantage that for the first time in Bulgaria there can be observed a conscious and systematic construction of a leftist identity outside of the BSP coordinate system and without references to its organizational and intellectual 'genetic code'. Another point that the authors of the survey have made could be provisionally called the 'elitism' of the new leftists. As a matter of fact, they are indeed concentrated foremost in capital Sofia, even though examples such as the Solidarity Center in Varna or the United group in Veliko Tarnovo suggest a broader geographical spread. In all accounts, the bonds of the new leftists with intellectual or academic circles are much more marked than those with labour. Partner relations with trade unions are almost absent. This is not so strange, given that since the very start of the democratic period, Bulgarian trade unions have been accused in ad hoc work, inordinately close ties with the political and economic elite, and a significantly weak degree of intervention in protecting labour during the course of economic transformations in the country. As I have partially shown, the 'new left' have maintained an impressively rich variety of positions on topics in Bulgaria's public and political agenda, but in spite of this they have not found it needed to enter the stage of institutional politics. Some of them have tended to think that this stage is indeed a trap steeped in false dilemmas and creating a false feelings of alternatives for society, while actually remaining a façade for a political and economic status quo and a mere theatre of representation. The radical vision of such activists excludes the option of a 'repair of the system' and presupposes instead only that system's 'dismantling' as a road to achieving their goals. Such a view has two consequences. First, most new left groups have avoided their formal founding and have no legal existence, binding internal rules, or executive organs, and because of this they do not project an image of homogeneity and unambiguous causes. Of course, there are exceptions to these generalizations when NGOs come to be created on the basis of those groups, most of all in view of applying for projects for financing. And second, the diversity of their activities also tends to come outside the sphere of current political life and most often can be reduced to political education in its varieties, including journalism, public discussions, but also publishing, talks, lectures, and viewing of films (Ferrario and Modesti 2014: 4).

The stormy events in Bulgaria during 2013 and the three grand protest waves in February, June, and November that year had their catalytic effect on the new left groups, to a great extent bringing them 'to the surface'. Their positions and points of view made it to 'official media', including on the internet. Different and much more popular 'public spokespersons' started to lead more or less active disputes with representatives of the 'new left'. Thus, the latter achieved a new higher level of public recognizability. Again, we can talk about two trends as a result of the catalytic effect of 2013. The first registers, perhaps paradoxically, an even more distinct division among separate groups instead of their unification under some common banner. The second opposes them, even more markedly than before, to the Socialist Party still dominating the left space.

The attitudes towards the 2013 protests are something that differentiates the separate groups. Some of them were entirely positive. Those groups stressed that we could now see a potential for developing protest culture in Bulgaria and to additionally discredit the existing model, opening the road to new horizontal forms of action (the Adelante Social Centre). According to another standpoint, the protests were an expression of direct democracy, and they have to always be supported by proponents of direct democracy, because they bring constructive energy for the future, no matter where there are economic interests involved or not (Solidarity Centre Varna). Some of the positions were more nuanced. Protests have to be supported, but only as a first step, after which a second is necessary—namely, to formulate an alternative to the rejected model (Life After Capitalism). In contrast, still others were not convinced in the possibility for a second step, claiming that protesters demanded only a repair of the system, but not its abolition, and so were not radical enough (Federation of Anarchists in Bulgaria). There were also groups that were internally divided in their attitude. They were taken aback by the anti-communist messages of protests and what they saw as an abstract morality propounded by protestor spokespeople, but still they thought that a critical reflection on protests on the part of participants could be a very useful step (Xaspel Social Centre). Voices 'against' provided the argument that protests in fact served certain dishonest party calculations (Priziv Student Movement) and refused to go to the economic foundations of oligarchy, which made them insincere in their ambition to overthrow it (Solidary Bulgaria). A completely categorical rejection was also voiced, based on the thesis that the protest manifested an unambiguously anti-social, elitist, pro-capitalist, and pro-neoliberal character (No Logo).

Difference on the issue regarding the meaning and directions of civic activity among new left groups has been coexisting with an ever more clearly articulated and expressed rejection of BSP as a pretender to the leftist crown in the Bulgarian political process. The role of the party has been many times commented in the public statements of representatives of those groups. For instance, Solidary Bulgaria has admitted that it owes its very origin to the "disappointment with BSP's radically rightist policies". This movement has concentrated the sharpest critique against BSP: that the party does not give political representation to leftists in Bulgaria, that its oligarchic behaviour has filled the very concept of left with negative content in the public's eyes, that its unprincipled compromises with its ideological core have turned the party into a "plug obstructing the formation of a new democratic left in Bulgaria". Disagreement with the claim that BSP is a leftist party is to a large degree a common denominator of the new left groups. They have resolutely refused to see in it a possible partner, viewing it, to the contrary, as a foe that hinders their own activity because delegitimizing with its political course everything left. The Xaspel Social Centre has formulated an assessment of BSP's ideological character: extremely conservative culturally and extremely neo-liberal economically. New Left Perspectives's manifesto has expanded on this type of argument. It has defended the need for a new left with the thesis that leftist politics in Bulgaria has been monopolized by BSP and reduced to absurd rightist economic measures. BSP has been interpreted as a 'traditional left', internally split into two—a liberal-oligarchic and a conservative-paternalistic part. The first stems from the rightist practice of the transition's neo-liberalism; the second, from the rightist legacy of state socialism. The task of the new left, according to the manifesto, is to strip the left of partisanship and nostalgia. Only then could Bulgaria get its true left.

The 'new left' are quite far from BSP not only verbally. In most of their positions, they have also diverged in practice. With the entire risk of generalizations and with the qualification that it is very hard for the diversity of such groups to be reduced to common characteristics, it is still possible to give the following comparison between the 'new left' and BSP (see Table 4.2.1).

Table 4.2.1.
Views of BSP and the new left on leading political, economic and cultural issues

	BSP	New left groups
View on the economy	State regulated market economy	Priority of social communities and solidarity in economic processes
Support for religion and the church	partial	no
Emphasis on the rights of minorities	partial	strong
View on generation change	conservative	radically positive
View on culture	conservative	liberal
Principal agent of social change	the state	social capital
View on conventional political participation	positive	skeptical

An impression could be created that the 'new left' do not pose a real challenge for BSP's political presence, for they, so to speak, run in different tracks. The new groups are not part of the race for voters and MPs seats, or for participation in the institutions of European, national, or municipal power. They are unquestionably fragmented, and practice has shown that situations of political crisis do not tend to bring them together, contributing instead to an additional distance apart. There is also a certain intellectual closedness although some of those groups have invested efforts to overcome it through specific initiatives in circles and professional communities far from intelligentsia. The educational system pushes the representatives of those groups up, instead of holding them on more down to earth where they could more immediately and efficiently influence people.

This self-imposed political marginal standing could be explained in part with ideological radicalism. Most 'new left' have attracted significant numbers of new supporters only with difficulty, after declaring that they want 'a change of the system' and nothing short of that. As we have noted, their ties with wage labour have been limited, for which part of the reasons are to be seen in the situation of the trade union movement in Bulgaria. The 'new left' have been quite active on environmental issues, which are questions that have tended to attract the attention of a significant part of society. At the same time, the unusual rightist self-identification of Bulgarian environmental organizations has tended to distance them from the messages of leftist groups. We should not forget that environmental structures in Bulgaria are a very well developed sector and enjoy ample public recognition, notwithstanding their modest electoral results (Krastanova 2012).

After all, the fact remains that the spontaneous emergence of new left groups has not led to a waning of enthusiasm and gradual decline. Most of them have preserved themselves and continued their activities. Their collectives are often highly educated and very adaptive to the contemporary situations; they have close contacts with similar structures outside Bulgaria and have managed to find financing for their initiatives by applying with different projects. It is true that at this point of time they have not achieved a broad public popularity[59], but in circles in which they are known, they have retained their positive image. This has created preconditions for young people of leftist beliefs to recognize them as their own and to seek answers for the questions troubling them with those groups, rather than with political parties of leftist orientation. We should not also underestimate the circumstance that a large part of the new left groups have been consistently and resolutely presenting themselves as the 'new' left, in contrast with the 'old', embodied by BSP, and in this way have contributed to the erosion of BSP's public image as a party that is capable of looking forward and not only back.

The political outlook for 'new left' however appears to be disheartening. As things stand, those groups appear to be just one of the (not too likely) options for an impulse of development of the Bulgarian left. However, we should bear in mind that in situations of crisis and dramatic drift of social layers, unexpected perspectives might open up for seemingly marginal phenomena.

---

59 However, we can say that this popularity is slowly rising. An example of this is the monthly magazine A-Specto which was initiated in March 2014. It brought together a bunch of Bulgarian leftist intellectuals and was soon to become an influential tribune for analyses and comments in a leftist and anti-globalist vein.

4.3 The Challenge of the 'Protest Year' 2013

2013 came to be among the peak years of global social discontent. With different scale and numbers, agenda and causes, duration and intensity, a string of civic protests swept the streets in cities in and outside of Europe. From Brazil to Thailand, in Spain and Slovenia, Russia and Ukraine, Turkey and Bosnia and Herzegovina, thousands of citizens openly voiced their dissent with government decisions or with governments themselves, with politicians and parties, with the economic model or the geopolitical orientation of their countries. Almost a quarter of a century after the start of democratic changes, Bulgaria, too, was not spared from powerful eruptions of protest activity unseen in the country at least since the dramatic 1996–97 winter and the collapse of the socialist Zhan Videnov cabinet.

2013 was without doubt a 'protest year' for Bulgaria not just because of the intensity with which citizens took to the street. Protests gripped large groups of Bulgarian society and claimed to be expressing their attitudes and demands. During the preceding decade and a half, people had often rallied, but their discontent had almost always been of a 'sectoral' nature. Their agenda involved the defence of rights and interests of separate groups. Ad hoc unions, civic movements, professional organizations, economic corporations had all been agents of those actions, which were carried out without a leading role for political parties and without, to a large degree, an involvement of networks of civic organization 'from below'. An impression was created that what society wanted was not a change of political power, but rather a change of policy with respect to a specific group or specific issue—not resignations, but rather solutions. In most cases, we could hardly speak of a more or less common public interest. To the contrary, protest activity was diverse. The phenomenon appeared of 'protests against protests'—certain groups standing up against others. Bulgaria's EU membership (2007) played the role of a context for different protest agents. There was no 'big' cause for everyone, apart from the country's European perspective in its manifold manifestations—from rule of law to a worthy life. Time belonged to 'small' causes (Popivanov 2008*b*).

In 2013, demands appeared to be much more global. Discontent addressed not separate policies, but rather the model of government as a whole. Not only those in power but also the opposition was targeted. People no longer accepted that political parties truly represent them, and that made them turn against the very bearers of power rather than against certain of their moves (Krastev 2014: 8–32). Citizens' anger was directed against the irresponsibility of political elites, against unprincipled behaviour that was destroying transparency and answerability, rendering politics oligarchic and undermining the quality of democracy in Bulgaria (Ganev 2014). The radicalization of Bulgarian society might perhaps appear unexpected against the backdrop of the relative social tranquillity of previous years. Without doubt, what we had was a flaming up of problems that had been long accumulating and that needed only a sparkle to explode.[60]

The first large protests in February 2013 led to the resignation of the centre-right GERB cabinet of PM Boyko Borissov. In itself, this is a remarkable fact. For the first time after February 1997 in Bulgaria, a cabinet stepped down before the end of its term. The country entered in a lasting political crisis. A period of less than two years (from February 2013 to November 2014) saw three parliaments and five cabinets (including two temporary caretaker governments entrusted only with conducting early general elections). Civic unrest and street pressure, the creation and collapse of ideologically unusual coalitions, economic hardships and banking tremors, new records of low trust in institutions and parties, and a blossoming of new political entities were all present during that period. There was an almost universally shared perception that a critical moment in the development of Bulgarian democracy had come that required a reformulation of the positions and roles of the political forces.

We could conditionally isolate three large protest waves in Bulgaria during 2013—in February, June, and November. But insofar as the November wave that culminated with student occupations of universities continued and further articulated the messages of the June wave, Bulgarian society was facing two major protests—a 'winter' and a 'summer' wave. Their characters were quite different. The winter protest was sharply social,

---

[60] Impulses and models of imitation were also coming from the outside. The protests in Greece in 2011 and after were often commented in Bulgarian media and society, upon which as a rule a negative comparison was being made between 'wakeful' Greeks and 'sleeping' Bulgarians. The second wave of the 2013 protests in Bulgaria, which surged in June, started just two weeks after the stormy thousands-strong demonstrations in Turkey that had burst out 28 May 2013 after authorities' decision to change development plans for Gezi Park in Istanbul. It is well-grounded to consider that the wide media coverage of events in Turkey also influenced the attitudes of the Bulgarian public.

starting from mass indignation with high and unpalatable electricity bills during the heating season, and then growing into rallies against monopolies in the energy sector, but also against big capital in general, and against the lack of efficient social protection for working people. The summer protest raised predominantly moral slogans and was provoked by the appointment of a major media mogul of dubious reputation at the head of Bulgaria's national security agency. Protesters stood up against the trampling down of democratic standards and the subjection of politics and law to shady economic interests. Within the time separating the two waves, parliamentary elections had been held. The winter protest was in the end directed against the rule of rightists. Its summer counterpart was in its very first weeks already attacking the new centre-left government. The similarities and differences between the two waves are debatable, but it can be claimed that they had a common denominator in the resolute rejection of business dependencies in Bulgarian politics.

Both protests, each in its own way, walked past the leading force in the Bulgarian leftist space, BSP. The February congress of the Socialists, which took place literally one day before the start of unrest, proclaimed a resolute "left turn" and formulated much more social and leftist messages than had been put forth by the left during the preceding decade. But still, under no form whatsoever did BSP succeed in becoming an exponent of the winter protest's demands, even though it attempted to legitimize itself as the main opponent of rightists GERB and the close to four years of relentless austerity policies they had carried out. There were common points between the Socialist Party's theses and those of the protesters, but the perception was never alive that the latter were placing hopes for the fulfilment of their demands on the former.

The May 2013 early general elections led to the formation of a coalition cabinet of BSP and DPS. But the cabinet was not the product of an election victory. Polls gave the first spot to none other but the GERB party, which had just been brought down by the protests. For the first time in the history of the Bulgarian democracy, the victor party did not come to take part in the executive. From this perspective, the centre-left cabinet could be interpreted as just an opportunity to demonstrate a government different from that which GERB had offered rather than as a green light for policies freely chosen by the leaders of the now ruling parties. Protests against the coalition cabinet, which continued on a daily basis for months, succeeded in eroding the claim that we were witness to a 'different kind of rule'. The voiced demands, steeped in moral pathos and lacking in social issues, led to a limiting of the social basis of the protest. The movement relatively quickly closed itself within the confines of capital Sofia and its central areas, acquiring a strong elitist tinge. The opportunity opened for BSP to establish itself in public opinion as a 'leftist antithesis' of the 'rightist protest' and to re-legitimize itself as a left party using the simplest mechanism of opposition. Logically speaking, things could sound that way: if you're against the right, then you belong to the left. But in practice this did not work out. The accusations that BSP is, in fact, a pro-oligarchic formation resonated much more widely in the media and society than its vows to be making a 'left turn'.

Why did that happen? We should recall again that the protests were aimed against the political elite and what came to be more and more frequently called 'the status quo' as such. Together with many other motives, a discontent surfaced with the result of the democratic transition, in which BSP had undoubtedly played an active part. Doubts that the Socialist Party constitutes a 'left alternative' to what was happening were widespread. The term in opposition turned out to have been insufficient for the party to 'clean up' the residue of the negative image it had acquired during the time of the Three-Way Coalition (2005–09), which came to be lastingly associated with rightist policies and corruption. The cabinet formed in 2013 was a new chance for a clean-up of that image and for change. But we can say that this opportunity was squandered. Street protests, sympathetic media and opposition formations managed to additionally 'package' public perceptions of the Socialists with elements such as corruption, business dependencies, and social indecision. On its part, the Socialist Party of course also carries a large part of the blame for that negative trend.

In spite of being in power after May 2013, BSP quickly fell into public and political isolation. A number of factors—many of which had already had a lasting one-way effect—combined in acting to shape the parameters of the incipient crisis of the leftist party.

There was an absence of a sufficiently broad public space for BSP's messages. This concerns most of all the media sphere. With the exception of a party daily of limited circulation and with influence almost exclusively on the hardline supporters of the party, practically no mass printed or electronic media can be named that exhibited a sympathetic stance on BSP's actions and messages.[61] BSP could not boast of a large number of sympathetic public speakers, either, i.e., people of authority whose words could have weight to attract the public's attention to the problems and solutions as defined by the party. Insofar as such speakers were present, they belonged to BSP and the public was treating their points of view much more as partisan than as personal or expert. This unenviable position of the party can be partially explained with the lack of desire on the part of Socialist leaders to create a parallel centre of leftist power based in the media space. But another important point was also the lack of a truly committed policy towards the intelligentsia and its needs during the entire democratic period.

There was an absence of working ties with civic structures. BSP had almost no close NGOs that it could work with. Bulgaria's civil society sector had in its major part built itself in opposition to the policies and image of the former communist party. It came to be established as a bearer of liberal and neo-liberal messages, traditionally rejecting 'leftist' theses as nostalgically dangerous or populistically impossible. And since the main donors of Bulgarian NGOs have tended to come from abroad, most of all the US but also Western Europe, one could expect that NGOs would be additionally reproducing the sceptical attitude of the so-called West towards the CSPs. Thus we reached a situation which has repeated itself with lawlike regularity, in which we tend to associate independent and expert positions with a critique of the left, and, in turn, we tend to associate leftist positions with partisanship and not independence, civic freedom, or expert understanding.

It can be argued that what is seen as the prestigious discourse of the Bulgarian post-socialist transformation is the rightist and liberal discourse. First, because the positive sign in that transformation is carried by change; and change has come with advancing rightist liberalism, against retreating communism. And second, because the former communist party itself has almost officially admitted that the transition had a 'rightist' character and has not succeeded in developing or applying a 'leftist project' for the devel-

---

61 Disagreement and non-acceptance in a number of cases, especially during the last few years, came to spread out to cover leftist talk as such. An indicative phenomenon here is the 2014 campaign against a Bulgarian National Radio journalist that demanded that his show be stopped from airing because of defending one-sidedly leftist views.

opment of the country. Thus during all years after 1989 BSP remained 'non-prestigious'. In contrast with, say, the 1920s or 1930s, it was no longer 'fashionable' to be leftist or socialist. The sole potential 'prestige' of the socialists, and that not in the minds of the entire society, can be reduced to the period of the communist regime. In this way, a quarter of a century after Zhivkov, it was possible for BSP—which had come a long way from its communist legacy—to be producing anti-communism as a reaction against itself, and for anti-communism to be a driving force in Bulgarian politics.

There was an absence of palpable ties with labour. The left in Europe had emerged a century and a half earlier in close co-operation with the trade union movement defending the rights of workers in the economic sphere. This relationship has remained standing till this very day. The main West European leftist parties have maintained close relations with trade unions. Historically, the Bulgarian left was no exception. Among the reasons for its ascent after World War I was its skill to integrate itself in the trade union structures, which were on the rise. The democratic transition overturned this picture. Both the trade union formerly sanctioned by formal communist power and the trade union that entered in the opposition SDS bloc (Podkrepa) took up a clear anti-communist stance. For a quarter of a century, Bulgarian trade unions were more or less hostile to the left.[62] But the point does not concern only organized forms of labour protection. Problems with the conditions and remuneration of labour in Bulgaria, which were acquiring drastically scandalous forms in the context of privatization and the lack of efficient control mechanisms, appeared to leave BSP unconcerned. In the course of the short 2013–14 term in power, the ruling Socialist Party again did not find the strength to show intolerance to injustice in the social sphere.[63]

There was an absence of efficient ties with the youth. This problem had followed the entire democratic stage of the Socialist Party. The advancing medium age of its members and voters, made manifest by opinion polls, speaks of itself about an extremely weak potential to attract young people.

---

62 This has found an expression in, for instance, trade unions' refusal to celebrate the traditional European trade union holiday, Labour Day on 1 May, only because on the same date BSP traditionally holds its own rallies.

63 During that very short period, there were a number of dramatic cases such as the chronic failure to pay out due wages in the weapons factories in the town of Sopot and the terrible working conditions that led to the tragic death of miners in the Oranovo mines.

In Bulgaria, there is no significant political party with such a low share of young electorate. The Socialists did not invest meaningful efforts in building a youth policy that could assess the needs and attitudes of young people in Bulgaria and offer them answers adequate to their worldviews. BSP is to be noted neither with an active course in support of the professional fulfilment of young people nor with a strategy for engaging them in politics via party mechanisms. Together with the stereotypes of BSP as a party turned towards the past, all of that has helped solidify the impression that any young people who orient themselves to the Socialists tend to do so due to family tradition, or due to carrier or business considerations—but not so much inspired conviction. Indeed, the ascent of new left groups of a predominantly youthful profile would have hardly been possible had the above been otherwise. And BSP itself seemed to not allow to its own youth structure to unfold its full potential to offer policies and messages. The public presence of this entity has been mostly unconvincing and has involved most of all artistic or 'voiceless' activities, but has not given much input on the roads of development of the Bulgarian state and politics.

Yet again, there was an absence of inspiring goals for government. BSP came back to power in 2013 with the slogan "Bulgaria Back to the People", but did not succeed in formulating a programme that could flesh it out. What is more, after the cabinet's constitution, The Socialist representatives refrained from referring to the goals set out by the Socialist Party itself, preferring instead to talk about the tasks set by the cabinet, which was composed together with a partner party from another ideological family and chaired by an expert PM.[64] BSP's motivation was presented in a way that was too pragmatic, ad hoc, and without a desire to offer a more sweeping vision or cause, remaining in the perception of many as the mere ambition to give meagre social benefits to the most needy. Much needed doors to the active layers of society, the people of intellectual labour, and those who praise toleration, social order, progress, and Europe (Penev 2010: 162–164) were to remain close.

---

64 PM Plamen Oresharski, nominated by BSP, has never been a party member, but, moreover, 10 years before he served as vice-chair of the main anti-communist force, SDS.

The internal divisions and splits that set in after May 2013 only naturally created a perception of instability of the party in power.[65] Without doubt, in most cases there was a strong personal moment involved, together with vested interests, career discontent, or economic motives, but still those shake-ups were noted in the public debate with the moral issues their raised (no matter how earnest their motives were). Those included questions about the personal wealth of specific figures in the BSP executive, their being part of oligarchic networks, their dependencies on the will and interests of Bulgarian and foreign companies, as well as questions regarding the domination of family and clan circles in the party's decision making.[66] The statements, declarations and disclosures of facts stimulated public opinion to perceive BSP as a corporation or a joint stock company with the balances and dividends of separate shareholders rather than as a political party with all of its possible advantages and faults.[67]

Real or exaggerated, BSP's dependence on DPS turned into a fact in the minds of the public, including many of the Socialists' members and supporters. It was as if there was a true revival of the times of the Three-Way Coalition (2005–09) when the systematic insinuation reigned that the cabinet was standing at the mercy of DPS's will, and this most junior partner in the coalition was receiving a disproportionally large share of power in decision making. The sense of a déjà-vu was sufficiently strong to make home that no lessons have been learned from the past. In 2013–14, accusations against BSP of serving DPS's interests grew considerably. The Socialists' opponents, just as 5 years ago, were incessantly talking that the once powerful 100-year old party was participating in the cabinet in the mere role of a servant of someone else's intentions. But this was an opinion also shared by a significant part of the BSP political elite and by separate local organizations inside the party; that is, it did not come only from the outside.

---

65 As early as July 2013, BSP supporters, among whom members of its executive, gathered on a rally in front of the party's headquarters to protest against its personnel policy. And in January 2014, the most popular politician of Bulgaria's left, former President Georgi Parvanov, announced his wholesale rejection of the party's course, declaring his intention to present his own candidates' list at the upcoming European elections (see above, Section 4.1).

66 Accusations in lack of transparency and corruption did not stop at 'lower levels'. Some of them targeted directly then party leader Sergei Stanishev and his family.

67 BSP vice-chair and former Parliament Speaker Georgi Pirinski, for instance, has explicitly referred to the party as a "holding".

Let us recall that for long years during its communist period, this party had been actively defending and helping entrench anti-Turkish attitudes via the education system and the media. Existing negative prejudices in Bulgarian society against Turks only solidified this picture. To this, we might add the problem with the unfulfilled election commitments on the part of BSP, which include some central ones—from the unfreezing of the project for a second nuclear power plant to the abolition of the flat tax rate. Attempts at excuse with citing the disagreement of the coalition partner had been already played out during 2005–09. Now the coalition partner was the same party. That is why many people started to question the point of a self-standing election platform if the party's central positions can be easily sacrificed at the coalition altar, without a preceding internal discussion or a serious supporting argument.

The resultant force of those factors involves the erosion of fundamental features of BSP's public image in the Bulgarian society. In play here is a process that had started long ago and that had gathered momentum during the term in office of the Three-Way Coalition to hold full sway in the course of the short lived 2013–14 cabinet in the guise of something already experienced that was only repeating and deepening the same errors and same negative characteristics.

BSP stopped looking like a driving force of the Bulgarian political process. It was no longer perceived the way it was—for good or for bad—by many during a significant part of the democratic period. The party seemed to lack its own specific offer to the Bulgarian society or will to change it in a well-formulated direction. Shortly put, the Socialist Party was no longer giving reasons to be seen as a party of the future. Its positions in the political debate came to be defensive and in a certain sense even appeared to be seeking excuse. To some extent, this could be seen as justified by the 'siege' situation in which the party was placed by the mass protests and the fact that it had to formulate policies under street pressure. And still, there was no a convincing impression that the Socialist Party had a resolute desire to take the initiative and be a party that sets the agenda rather than react to an agenda set by others. From a political force that by virtue of its Marxist roots ought to be a party of historic optimism, with time BSP was turning into a party of historic pessimism, and this bore the fruit of apocalyptic passiveness or conformist flexibility in the public debate.

BSP seemed to be losing the moral fight to be a party that resolutely stands behind the poor individual in the Bulgarian society—behind the people who lost from social and economic transformations, behind the vulnerable and all those who felt their perspectives dammed. The anti-oligarchic rhetoric of the protests and the moralizing propaganda of internal and external opponents enflamed lasting problems for the Socialists and demonstrated, if I am allowed to use Andersen's metaphor, that 'the emperor is wearing nothing'. If BSP was once associated with statism, or the view that state regulation is needed for public and economic processes, this line of thinking was growing gravely weaker and torn. Many reasons, part of them discussed above, led to the perception that BSP's 2013–14 term in power left a weak state controlled by and serving big capital rather than its citizens.[68]

Another traditional stereotype regarding the Socialist Party was also put under question—the belief that it is capable of being an agent of the project for modernization of the Bulgarian society. The Socialist Party's modernization views in the 2013–14 period did not come to be articulated in the shape of effective state policy and were left with the stamp of indecisiveness and unpersuasiveness. With the intent of overcoming Bulgaria's economic stagnation in early 2014, BSP put forward the slogan of reindustrializing Bulgaria, which included creating productive enterprises to compensate the collapse of the country's industrial economy under the pressure of privatization. But this bid did not come to be filled with adequate content. BSP attempted to set into motion major infrastructure projects such as the construction of a new nuclear power unit and the building of the Bulgarian section of the South Stream gas pipeline. The result was that the party yielded nothing but empty strokes and constant scandals for more than one year. International factors can be said to have played an important role

---

68 A certain, albeit not leading role in the initial formation of those attitudes was played by the judiciary during the whole democratic period. Its messages were traditionally very close to the anti-communist forces' accusations in corruption and abuse of power directed at the former communists. This was something at time facilitated by the cadre developments in the higher levels of the judicial system. A number of key figures, who by definition should be independent, such as Ivan Tatarchev, Bulgaria's Chief Persecutor at the onset of transitions, or Ivan Grigorov, a later President of the Supreme Court of Cassation, were not hiding their belonging to anti-communist organizations and were voicing markedly negative views of BSP.

for the failure of the Socialists's modernization programme—but that does not make it a lesser failure.

In its capacity of a successor of the former communist party, BSP was strongly reliant on the votes of those Bulgarian citizens who tended to assess positively the socialist period and who identified with its achievements. But it turned out that the Socialists gradually lost their position of a party with a monopoly on nostalgia. On this terrain, their main rightist opponent GERB was treading with a steady step. And that was nothing unexpected. In contrast with the initial anti-communist right in the new Bulgarian democracy, the SDS who mounted a wholesale rejection of the age of socialism and its political elite, GERB were striving to draw part of their legitimacy from the memory of the communist past[69]. Traditionalism, patrimonial messages, references to the scope for construction of the old regime all became a trademark for GERB. That is how the high estimation for the socialist period among large groups of Bulgarian society (something measured by opinion polls) no longer transforms into electoral support for the communists' successors. It turns out that many in Bulgaria strongly like the communist regime and the person of Zhivkov, but resolutely reject the contemporary BSP and do not even consider themselves to be leftists.[70]

If in the past BSP had been drawing part of its legitimacy from nationalism and Russophilia, these two stereotypes gradually started to contradict the party's behaviour and messages and the forms in which those were being presented to the public by media. There was no way that long-time active partnership with DPS could be interpreted as an expression of nationalism. On the other hand, the 2013–14 configuration in the Bulgarian Parliament was such that the BSP-led cabinet had to rely on the presence of nationalist party Ataka MPs at parliament sittings. Domestic and international criticisms of this situation led to systematic attempts on the part of BSP to distance itself from Ataka and nationalism. 'The Russian link', also very strong

---

69 GERB was founded in 2006 and is still chaired by Boyko Borissov, a former bodyguard of the communist head of state Todor Zhivkov.
70 According to very recent opinion poll data, the share of positive assessment of the socialist period in Bulgarian history is higher than that of the negative assessment in all (!) age groups, except the 28–40 year old segment where the two are equal. Among older generations, this positive assessment surpasses the negative more than 5 times (Mitev and Kovacheva 2014: 137). It is not hard to see that those with a positive assessment are twice as many as BSP's voters and the people who identified themselves as ideologically leftist.

in the past, was put under pressure during the time of the Three-Way Coalition with the decision of the Socialist-dominated cabinet to allow the building of US military bases on Bulgarian territory. Harder blows were served by the consequences of the worsened 2013–14 international situation, especially in the light of the anti-Russian protests in Ukraine and Russia's annexation of Crimea. Tense relations between Russia and the West called for separate European countries to 'make their stand'. Bulgaria, then ruled by BSP, was among the countries that took a position critical of Russia's behaviour.[71] Against the backdrop of categorically pro-Russian messages of the Ataka party, this exerted a manifest effect upon BSP's image as a Russophile entity. Further actions on the part of the Socialists attempting to decrease this impression failed to bring immediate change.

That is how BSP found it to be extremely hard to find for itself an image that could be seen as positive by large groups of society. The natural result from this was the sequence of two heavy defeats at elections for European Parliament in May 2014 and Bulgarian National Assembly in October that same year. In May 2013, elections had given Socialists the chance to make amends. A year later it was evident that amends had not been made. Dilemmas regarding BSP's future were now looming large.

In the end of the day, the Bulgarian political process should not be viewed as separated of the European processes and the dynamics of CEE events. In the early 21st century, BSP was less and less often making attempts to develop its own strategies, starting to increasingly depend on PES messages instead. The Bulgarian socialists were apparently re-adopting the old Blagoev's thesis that the future of the left in Bulgaria is conditional three fourths on the situation abroad and only one fourth on the situation at home. Thus the incipient insecurity of the European left came to be reflected in Bulgaria. Ahead of 2014 European elections, PES came forth with slogans for more jobs, fight against youth unemployment, and a new industrialization for Europe, and BSP attempted something similar in Bulgaria.[72] After May 2014, PES quietly backed off on most of its ideas. The same happened to BSP, which appeared to be trapped in the cul-de-sac of

---

71 Minister of Foreign Affairs Kristian Vigenin, who was also a member of BSP's highest executive, was one of the first EU statespersons who visited Kiev to talk with new anti-Russian authorities as early as March 2014, only one week after the deposition of President Viktor Yanukovych.

72 A useful analysis of this point has been offered by Kaneva (2014: 115–119).

the European left. And that is to some extent understandable if we take into account the tradition in accordance with which we are to think of the potential goal of the leftist project as international and not achievable in a separate country. By definition, leftist projects should be changing the economic environment for the functioning of society and politics, and in the globalized world this environment is international to a much greater degree. Thus, leftist parties, BSP included, have come to be dependent on decisions of the left at the supranational level. And during the years after the 2008 world economic crisis, the supranational EU level was oriented to what have been in effect rightist policies. Critics reduced European institutions' efforts to ambitions to save banks and major capital from the blows of the crisis and nothing more. It was not the regulations and general conditions of labour but fiscal stability that received predominance. There appeared to be no place for the left here. And BSP's dependence on PES's impasse was rendered even more perceptible due to the de facto refusal on the part of the Bulgarian Socialists to look for a version of their own that could be adequate to the situation of the EU's poorest member, where social distances are greatest and most painful, and too many people have to lead a daily struggle for survival.[73]

The fate of CSPs in CEE offers another context that is hardly more comforting for Bulgarian Socialists. The second decade of the new century has found those parties almost everywhere on the retreat. This is something most clearly expressed in Poland and Hungary. The Polish Democratic Left Alliance has been steadily and relentlessly losing positions, leaving the political stage to the clash between a moderate right (economically liberal and culturally conservative) and an openly populist religious-conservative right. The Hungarian Socialist Party, after the shake-ups of the 2000s, is not giving any signs of recovery, but is also losing influence in the competition between social-nationalistic populism and purely nationalistic populism. In Slovakia SMER has retained its stable standing, but could only with difficulty be perceived in the traditions of the post-

---

73 Statistical data on current European indexes show that in 2012 the relative share of Bulgarian citizens under the poverty line was 21.2%, with the share of those who are in danger of poverty and social exclusion—49%. In both respects Bulgaria was in the gravest condition among EU member states. There is a trend for this feature to turn into a stable characteristic of Bulgaria's population (see e.g. Ganchev 2014: 25–26). It goes without saying that this sorry picture makes for a not inconsiderable potential political space for leftist formations, at least theoretically.

communist left. In Romania social democrats have been very strong electorally and politically, but it is debatable to what degree that is due to their leftist profile, which has quite evolved in the direction of social populism and conservative nationalism, becoming even less distinct after a number of coalitions with rightist and liberal formations. Germany and the Czech Republic are special cases. The CSPs there have registered an advance rather than decay—a trend expressed more clearly in Germany and more weakly in the Czech Republic. However, one should not forget that after democratic changes those parties have not participated in state government and have never been considered part of the liberal consensus for the development of their countries.

In the first chapter of this book, I tried to show that post-communist left parties in CEE have walked different roads of transformations and development, shaped in part by their role and goals in the former socialist societies, and the traditions of the countries in which they exercised power. The common Eastern Bloc framework notwithstanding, ruling parties turned out to be surprisingly different, and what happened with them after is directly related to this 'being different'. What is perhaps paradoxical is that after a quarter of a century of liberal democracy—which gives much richer opportunities for political development—those parties in their major part had to face not different but rather similar crises more or less having to do with the issue of their identities and the biographies of their relations to rightist and liberal policies, their belonging to specific consensus situations in political life, and the fact that they have come to be seen as an elite in the implementation of reforms. When, as a leftwing force, you have a hard time explaining in the name of just what you are an elite, the possibility is growing that you will become the target of anti-elitist attacks.

The populist Zeitgeist, using the expression of Cas Mudde (2004), has dried out the political force of leftist formations. Widespread distrust in the left's capacity to solve problems transformed itself in hopes for leadership (in line with US patterns that were becoming more and more popular), and for pragmatism pretending to lead beyond left and right. Such attitudes are sufficiently popular in Bulgaria, too, strengthened by an alarmingly low level of trust in parties and institutions. In fact, the populist wave turned out to be much more fatal for the left than for the right because behind the messages for pragmatism and concern for the people it was reproducing the economic and social order of rightwing liberalism in CEE.

In political life, BSP has fallen in the shadow of the rising populism. In leftist space, it has fallen in the shadow of formations such as ABV or Movement 21, which have shown a desire to participate in the partitioning of the Socialists' assets and which have enjoyed a much better media presence. To a smaller degree, the old party has also fallen in the shadow of new left groups, which do not compete for voters, but which have systematically undermined BSP's left image and have become a more and more wanted partner on the part of NGOs, media, and foreign actors.

The crisis of the Bulgarian Socialist Party after October 2014 does not automatically mean a transfer of some of the left's symbolic capital in another direction. The crisis of BSP is a crisis of the Bulgarian left taken as a whole, a crisis requiring a thoroughgoing re-formulation of the left's place, role, and perspectives. The old reflexes and decisions, the old ways of mobilization and public presence are becoming less and less effective.

The old gods are already dead, and others are not yet born.

In Lieu of a Conclusion

In this book, I have attempted to show the following:
- ✓ The Bulgarian left possesses specific national characteristics significantly differentiating it from the manifestations and issues of the left in post-socialist CEE: characteristics that brought the Bulgarian communist successor party to the fore in the processes of the country's democratic transformation after 1989.
- ✓ The Bulgarian left has existed in different forms, but the society is bound by lasting ties to the functioning of a specific party—communist in the past, socialist nowadays—and that party's projects for a radical change of the trajectory of the Bulgarian national development.
- ✓ The public and political role of the Bulgarian left can be understood above all in a retrospective view, as part of a long historical tradition that gradually shaped the left's image and the stereotypes and expectations following from that image.
- ✓ In the new democratic situation, the Bulgarian left, in spite of its strong tradition, did not succeed in formulating a leftist project for the country's development and took the course of compromise with dominant rightist liberal trends.
- ✓ In this way, a crisis of identity has naturally ensued, which requires a thoroughgoing reassessment of the notion of leftist ideas and leftist policies in Bulgaria, in spite of, and perhaps even because of, the presence of strong leftist attitudes in society.
- ✓ In the end, the image of the left in Bulgaria has often turned out to be more important that the left's policies. The messages and beliefs suggested by the Bulgarian left have often exercised a stronger attractive power than the actual mechanisms of protection of social or class interests—especially in the country's most recent democratic history.

That is why, in my view:

There is undoubtedly a solid ground for a stronger left in Bulgaria, the poorest EU member. In the historical road it walked, the leading Bulgarian leftist party has been instrumental in developing and shaping certain value and worldview attitudes among a significant part of Bulgarian society. This party is now facing its most serious challenge for the last 25 years, and its dominant position is shaken by new leftist projects 'from above' and new left groups 'from below', by political populism 'at the top' and social apathy 'at the bottom'. Notwithstanding the fate of this party, the attitudes it helped shape are here to stay and they are bound to seek political agency to find their expression.

Bibliography

ABV 2014a. *Patjat na Balgarija v novija vek. Programna deklaracija na Politicheska partija ABV* [*The Path of Bulgaria into the New Century. Programme Declaration of the Alternative for Bulgarian Revival Political Party*] www.abv-alternativa.bg/documents.html?file=files/upload/docs/ProgramaABV.doc (Jan., 2015)

ABV 2014b. *Za obstanovkata v stranata i izhoda ot politicheskata kriza. Rezoljucija na uchreditelnata konferencija na PP ABV* [*On the Situation in the Country and the Exit From the Political Crisis. Resolution of the ABV Foundational Conference*] www.abv-alternativa.bg/documents.html?file=files/upload/docs/ABV_resolution.doc (Jan., 2015)

Andreev, Svetlozar 2009. "The Unbearable Lightness of Membership: Bulgaria and Romania after the 2007 EU Accession". *Communist and Post-Communist Studies* 42(3): 375–393

Backes, Uwe and Patrick Moreau (eds.) 2008. *Communist and Post-Communist Parties in Europe*. Göttingen: Vandenhoeck&Ruprecht.

Baeva, Iskra 2010. Balgarskijat socializam sled Vtorata svetovna vojna kato izsledovatelski problem [The Bulgarian Socialism after the World War II as a Research Problem]. In *Izsledvaniya po istoriya na socializma v Balgariya 1944–1989* [*Studies on the history of socialism in Bulgaria 1944–1989*], edited by Evgeny Kandilarov, 7–24. Sofia: Friedrich Ebert Stiftung.

Bell, John D. 1977. *Peasants in Power. Alexander Stamboliski and the Bulgarian Agrarian National Union 1899–1923*. Princeton NJ: Princeton University Press.

Bell, John D. 1986. *The Bulgarian Communist Party from Blagoev to Zhivkov*. Stanford: The Hoover Institution.

Berglund, Sten and Joakim Ekman 2010. Cleavages and Political Transformations. In *Handbook of European Societies: Social Transformations in the 21st century*, edited by Stefan Immerfall and Göran Therborn, 91–110. New York and Dordrecht: Springer.

Betz, Hans-Georg and Helga A. Welsh. "The PDS in the New German Party System". *German Politics* 4(3): 92–111

Blagoev, Dimitar 2010. *Nashite apostoli* [*Our apostles*]. Sofia: Zahary Stoyanov.

Blair, Tony and Gerhard Schröder 1999. Europe: The Third Way/Die Neue Mitte. http://web.archive.org/web/19990819090124/ http://www.labour.org.uk/views/items/00000053.html (Jan., 2015)

Bozóki, András 2005. The Image of Europe: The European Integration and the New Central Europe. In *Changing Faces of Federalism: Political Reconfiguration of Europe from East to West*, edited by Sergio Ortino, Mitja Zagar and Vojtech Mastny, 85–106. Manchester: Manchester University Press.

Bozóki, András and John T. Ishiyama (eds.) 2002. *The Communist Successor Parties of Central and Eastern Europe*. New York: M.E.Sharpe.

Branković, Srbobran 2002. The Yugoslav 'Left' Parties: Continuities of Communist Tradition in the Milošević Era. In *The Communist Successor Parties of Central and Eastern Europe*, edited by András Bozóki and John T. Ishiyama, 206–223. New York: M.E.Sharpe.

Brunnbauer, Ulf 2007. *Die sozialistische Lebensweise. Ideologie, Gesellschaft, Familie und Politik in Bulgarien (1944–1989)*. Wien: Böhlau.

BSP 2008a. *Programno razvitie na BSP. Sbornik dokumenti 1990–2005.* [*Programme development of BSP. A collection of documents 1990–2005*]. Sofia: Centar za istoricheski i politologicheski izsledvaniya.

BSP 2008b. *Za Balgarija—svobodni grajdani, spravedliva darjava, solidarno obshtestvo. Programa na Balgarskata socialisticheska partija* [*For Bulgaria—Free Citizens, Just State, Solidary Society. Programme of the Bulgarian Socialist Party*] www.bsp.bg/public/files/docs/nova-programana-bsp-1.doc (Jan., 2015)

BSP 2010. *Balgarija 2020—evropejska socialna darjava. Osnovni parametri na levija proekt. Deklaracija na 47-ija kongres na BSP* [*Bulgaria 2020—a European Welfare State. Chief Parameters of the Leftist Project. Declaration of the 47th congress of the Bulgarian Socialist Party*] www.bsp.bg/public/files/docs/tezisi-bg-2020.doc (Jan., 2015)

Cholova, Blagovesta 2008. The Europeanization of the Bulgarian Party System. In *New Perspectives for the EU Team Presidencies: New Members, New Candidates and New Neighbours*, edited by Atilla Ágh and Judit Kis-Varga, 185–206. Budapest: 'Together for Europe' Research Centre.

Collignon, Stefan 2012. The Preconditions of Social Europe and the Tasks of Social Democracy. In *The Future of European Social Democracy: Building the Good Society*, edited by Henning Meyer and Jonathan Rutherford, 39–55. Basingstoke: Palgrave Macmillan.

Cotta, Maurizio 1996. Structuring the New Party Systems after the Dictatorship: Coalitions, Alliances, Fusions and Splits during the Transition and Post-Transition Stages. In *Stabilizing Fragile Democracies. Comparing New Party Systems in Southern and Eastern Europe*, edited by Geoffrey Pridham and Paul G. Lewis, 69–99. London: Routledge.

Crampton, R.J. 2005. *A Concise History of Bulgaria*. 2nd edn. Cambridge: Cambridge University Press.

Curry, Jane Leftwich 2003. Poland's Ex-Communists: From Pariahs to Establishment Players. In *The Left Transformed in Post-Communist Societies. The Cases of East-Central Europe, Russia and Ukraine*, edited by Jane Leftwich Curry and Joan Barth Urban, 19–60. Rowman&Littlefield Publishers.

Curry, Jane Leftwich and Joan Barth Urban (eds.) 2003. *The Left Transformed in Post-Communist Societies. The Cases of East-Central Europe, Russia and Ukraine*. Rowman&Littlefield Publishers.

D21 2014. *Politicheska programa na PP Dvijenie 21* [Political Programme of the Movement 21 Political Party] http://d21.bg/wp-content/uploads/2014/09/D21_programa_izbori_2014.pdf (Jan., 2015)

Dainov, Evgeny 1995. Dihotomnata revoljuciya ili 'lyavo' i 'dyasno', krivo i pravo, novo i staro [The dichotomous revolution, or 'left' and 'right', wrong and right, new and old]. In *Mahaloto na Darendorf: 'Lyavo' i 'dyasno' v balgarskiya politicheski jivot [Dahrendorf's pendulum: 'Left' and 'right' in the Bulgarian political life]*, edited by Ivan Krastev, 7–26. Sofia: Friedrich Naumann Stiftung.

Damianova, Zhivka 1990. Bulgaria. In *Formation of Labour Movements 1870–1914. An International Perspective*, edited by Marcel van der Linden and Jürgen Rojahn, 393–420. Leiden: Brill.

Daskalov, Roumen 2011. *Debating the Past. Modern Bulgarian History from Stambolov to Zhivkov*. Budapest: Central European University Press.

Dauderstädt, Michael 2005. "The Communist Successor Parties of Eastern and Central Europe and European Integration". *Communist Studies and Transition Politics* 21(1): 48–66

De Waele, Jean-Michel and Sorina Soare 2011. The Central and Eastern European Left: A Political Family under Construction. In *What's Left of the Left: Democrats and Social Democrats in Challenging Times*, edited by James Cronin, George Ross and James Shoch, 290–318. Durham, NC and London: Duke University Press.

Detrez, Raymond 2006. *Historical Dictionary of Bulgaria*. 2nd edn. Oxford: The Scarecrow Press.

Dimitrov, Vesselin 2001. *Bulgaria: The Uneven Transition*. London: Routledge.

Dimitrova, Antoaneta 2002. Bulgaria. In *Post-Communist Democratization. Political Discourses across Thirteen Countries*, edited by John S. Dryzek and Leslie Templeman Holmes, 206–221. Cambridge: Cambridge University Press.

Dimou, Augusta 2009. *Entangled Paths Towards Modernity. Contextualizing Socialism and Nationalism in the Balkans*. Budapest and New York: CEU Press.

Drezov, Kyril 2000. Bulgaria: Transition Comes Full Circle 1989–1997. In *Experimenting with Democracy: Regime Change in the Balkans*, edited by Geoffrey Pridham and Tom Gallagher, 195–218. London and New York: Routledge.

Dullien, Sebastian, Hansjörg Herr and Christian Kellermann 2012. A Decent Capitalism for a Good Society. In *The Future of European Social Democracy: Building the Good Society*, edited by Henning Meyer and Jonathan Rutherford, 57–73. Basingstoke: Palgrave Macmillan.

Elster, Jon, Claus Offe and Ulrich K. Preuss 1998. *Institutional Design in Post-Communist Societies: Rebuilding the Ship at Sea*. Cambridge: Cambridge University Press.

Fakel 2004. *Vechna drujba. Sekretni stenogrami. [Eternal friendship. Secret transcripts of conversations between M. Gorbachev and Bulgarian state and party leaders 1987–1991]*. Fakel 25(3): 298–368

Feiwel, George R. 1982. Economic Development and Planning in Bulgaria in the 1970s. In *The East European Economies in the 1970s*, edited by Alec Nove, Hans-Hermann Hohmann and Gertraud Seidenstecher, 215–252. London: Butterworths.

FAB 2007. *Federacija na anarhistite v Balgarija. Deklaracija na principite, celite i sredstvata [Federation of the Anarchists in Bulgaria. Declaration of the Principles, Ends, and Means]*. http://anarchy.bg/?p=98 (Jan., 2015)

Ferrario, Andrea and Paolo Modesti 2014. *Inchiesta sui gruppi alternativi di sinistra e/o antiautoritari in Bulgaria*. Crisi Globale.

Fisher, Sharon 2002. The Troubled Evolution of Slovakia's Ex-Communists. In *The Communist Successor Parties of Central and Eastern Europe*, edited by András Bozóki and John T. Ishiyama, 116–140. New York: M.E.Sharpe.

Fleckenstein, Timo 2011. *Institutions, Ideas and Learning in Welfare State Change: Labour Market Reforms in Germany*. Basingstoke: Palgrave Macmillan.

Ganchev, Gancho T. 2014. Problemi na borbata s bednostta v Balgarija (2014) [Problems of the fight against poverty in Bulgaria (2014)]. In *Borbata s bednostta v Balgarija: makroikonomika, etnicheski aspekti, evrointegracija, roljata na turizma [The Fight against Poverty in Bulgaria: Macroeconomics, Ethnic Aspects, European Integration, the Role of Tourism]*, edited by Gancho T. Ganchev, 11–36. Sofia: Friedrich Ebert Stiftung.

Ganev, Venelin I. 2014. "Bulgaria's Year of Civic Anger". *Journal of Democracy* 25(1): 33–45

Genov, Nikolai and Anna Krasteva (eds.) 2001. *Recent Social Trends in Bulgaria 1960–1995*. Montreal: McGill-Queen's University Press.

Giatzidis, Emil 2002. *An Introduction to Post-Communist Bulgaria: Political, Economic and Social Transformation*. Manchester: Manchester University Press.

Gorbachev, Mikhail 1989. *The Socialist Idea and the Revolutionary Perestroika*. Moscow: Novosti Press. [originally published in *Pravda*, 26 November 1989]

Grzymala-Busse, Anna M. 2002. *Redeeming the Communist Past. The Regeneration of Communist Parties in East Central Europe.* Cambridge: Cambridge University Press.

Grzymala-Busse, Anna M. 2006. "Authoritarian Determinants of Democratic Party Competition: The Communist Successor Parties in East Central Europe". *Party Politics* 12(3): 415–437

Guentchev, Dimitar 2008. Teoretichno i programno razvitie na balgarskata socialdemokracija 1891–1919 [Theoretical and Programme Development of the Bulgarian Social Democracy 1891–1919]. In *Izsledvanija po istorija na socializma v Balgarija 1891–1944* [Studies on the History of Socialism in Bulgaria 1891–1944], edited by Evgeny Kandilarov, 30–69. Sofia: Friedrich Ebert Stiftung.

Hanley, Sean 2002. The Communist Party of Bohemia and Moravia after 1989: 'Subcultural Party' to Neocommunist Force? In *The Communist Successor Parties of Central and Eastern Europe*, edited by András Bozóki and John T. Ishiyama, 141–165. New York: M.E.Sharpe.

Heffernan, Richard 2011. "Labour's New Labour Legacy: Politics after Blair and Brown". *Political Studies Review* 9(2): 163–177

History 1981. *Istoriya na Balgarskata komunisticheska partiya* [History of the Bulgarian Communist Party]. Edited by Ruben Avramov et al. Sofia: Partizdat.

Hough, Dan 2001. *Fall and Rise of the PDS in Eastern Germany.* Birmingham: The University of Birmingham Press.

Hough, Dan 2005. "Third Ways or New Ways? The Post-Communist Left in Central Europe". *The Political Quarterly* 76(2): 253–263

Hough, Dan, Michael Koss and Jonathan Olsen 2007. *The Left Party in Contemporary German Politics.* Basingstoke: Palgrave Macmillan.

Hough, Dan, William E. Paterson and James Sloam (eds.) 2006. *Learning from the West? Policy, Transfer and Programmatic Change in the Communist Successor Parties of Eastern and Central Europe.* New York: Routledge.

Hudson, Kate 2012. *The New European Left: A Socialism for the Twenty-First Century?* Basingstoke: Palgrave Macmillan.

Inglot, Tomasz 2008. *Welfare States in East Central Europe 1919–2004.* Cambridge: Cambridge University Press.

Ishiyama, John T. (ed.) 1999. *Communist Successor Parties in Post-Communist Politics.* Commack, NY: Nova Science Publ.

Ishiyama, John T. 1998. "Strange Bedfellows; Explaining Political Cooperation between Communist Successor Parties and Nationalists in Eastern Europe". *Nations and Nationalism* 4(1): 61–85

Ishiyama, John T. 2001. "Party Organization and the Political Success of the Communist Successor Parties". *Social Science Quarterly* 82(4): 844–864

Kalinova, Evguenia and Iskra Baeva 2001. *La Bulgarie contemporaine entre l'Est et l'Ouest*. Paris: L'Harmattan.

Kandilarov, Evgeny 2010.Ot 'realen' kum 'demokratichen' socializam. [From 'real' towards 'democratic' socialism]. In *Izsledvaniya po istoriya na socializma v Balgariya 1944–1989* [*Studies on the history of socialism in Bulgaria 1944–1989*], edited by Evgeny Kandilarov, 64–157. Sofia: Friedrich Ebert Stiftung.

Kandilarov, Evgeny 2011. Otnoshenieto na BSP kum socialisticheskoto minalo [The attitude of BSP towards the socialist past]. In *Izsledvaniya po istoriya na socializma v Balgariya. Prehodat* [*Studies on the history of socialism in Bulgaria. The transition*], edited by Lilyana Kaneva, Maxim Mizov and Evgeny Kandilarov, 338–376. Sofia: Friedrich Ebert Stiftung.

Kanev, Dobrin 1996. Bulgaria: "Left" and "Right" in the Emerging Party System. In *Grappling with Democracy: Deliberations on Post-Communist Societies (1990–1995)*, edited by Elzbieta Matynia, 176–188. Prague: Sociologické Nakladatelství.

Kanev, Dobrin 2001. Lyavoto politichesko prostranstvo v Balgarija—problemi i perspektivi. [The Left Political Space in Bulgaria—problems and perspectives] In *Politicheskite partii v Balgarija i Avstrija pred novi predizvikatelstva* [*The Political Parties in Bulgaria and Austria Facing New Challenges*], edited by Georgi Karasimeonov, 10–33. Sofia: GorexPress.

Kanev, Dobrin 2002. La transformation du parti commmuniste bulgare. In *Partis politiques et démocratie en Europe centrale et orientale*, edited by Jean-Michel De Waele, 83–99. Bruxelles: Editions de l'Université de Bruxelles.

Kanev, Dobrin 2011. Trudnijat pat na transformacija na BSP [The Difficult Path of Transformation of the Bulgarian Socialist Party]. In *Izsledvaniya po istoriya na socializma v Balgariya. Prehodat* [*Studies on the history of socialism in Bulgaria. The transition*], edited by Lilyana Kaneva, Maxim Mizov and Evgeny Kandilarov, 217–247. Sofia: Friedrich Ebert Stiftung.

Kaneva, Liliana 2014. Obnovlenie na osnovnite cennosti i principi na socialdemokracijata [A Renewal of the Main Values and Principles of Social Democracy]. In *Socialnata alternativa za Evropa* [*The Social Alternative for Europe*], edited by Dobrin Kanev, 105–119. Sofia: Friedrich Ebert Stiftung.

Karasimeonov, Georgi (ed.) 1997b. *The 1990 Election to the Bulgarian Grand National Assembly and the 1991 Election to the Bulgarian National Assembly: Analyses, Documents and Data*. Berlin: Edition Sigma.

Karasimeonov, Georgi 1996. Bulgaria's New Party System. In *Stabilizing Fragile Democracies. Comparing New Party Systems in Southern and Eastern Europe*, edited by Geoffrey Pridham and Paul G. Lewis, 254–265. London: Routledge.

Karasimeonov, Georgi 1997a. "The development of Political Science in Bulgaria: A Discipline in Transition". *European Journal of Political Research* 31(4): 519–532.

Karasimeonov, Georgi 2010. *Partiinata sistema v Bulgaria. 3-o izd. [The Party System in Bulgaria. 3rd edn.]*. Sofia: GorexPress.

Karasimeonov, Georgi and Milen Lyubenov 2013. Bulgaria. In *The Handbook of Political Change in Eastern Europe. 3rd edn*, edited by Sten Berglund et al., 407–429. Edward Elgar Publishing.

Kassaiye, Berhanu 1998. "The Evolution of Social Democracy in Reforming Bulgaria". *Journal of Communist Studies and Transition Politics* 14 (3): 109–125.

Kaufmann, Franz-Xaver 2012. *European Foundations of the Welfare State*. New York and Oxford: Berghahn Books.

Kitschelt, Herbert 1995. "Formation of Party Cleavages in Post-Communist Democracies: Theoretical Propositions". *Party Politics* 1(4): 447–472

Kitschelt, Herbert, Dimitar Dimitrov and Assen Kanev 1995. "The Structuring of the Vote in Post-Communist Party Systems: The Bulgarian Case". *European Journal of Political Research* 27(2): 143–160

Kolarova, Rumyana and Dimitr Dimitrov 1996. The Roundtable Talks in Bulgaria. In *The Roundtable Talks and the Breakdown of Communism*, edited by Jon Elster, 178–212. Chicago: University of Chicago Press.

Körösényi, András 1999. *Government and Politics in Hungary*. Budapest: CEU Press.

Kouvelakis, Stathis 2011. "The Greek Cauldron". *New Left Review* 72 (November/December): 17–32

Krastanova, Radosveta 2012. *The Green Movement and the Green Parties in Bulgaria: Between System Integration and System Change*. Sofia: Friedrich Ebert Stiftung.

Krastev, Ivan 2014. *Democracy Disrupted: The Global Politics of Protest*. Philadelphia: University of Pennsylvania Press.

Kuzio, Taras 2008. "Comparative Perspectives on Communist Successor Parties in Central-Eastern Europe and Eurasia". *Communist and Post-Communist Studies* 41(4): 397–419

Lavelle, Ashley 2008. *The Death of Social Democracy: Political Consequences in the 21st century*. Aldershot: Ashgate.

Lévesque, Jacques 2010. The East European Revolutions of 1989. In *The Cambridge History of the Cold War. Volume III: Endings*, edited by Melvyn P. Leffler and Odd Arne Westad, 311–332. Cambridge: Cambridge University Press.

Levicata 2009. *Programni dokumenti na politicheska partija Balgarskata levica* [Programme documents of the Bulgarian Left Political Party] www.levicata.org/bg/about/ (Jan., 2015)

Lubecki, Jacek 2004. "Echoes of Latifundism? Electoral Constituencies of Successor Parties in Post-Communist Countries". *East European Politics and Societies* 18(1): 10–44

Lyubenov, Milen 2011. *Balgarskata partijna sistema: grupirane I strukturirane na partijnite predpochitanija 1990–2009* [The Party System of Bulgaria: Grouping and Structuring of Party Preferences 1990–2009]. Sofia: St. Kliment Ohridski University Press.

Malinov, Svetoslav 2010. *The Bulgarian Center Right—Victories, Defeats, Transformations*. Sofia: Friedrich Ebert Stiftung.

Manifest 2006. *Manifest na levicata v BSP 2006* [Manifesto of the BSP Left]. http://bsp1891.org/ (Jan., 2015)

Markowski, Radoslaw 2002. The Polish SLD in the 1990s: From Opposition to Incumbents and Back. In *The Communist Successor Parties of Central and Eastern Europe*, edited by András Bozóki and John T. Ishiyama, 51–88. New York: M.E.Sharpe.

Matonyte, Irmina 2009. "Ex-nomenklatura and Ex-dissidents in the Post-communist Parliaments of Estonia, Latvia, Lithuania and Poland". *Viešoji Politika ir Administravimas* 29: 28–39

Mineva, Emilia 2001. On the Reception of Marxism in Bulgaria. *Studies in East European Thought* 53(1/2): 61–74

Mitev, Petar-Emil 1987. "Gradivnata energija na doverieto" ["The Creative Energy of Trust"]. *Narodna kultura* 32–33.

Mitev, Petar-Emil 1992. *Ot komunizam kum demokracija: Problemat za novite eliti v konteksta na socialnite promeni*. Doklad pred mejdunarodnata konferencija "Novite eliti. Socialna stratifikacija I socialna mobilnost v uslovijata na antinomenklaturni revoljucii" (29–30 maj) [*From Communism towards Democracy: The problem of the new elites in the context of the social change*. Paper presented at the international conference "The New Elites. Social Stratification and Social Mobility during Anti-Nomenklatura Revolutions' (29–30 May)]

Mitev, Petar-Emil 1996. *Levicata v bulgarskjya prehod*. Doklad pred mejdunarodnata konferencija "Evropejskata socialdemokracija i bulgarskata levica" (22–23 januari) [*The Left in the Bulgarian Transition*. Paper presented at the international conference "The European Social Democracy and the Bulgarian Left" (22–23 January)].

Mitev, Petar-Emil 2011. Prehodat i poukite za balgarskata levica [The Transition and the Lessons for the Bulgarian Left]. In *Izsledvaniya po istoriya na socializma v Balgariya. Prehodat* [*Studies on the history of socialism in Bulgaria. The transition*], edited by Lilyana Kaneva, Maxim Mizov and Evgeny Kandilarov, 16–59. Sofia: Friedrich Ebert Stiftung.

Mitev, Petar-Emil 2013. Enigmata Marx [The Marx Enigma]. In *Karl Marx. Chovekat i budeshteto. Izbrano* [*Karl Marx. Man and the Future. Selected Works*], edited by Bernard Muntian, Petar-Emil Mitev and Boris Popivanov, 643–683. Sofia: Iztok-Zapad.

Mitev, Petar-Emil and Siyka Kovacheva 2014. *Young People in European Bulgaria: A Sociological Portrait 2014*. Sofia: Friedrich Ebert Stiftung.

Moore, Patrick 1984. Bulgaria. In *Communism in Eastern Europe, 2nd edn.*, edited by Teresa Rakowska-Harmstone, 186–212. Bloomington, IN: Indiana University Press.

Mudde, Cas 2004. "The Populist Zeigeist". *Government and Opposition* 39(4): 542–563

Mungiu-Pippidi, Alina 2002. The Romanian Postcommunist Parties: A Story of Success. In *The Communist Successor Parties of Central and Eastern Europe*, edited by András Bozóki and John T. Ishiyama, 188–205. New York: M.E.Sharpe.

Murer, Jeffrey S. 1999. Challenging Expectations: A Comparative Study of the Communist Successor Parties of Hungary, Bulgaria and Romania. In *Communist Successor Parties in Post-Communist Politics*, edited by John T. Ishiyama, 179–221. Commack, NY: Nova Science Publ.

Murer, Jeffrey S. 2002. Mainstreaming Extremism: The Romanian PDSR and the Bulgarian Socialists in Comparative Perspective. In *The Communist Successor Parties of Central and Eastern Europe*, edited by András Bozóki and John T. Ishiyama, 367–396. New York: M.E.Sharpe.

Muxel, Anne 2011. Loyalties, Mobilities, Abstentions. In *The New Voter in Western Europe. France and Beyond*, edited by Bruno Cautres and Anne Muxel, 27–56. Basingstoke: Palgrave Macmillan.

Nagle, John T. and Alison Mahr 1999. *Democracy and Democratization. Post-Communist Europe in Comparative Perspective*. London: SAGE Publications.

New Left 2012. *Novi levi perspektivi: ravenstvo i ljavo sled 1989 g. Manifest.* [*New Left Perspectives: Equality and the Left after 1989. Manifesto*]. http://novilevi.org/manifesto (Jan., 2015)

Njagulov, Blagovest 2014. Early Socialism in the Balkans. Ideas and Practices in Serbia, Romania and Bulgaria. In *Entangled Histories of the Balkans. Volume Two: Transfers of Political Ideologies and Institutions*, edited by Roumen Daskalov and Diana Mishkova, 199–280. Leiden and Boston: Brill.

O'Neill, William L. 2001. *The New Left: A History*. Wheeling, IL: Harlan Davidson.

Offe, Claus 2009. Epilogue: Lessons Learnt and Open Questions. In *Post-Communist Welfare Pathways: Theorizing Social Policy Transformations in Central and Eastern Europe*, edited by Alfio Cerami and Pieter Vanhuysse, 237–247. Basingstoke: Palgrave Macmillan.

Olsen, Jonathan 2002. "The Dilemmas of Germany's PDS". *German Policy Studies/Politikfeldanalyse* 2(2): 197–220

Oren, Nissan 1973. *Revolution Administered: Agrarianism and Communism in Bulgaria*. Baltimore, MD: Johns Hopkins University Press.

Orenstein, Mitchell 1998. "A Genealogy of Communist Successor Parties in East-central Europe and the Determinants of Their Success". *East European Politics and Societies* 12(3): 472–499

Palier, Bruno 2010. The Long Conservative Corporatist Road to Welfare Reforms. In *A Long Goodbye to Bismarck? The Politics of Welfare Reforms in Continental Europe*, edited by Bruno Palier, 333–388. Amsterdam: Amsterdam University Press.

Parvanov, Georgi 2010. *ABV e nepartien, no ne i antipartien proekt* [ABV is a non-party, however not an anti-party project] Dnevnik Daily, 11 November http://www.dne vnik.bg/bulgaria/2010/11/11/991944_purvanov_abv_e_nepartien_no_ne_e_antiparti en_proekt/ (Jan., 2015)

Penev, Vassil 1991. "Ideologicheskoto prostranstvo v Bulgaria" ["The ideological space in Bulgaria"]. *Izbor* 3–4: 7–12.

Penev, Vassil 1992. "Political Parties in Bulgaria after 1989: Establishing, Functions, Organizational Structures and Interactions". *Bulgarian Quarterly* 2(3/4): 50–64.

Penev, Vassil 2010. Logichni i haotichni tezisi za balgarskata levica i BSP [Some Logical and Chaotical Theses on the Bulgarian Left and the Bulgarian Socialist Party]. In *Demokracijata v Balgarija prez XXI vek* [*The Democracy in Bulgaria in the 21st Century*], edited by Antony Todorov, 161–165. Veliko Tarnovo: Evropejski informacionen centar.

Penev, Vassil and Boris Popivanov 2012. Traditional and Modern in the Ideological Development and the Social Perception of the Bulgarian Left. In *Tradition, Modernization, Identities. The Traditional and the Modern in the Culture of Serbian and the Balkan Nations*, edited by Ljubinko Milosavljević, Branislav Stevanović and Gordana Stojić, 533–547. Nis: University of Nis.

Penev, Vassil and Boris Popivanov 2013. Orthodoxy and Ideology in Modern Bulgaria: The Impact of the Bulgarian Orthodox Church on Politics and Society. In *Tradition, Modernization, Identities. Dialogue of Cultures and Partnership of Civilizations in the Balkans*, edited by Ljubiša Mitrović, Danijela Gavrilović and Mirjana Kristović, 317–331. Nis: University of Nis.

Pirgova, Maria 1992. "Political Models Shaping the Pluralistic Political System in Bulgaria". *Bulgarian Quarterly* 2(3/4): 65–72.

Pirgova, Maria 2002. *Balgarskijat parlamentarizam v uslovijata na globalnija prehod* [*The Bulgarian Parliamentarism in the Global Transition*]. Sofia: Paradigma.

Pirgova, Maria 2011. Parlamentarizmat i levicata v balgarskija prehod [The Parliamentarism and the Left in the Bulgarian Transition]. In *Izsledvaniya po istoriya na socializma v Balgariya. Prehodat* [*Studies on the history of socialism in Bulgaria. The transition*], edited by Lilyana Kaneva, Maxim Mizov and Evgeny Kandilarov, 128–145. Sofia: Friedrich Ebert Stiftung.

Pirgova, Maria 2013. Socialnata darjava kato teoretichen problem za BSP v godinite na prehoda i dnes [The Welfare State as a Theoretical Problem for the Bulgarian Socialist Party in the Years of the Transition and Now]. In *Izsledvanija po istorija na socializma v Balgarija. Prehodat II* [*Studies on the history of socialism in Bulgaria. The transition II*], edited by Lilyana Kaneva, Maxim Mizov and Evgeny Kandilarov, 43–60. Sofia: Centar za istoricheski i politologicheski izsledvanija.

Pop-Elecheș, Grigore 2008. "A Party for All Seasons: Electoral Adaptation of Romanian Communist Successor Parties". *Communist and Post-Communist Studies* 41(4): 465–479

Popivanov, Boris 2008a. Toward the Idea of Political Representation of the Bulgarian Peasants. In *Village in Transition*, edited by Đura Stevanović, 370–377. Beograd and Vlasotince: Serbian Rural and Agricultural Sociology Association.

Popivanov, Boris 2008b. "Citizenship and Civic Activity in Contemporary Bulgaria: (Non-)European Dimensions". *Sociologija. Mintis ir veiksmas* 23(3): 47–57

Raichev, Andrey and Kantcho Stoychev 2008. *Kakvo se sluchi? Razkaz za prehoda v Bulgaria I malko sled nego* [What happened? A Story about the Transition in Bulgaria and Shortly Afterwards]. Sofia: Trud.

Rothschild, Joseph 1959. *The Communist Party of Bulgaria: Origins and Development 1883–1936*. New York: Columbia University Press.

Roussopoulos, Dimitrios (ed.) 2007. *The New Left: Legacy and Continuity*. Montréal: Black Rose Books.

Schröder, Gerhard 2003. *Courage for Peace and Courage for Change*. http://gerhard-schroeder.de/en/2003/03/14/speech-agenda-2010/ (Jan., 2015)

Septemvri 2006. *Dvijenie za saprotiva "23 septemvri". Principi*. [Movement for Resistance "23 September". Principles]. www.septemvri23.com/principle.htm (Jan., 2015)

Siani-Davies, Peter 2005. *The Romanian Revolution of December 1989*. Ithaca: Cornell University Press.

Sloam, James 2005. "West European Social Democracy as a Model for Transfer". *Journal of Communist Studies and Transition Politics* 21(1): 67–83

Smith, Gordon 1990. *Politics in Western Europe*. 5th edn. New York: Holmes and Meyer Publishers.

Spirova, Maria 2008. "The Bulgarian Socialist Party: The Long Road to Europe". *Communist and Post-Communist Studies* 41(4): 481–495

Spirova, Maria 2010. Bulgaria since 1989. In *Central and Southeastern Europe since 1989*, edited by Sabrina P. Ramet, 401–421. Cambridge: Cambridge University Press.

Spirova, Maria 2012. 'A Tradition We Don't Mess With': Party Patronage in Bulgaria. In *Party Patronage and Party Government in European Democracies*, edited by Petr Kopecký, Peter Mair and Maria Spirova, 54–73. Oxford: Oxford University Press.

Staar, Richard F. 1982. *Communist Regimes in Eastern Europe*. 4th edn. Stanford: The Hoover Institution

Stanishev, Sergei 2002. *Politicheski doklad na predsedatelja na NS na BSP pred 45-ija kongres na BSP* (8 juni) [*Political Report by the Chairman of the NC of the BSP to the 45th BSP Congress* (8 June)].

Stanishev, Sergei 2008. *Zashtoto sme socialisti* [*Because We Are Socialists*]. Sofia: Duma

Stanishev, Sergei 2009. *Politicheski doklad na predsedatelja na NS na BSP pred sedmoto zasedanie na 47-ija kongres na BSP* (18 oktomvri) [*Political Report by the Chairman of the NC of the BSP to the seventh sitting of the 47th BSP Congress* (18 October)]. http://www.bsp.bg/bg/novini/view/politicheski-doklad-na-predsedatelja-na-ns-na-bsp-sergej-stanishev-pred-sedmoto-zasedanie-na-47-mija-kongres-na-bsp/977 (Jan., 2015)

Strmiska, Maximilian 2002. "The Communist Party of Bohemia and Moravia: A Post-Communist Socialist or a Neo-Communist Party?". *German Policy Studies/ Politikfeldanalyse* 2(2): 40–60

Sykgelos, Yannis 2011. *Nationalism from the Left. The Bulgarian Communist Party during the Second World War and the Early Post-War Years.* Leiden and Boston: Brill.

Szczerbiak, Aleks 2001. *Poles Together? The Emergence and Development of Political Parties in Postcommunist Poland.* Budapest: CEU Press.

Tismăneanu, Vladimir 1999. "Understanding national Stalinism: reflections on Ceaușescu's socialism". *Communist and Post-Communist Studies* 32(2): 155–173

Todorov, Antony 2004. Un clivage centré sur le passé communiste. In *Les clivages politiques en Europe centrale et orientale*, edited by Jean-Michel De Waele, 257–268. Bruxelles: Editions de l'Université de Bruxelles.

Todorov, Antony 2010. *Grajdani, partii, izbori. Balgarija 1879–2009* [*Citizens, Parties, Elections. Bulgaria 1879–2009*]. Sofia: Iztok-Zapad.

Todorov, Antony 2013a. The Bulgarian Socialist Party. In *The Palgrave Handbook of Social Democracy in the European Union*, edited by Jean-Michel De Waele, Fabien Escalona and Mathieu Vieira, 401–415. Basingstoke: Palgrave Macmillan.

Todorov, Antony 2013b. *Kakva levica?* [*What Kind of Left?*] Personal blog. https://antoniytodorov.wordpress.com/2013/07/

Todorova, Maria 1995. The Course and Discourses of Bulgarian Nationalism. In *The Eastern European Nationalism in the Twentieth Century*, edited by Peter F. Sugar, 55–102. Washington DC: The American University Press.

Tóka, Gábor 1998. Hungary. In *Handbook of Political Change in Eastern Europe*, edited by Sten Berglund, Tomas Hellén and Frank H. Aarebrot, 231–274. Cheltenham: Edward Elgar.

Vachudová, Milada and Tim Snyder 1997. "Are Transitions Transitory? Two Types of Political Change in Eastern Europe since 1989". *East European Politics and Societies* 11(1): 1–35

Wahl, Asbjørn 2011. *The Rise and Fall of the Welfare State*. New York: Pluto Press.

Webb, Paul and Stephen White (eds.) 2007. *Party Politics in New Democracies*. Oxford and New York: Oxford University Press.

Whitefield, Stephen 2002. "Political Cleavages and Post-Communist Politics". *Annual Review of Political Science* 5: 181–200

Ziblatt, Daniel F. 1998. "The Adaptation of Ex-Communist Parties to Post-Communist East Central Europe: A Comparative Study of the East German and Hungarian Ex-Communist Parties". *Communist and Post-Communist Studies* 31(2): 119–137

Zubek, Voytek 1994. "The Reassertion of the Left in Post-communist Poland". *Europe-Asia Studies* 46(5): 801–837

SOVIET AND POST-SOVIET POLITICS AND SOCIETY

Edited by Dr. Andreas Umland

ISSN 1614-3515

1   Андреас Умланд (ред.)
    Воплощение Европейской
    конвенции по правам человека в
    России
    Философские, юридические и
    эмпирические исследования
    ISBN 3-89821-387-0

2   Christian Wipperfürth
    Russland – ein vertrauenswürdiger
    Partner?
    Grundlagen, Hintergründe und Praxis
    gegenwärtiger russischer Außenpolitik
    Mit einem Vorwort von Heinz Timmermann
    ISBN 3-89821-401-X

3   Manja Hussner
    Die Übernahme internationalen Rechts
    in die russische und deutsche
    Rechtsordnung
    Eine vergleichende Analyse zur
    Völkerrechtsfreundlichkeit der Verfassungen
    der Russländischen Föderation und der
    Bundesrepublik Deutschland
    Mit einem Vorwort von Rainer Arnold
    ISBN 3-89821-438-9

4   Matthew Tejada
    Bulgaria's Democratic Consolidation
    and the Kozloduy Nuclear Power Plant
    (KNPP)
    The Unattainability of Closure
    With a foreword by Richard J. Crampton
    ISBN 3-89821-439-7

5   Марк Григорьевич Меерович
    Квадратные метры, определяющие
    сознание
    Государственная жилищная политика в
    СССР. 1921 – 1941 гг
    ISBN 3-89821-474-5

6   Andrei P. Tsygankov, Pavel
    A. Tsygankov (Eds.)
    New Directions in Russian
    International Studies
    ISBN 3-89821-422-2

7   Марк Григорьевич Меерович
    Как власть народ к труду приучала
    Жилище в СССР – средство управления
    людьми. 1917 – 1941 гг.
    С предисловием Елены Осокиной
    ISBN 3-89821-495-8

8   David J. Galbreath
    Nation-Building and Minority Politics
    in Post-Socialist States
    Interests, Influence and Identities in Estonia
    and Latvia
    With a foreword by David J. Smith
    ISBN 3-89821-467-2

9   Алексей Юрьевич Безугольный
    Народы Кавказа в Вооруженных
    силах СССР в годы Великой
    Отечественной войны 1941-1945 гг.
    С предисловием Николая Бугая
    ISBN 3-89821-475-3

10 Вячеслав Лихачев и Владимир
    Прибыловский (ред.)
    Русское Национальное Единство,
    1990-2000. В 2-х томах
    ISBN 3-89821-523-7

11 Николай Бугай (ред.)
    Народы стран Балтии в условиях
    сталинизма (1940-е – 1950-е годы)
    Документированная история
    ISBN 3-89821-525-3

12 Ingmar Bredies (Hrsg.)
    Zur Anatomie der Orange Revolution
    in der Ukraine
    Wechsel des Elitenregimes oder Triumph des
    Parlamentarismus?
    ISBN 3-89821-524-5

13 Anastasia V. Mitrofanova
    The Politicization of Russian
    Orthodoxy
    Actors and Ideas
    With a foreword by William C. Gay
    ISBN 3-89821-481-8

14 *Nathan D. Larson*
    Alexander Solzhenitsyn and the
    Russo-Jewish Question
    ISBN 3-89821-483-4

15 *Guido Houben*
    Kulturpolitik und Ethnizität
    Staatliche Kunstförderung im Russland der
    neunziger Jahre
    Mit einem Vorwort von Gert Weisskirchen
    ISBN 3-89821-542-3

16 *Leonid Luks*
    Der russische „Sonderweg"?
    Aufsätze zur neuesten Geschichte Russlands
    im europäischen Kontext
    ISBN 3-89821-496-6

17 *Евгений Мороз*
    История «Мёртвой воды» – от
    страшной сказки к большой
    политике
    Политическое неоязычество в
    постсоветской России
    ISBN 3-89821-551-2

18 *Александр Верховский и Галина
    Кожевникова (ред.)*
    Этническая и религиозная
    интолерантность в российских СМИ
    Результаты мониторинга 2001-2004 гг.
    ISBN 3-89821-569-5

19 *Christian Ganzer*
    Sowjetisches Erbe und ukrainische
    Nation
    Das Museum der Geschichte des Zaporoger
    Kosakentums auf der Insel Chortycja
    Mit einem Vorwort von Frank Golczewski
    ISBN 3-89821-504-0

20 *Эльза-Баир Гучинова*
    Помнить нельзя забыть
    Антропология депортационной травмы
    калмыков
    С предисловием Кэролайн Хамфри
    ISBN 3-89821-506-7

21 *Юлия Лидерман*
    Мотивы «проверки» и «испытания»
    в постсоветской культуре
    Советское прошлое в российском
    кинематографе 1990-х годов
    С предисловием Евгения Марголита
    ISBN 3-89821-511-3

22 *Tanya Lokshina, Ray Thomas, Mary
    Mayer (Eds.)*
    The Imposition of a Fake Political
    Settlement in the Northern Caucasus
    The 2003 Chechen Presidential Election
    ISBN 3-89821-436-2

23 *Timothy McCajor Hall, Rosie Read
    (Eds.)*
    Changes in the Heart of Europe
    Recent Ethnographies of Czechs, Slovaks,
    Roma, and Sorbs
    With an afterword by Zdeněk Salzmann
    ISBN 3-89821-606-3

24 *Christian Autengruber*
    Die politischen Parteien in Bulgarien
    und Rumänien
    Eine vergleichende Analyse seit Beginn der
    90er Jahre
    Mit einem Vorwort von Dorothée de Nève
    ISBN 3-89821-476-1

25 *Annette Freyberg-Inan with Radu
    Cristescu*
    The Ghosts in Our Classrooms, or:
    John Dewey Meets Ceauşescu
    The Promise and the Failures of Civic
    Education in Romania
    ISBN 3-89821-416-8

26 *John B. Dunlop*
    The 2002 Dubrovka and 2004 Beslan
    Hostage Crises
    A Critique of Russian Counter-Terrorism
    With a foreword by Donald N. Jensen
    ISBN 3-89821-608-X

27 *Peter Koller*
    Das touristische Potenzial von
    Kam''janec–Podil's'kyj
    Eine fremdenverkehrsgeographische
    Untersuchung der Zukunftsperspektiven und
    Maßnahmenplanung zur
    Destinationsentwicklung des „ukrainischen
    Rothenburg"
    Mit einem Vorwort von Kristiane Klemm
    ISBN 3-89821-640-3

28 *Françoise Daucé, Elisabeth Sieca-
    Kozlowski (Eds.)*
    Dedovshchina in the Post-Soviet
    Military
    Hazing of Russian Army Conscripts in a
    Comparative Perspective
    With a foreword by Dale Herspring
    ISBN 3-89821-616-0

29 Florian Strasser
    Zivilgesellschaftliche Einflüsse auf die
    Orange Revolution
    Die gewaltlose Massenbewegung und die
    ukrainische Wahlkrise 2004
    Mit einem Vorwort von Egbert Jahn
    ISBN 3-89821-648-9

30 Rebecca S. Katz
    The Georgian Regime Crisis of 2003-
    2004
    A Case Study in Post-Soviet Media
    Representation of Politics, Crime and
    Corruption
    ISBN 3-89821-413-3

31 Vladimir Kantor
    Willkür oder Freiheit
    Beiträge zur russischen Geschichtsphilosophie
    Ediert von Dagmar Herrmann sowie mit
    einem Vorwort versehen von Leonid Luks
    ISBN 3-89821-589-X

32 Laura A. Victoir
    The Russian Land Estate Today
    A Case Study of Cultural Politics in Post-
    Soviet Russia
    With a foreword by Priscilla Roosevelt
    ISBN 3-89821-426-5

33 Ivan Katchanovski
    Cleft Countries
    Regional Political Divisions and Cultures in
    Post-Soviet Ukraine and Moldova
    With a foreword by Francis Fukuyama
    ISBN 3-89821-558-X

34 Florian Mühlfried
    Postsowjetische Feiern
    Das Georgische Bankett im Wandel
    Mit einem Vorwort von Kevin Tuite
    ISBN 3-89821-601-2

35 Roger Griffin, Werner Loh, Andreas
    Umland (Eds.)
    Fascism Past and Present, West and
    East
    An International Debate on Concepts and
    Cases in the Comparative Study of the
    Extreme Right
    With an afterword by Walter Laqueur
    ISBN 3-89821-674-8

36 Sebastian Schlegel
    Der „Weiße Archipel"
    Sowjetische Atomstädte 1945-1991
    Mit einem Geleitwort von Thomas Bohn
    ISBN 3-89821-679-9

37 Vyacheslav Likhachev
    Political Anti-Semitism in Post-Soviet
    Russia
    Actors and Ideas in 1991-2003
    Edited and translated from Russian by Eugene
    Veklerov
    ISBN 3-89821-529-6

38 Josette Baer (Ed.)
    Preparing Liberty in Central Europe
    Political Texts from the Spring of Nations
    1848 to the Spring of Prague 1968
    With a foreword by Zdeněk V. David
    ISBN 3-89821-546-6

39 Михаил Лукьянов
    Российский консерватизм и
    реформа, 1907-1914
    С предисловием Марка Д. Стейнберга
    ISBN 3-89821-503-2

40 Nicola Melloni
    Market Without Economy
    The 1998 Russian Financial Crisis
    With a foreword by Eiji Furukawa
    ISBN 3-89821-407-9

41 Dmitrij Chmelnizki
    Die Architektur Stalins
    Bd. 1: Studien zu Ideologie und Stil
    Bd. 2: Bilddokumentation
    Mit einem Vorwort von Bruno Flierl
    ISBN 3-89821-515-6

42 Katja Yafimava
    Post-Soviet Russian-Belarussian
    Relationships
    The Role of Gas Transit Pipelines
    With a foreword by Jonathan P. Stern
    ISBN 3-89821-655-1

43 Boris Chavkin
    Verflechtungen der deutschen und
    russischen Zeitgeschichte
    Aufsätze und Archivfunde zu den
    Beziehungen Deutschlands und der
    Sowjetunion von 1917 bis 1991
    Ediert von Markus Edlinger sowie mit einem
    Vorwort versehen von Leonid Luks
    ISBN 3-89821-756-6

44 *Anastasija Grynenko in Zusammenarbeit mit Claudia Dathe*
Die Terminologie des Gerichtswesens der Ukraine und Deutschlands im Vergleich
Eine übersetzungswissenschaftliche Analyse juristischer Fachbegriffe im Deutschen, Ukrainischen und Russischen
Mit einem Vorwort von Ulrich Hartmann
ISBN 3-89821-691-8

45 *Anton Burkov*
The Impact of the European Convention on Human Rights on Russian Law
Legislation and Application in 1996-2006
With a foreword by Françoise Hampson
ISBN 978-3-89821-639-5

46 *Stina Torjesen, Indra Overland (Eds.)*
International Election Observers in Post-Soviet Azerbaijan
Geopolitical Pawns or Agents of Change?
ISBN 978-3-89821-743-9

47 *Taras Kuzio*
Ukraine – Crimea – Russia
Triangle of Conflict
ISBN 978-3-89821-761-3

48 *Claudia Šabić*
"Ich erinnere mich nicht, aber L'viv!"
Zur Funktion kultureller Faktoren für die Institutionalisierung und Entwicklung einer ukrainischen Region
Mit einem Vorwort von Melanie Tatur
ISBN 978-3-89821-752-1

49 *Marlies Bilz*
Tatarstan in der Transformation
Nationaler Diskurs und Politische Praxis 1988-1994
Mit einem Vorwort von Frank Golczewski
ISBN 978-3-89821-722-4

50 *Марлен Ларюэль (ред.)*
Современные интерпретации русского национализма
ISBN 978-3-89821-795-8

51 *Sonja Schüler*
Die ethnische Dimension der Armut
Roma im postsozialistischen Rumänien
Mit einem Vorwort von Anton Sterbling
ISBN 978-3-89821-776-7

52 *Галина Кожевникова*
Радикальный национализм в России и противодействие ему
Сборник докладов Центра «Сова» за 2004-2007 гг.
С предисловием Александра Верховского
ISBN 978-3-89821-721-7

53 *Галина Кожевникова и Владимир Прибыловский*
Российская власть в биографиях I
Высшие должностные лица РФ в 2004 г.
ISBN 978-3-89821-796-5

54 *Галина Кожевникова и Владимир Прибыловский*
Российская власть в биографиях II
Члены Правительства РФ в 2004 г.
ISBN 978-3-89821-797-2

55 *Галина Кожевникова и Владимир Прибыловский*
Российская власть в биографиях III
Руководители федеральных служб и агентств РФ в 2004 г.
ISBN 978-3-89821-798-9

56 *Ileana Petroniu*
Privatisierung in Transformationsökonomien
Determinanten der Restrukturierungs-Bereitschaft am Beispiel Polens, Rumäniens und der Ukraine
Mit einem Vorwort von Rainer W. Schäfer
ISBN 978-3-89821-790-3

57 *Christian Wipperfürth*
Russland und seine GUS-Nachbarn
Hintergründe, aktuelle Entwicklungen und Konflikte in einer ressourcenreichen Region
ISBN 978-3-89821-801-6

58 *Togzhan Kassenova*
From Antagonism to Partnership
The Uneasy Path of the U.S.-Russian Cooperative Threat Reduction
With a foreword by Christoph Bluth
ISBN 978-3-89821-707-1

59 *Alexander Höllwerth*
Das sakrale eurasische Imperium des Aleksandr Dugin
Eine Diskursanalyse zum postsowjetischen russischen Rechtsextremismus
Mit einem Vorwort von Dirk Uffelmann
ISBN 978-3-89821-813-9

60   *Олег Рябов*
       «Россия-Матушка»
       Национализм, гендер и война в России XX века
       С предисловием Елены Гощило
       ISBN 978-3-89821-487-2

61   *Ivan Maistrenko*
       Borot'bism
       A Chapter in the History of the Ukrainian Revolution
       With a new introduction by Chris Ford
       Translated by George S. N. Luckyj with the assistance of Ivan L. Rudnytsky
       ISBN 978-3-89821-697-5

62   *Maryna Romanets*
       Anamorphosic Texts and Reconfigured Visions
       Improvised Traditions in Contemporary Ukrainian and Irish Literature
       ISBN 978-3-89821-576-3

63   *Paul D'Anieri and Taras Kuzio (Eds.)*
       Aspects of the Orange Revolution I
       Democratization and Elections in Post-Communist Ukraine
       ISBN 978-3-89821-698-2

64   *Bohdan Harasymiw in collaboration with Oleh S. Ilnytzkyj (Eds.)*
       Aspects of the Orange Revolution II
       Information and Manipulation Strategies in the 2004 Ukrainian Presidential Elections
       ISBN 978-3-89821-699-9

65   *Ingmar Bredies, Andreas Umland and Valentin Yakushik (Eds.)*
       Aspects of the Orange Revolution III
       The Context and Dynamics of the 2004 Ukrainian Presidential Elections
       ISBN 978-3-89821-803-0

66   *Ingmar Bredies, Andreas Umland and Valentin Yakushik (Eds.)*
       Aspects of the Orange Revolution IV
       Foreign Assistance and Civic Action in the 2004 Ukrainian Presidential Elections
       ISBN 978-3-89821-808-5

67   *Ingmar Bredies, Andreas Umland and Valentin Yakushik (Eds.)*
       Aspects of the Orange Revolution V
       Institutional Observation Reports on the 2004 Ukrainian Presidential Elections
       ISBN 978-3-89821-809-2

68   *Taras Kuzio (Ed.)*
       Aspects of the Orange Revolution VI
       Post-Communist Democratic Revolutions in Comparative Perspective
       ISBN 978-3-89821-820-7

69   *Tim Bohse*
       Autoritarismus statt Selbstverwaltung
       Die Transformation der kommunalen Politik in der Stadt Kaliningrad 1990-2005
       Mit einem Geleitwort von Stefan Troebst
       ISBN 978-3-89821-782-8

70   *David Rupp*
       Die Rußländische Föderation und die russischsprachige Minderheit in Lettland
       Eine Fallstudie zur Anwaltspolitik Moskaus gegenüber den russophonen Minderheiten im „Nahen Ausland" von 1991 bis 2002
       Mit einem Vorwort von Helmut Wagner
       ISBN 978-3-89821-778-1

71   *Taras Kuzio*
       Theoretical and Comparative Perspectives on Nationalism
       New Directions in Cross-Cultural and Post-Communist Studies
       With a foreword by Paul Robert Magocsi
       ISBN 978-3-89821-815-3

72   *Christine Teichmann*
       Die Hochschultransformation im heutigen Osteuropa
       Kontinuität und Wandel bei der Entwicklung des postkommunistischen Universitätswesens
       Mit einem Vorwort von Oskar Anweiler
       ISBN 978-3-89821-842-9

73   *Julia Kusznir*
       Der politische Einfluss von Wirtschaftseliten in russischen Regionen
       Eine Analyse am Beispiel der Erdöl- und Erdgasindustrie, 1992-2005
       Mit einem Vorwort von Wolfgang Eichwede
       ISBN 978-3-89821-821-4

74   *Alena Vysotskaya*
       Russland, Belarus und die EU-Osterweiterung
       Zur Minderheitenfrage und zum Problem der Freizügigkeit des Personenverkehrs
       Mit einem Vorwort von Katlijn Malfliet
       ISBN 978-3-89821-822-1

75 Heiko Pleines (Hrsg.)
Corporate Governance in post-
sozialistischen Volkswirtschaften
ISBN 978-3-89821-766-8

76 Stefan Ihrig
Wer sind die Moldawier?
Rumänismus versus Moldowanismus in
Historiographie und Schulbüchern der
Republik Moldova, 1991-2006
Mit einem Vorwort von Holm Sundhaussen
ISBN 978-3-89821-466-7

77 Galina Kozhevnikova in collaboration
with Alexander Verkhovsky and
Eugene Veklerov
Ultra-Nationalism and Hate Crimes in
Contemporary Russia
The 2004-2006 Annual Reports of Moscow's
SOVA Center
With a foreword by Stephen D. Shenfield
ISBN 978-3-89821-868-9

78 Florian Küchler
The Role of the European Union in
Moldova's Transnistria Conflict
With a foreword by Christopher Hill
ISBN 978-3-89821-850-4

79 Bernd Rechel
The Long Way Back to Europe
Minority Protection in Bulgaria
With a foreword by Richard Crampton
ISBN 978-3-89821-863-4

80 Peter W. Rodgers
Nation, Region and History in Post-
Communist Transitions
Identity Politics in Ukraine, 1991-2006
With a foreword by Vera Tolz
ISBN 978-3-89821-903-7

81 Stephanie Solywoda
The Life and Work of
Semen L. Frank
A Study of Russian Religious Philosophy
With a foreword by Philip Walters
ISBN 978-3-89821-457-5

82 Vera Sokolova
Cultural Politics of Ethnicity
Discourses on Roma in Communist
Czechoslovakia
ISBN 978-3-89821-864-1

83 Natalya Shevchik Ketenci
Kazakhstani Enterprises in Transition
The Role of Historical Regional Development
in Kazakhstan's Post-Soviet Economic
Transformation
ISBN 978-3-89821-831-3

84 Martin Malek, Anna Schor-
Tschudnowskaja (Hrsg.)
Europa im Tschetschenienkrieg
Zwischen politischer Ohnmacht und
Gleichgültigkeit
Mit einem Vorwort von Lipchan Basajewa
ISBN 978-3-89821-676-0

85 Stefan Meister
Das postsowjetische Universitätswesen
zwischen nationalem und
internationalem Wandel
Die Entwicklung der regionalen Hochschule
in Russland als Gradmesser der
Systemtransformation
Mit einem Vorwort von Joan DeBardeleben
ISBN 978-3-89821-891-7

86 Konstantin Sheiko in collaboration
with Stephen Brown
Nationalist Imaginings of the
Russian Past
Anatolii Fomenko and the Rise of Alternative
History in Post-Communist Russia
With a foreword by Donald Ostrowski
ISBN 978-3-89821-915-0

87 Sabine Jenni
Wie stark ist das „Einige Russland"?
Zur Parteibindung der Eliten und zum
Wahlerfolg der Machtpartei
im Dezember 2007
Mit einem Vorwort von Klaus Armingeon
ISBN 978-3-89821-961-7

88 Thomas Borén
Meeting-Places of Transformation
Urban Identity, Spatial Representations and
Local Politics in Post-Soviet St Petersburg
ISBN 978-3-89821-739-2

89 Aygul Ashirova
Stalinismus und Stalin-Kult in
Zentralasien
Turkmenistan 1924-1953
Mit einem Vorwort von Leonid Luks
ISBN 978-3-89821-987-7

90 Leonid Luks
    Freiheit oder imperiale Größe?
    Essays zu einem russischen Dilemma
    ISBN 978-3-8382-0011-8

91 Christopher Gilley
    The 'Change of Signposts' in the
    Ukrainian Emigration
    A Contribution to the History of
    Sovietophilism in the 1920s
    With a foreword by Frank Golczewski
    ISBN 978-3-89821-965-5

92 Philipp Casula, Jeronim Perovic
    (Eds.)
    Identities and Politics
    During the Putin Presidency
    The Discursive Foundations of Russia's
    Stability
    With a foreword by Heiko Haumann
    ISBN 978-3-8382-0015-6

93 Marcel Viëtor
    Europa und die Frage
    nach seinen Grenzen im Osten
    Zur Konstruktion 'europäischer Identität' in
    Geschichte und Gegenwart
    Mit einem Vorwort von Albrecht Lehmann
    ISBN 978-3-8382-0045-3

94 Ben Hellman, Andrei Rogachevskii
    Filming the Unfilmable
    Casper Wrede's 'One Day in the Life
    of Ivan Denisovich'
    Second, Revised and Expanded Edition
    ISBN 978-3-8382-0044-6

95 Eva Fuchslocher
    Vaterland, Sprache, Glaube
    Orthodoxie und Nationenbildung
    am Beispiel Georgiens
    Mit einem Vorwort von Christina von Braun
    ISBN 978-3-89821-884-9

96 Vladimir Kantor
    Das Westlertum und der Weg
    Russlands
    Zur Entwicklung der russischen Literatur und
    Philosophie
    Ediert von Dagmar Herrmann
    Mit einem Beitrag von Nikolaus Lobkowicz
    ISBN 978-3-8382-0102-3

97 Kamran Musayev
    Die postsowjetische Transformation
    im Baltikum und Südkaukasus
    Eine vergleichende Untersuchung der
    politischen Entwicklung Lettlands und
    Aserbaidschans 1985-2009
    Mit einem Vorwort von Leonid Luks
    Ediert von Sandro Henschel
    ISBN 978-3-8382-0103-0

98 Tatiana Zhurzhenko
    Borderlands into Bordered Lands
    Geopolitics of Identity in Post-Soviet Ukraine
    With a foreword by Dieter Segert
    ISBN 978-3-8382-0042-2

99 Кирилл Галушко, Лидия Смола
    (ред.)
    Пределы падения – варианты
    украинского будущего
    Аналитико-прогностические исследования
    ISBN 978-3-8382-0148-1

100 Michael Minkenberg (ed.)
    Historical Legacies and the Radical
    Right in Post-Cold War Central and
    Eastern Europe
    With an afterword by Sabrina P. Ramet
    ISBN 978-3-8382-0124-5

101 David-Emil Wickström
    Rocking St. Petersburg
    Transcultural Flows and Identity Politics in
    the St. Petersburg Popular Music Scene
    With a foreword by Yngvar B. Steinholt
    Second, Revised and Expanded Edition
    ISBN 978-3-8382-0100-9

102 Eva Zabka
    Eine neue „Zeit der Wirren"?
    Der spät- und postsowjetische Systemwandel
    1985-2000 im Spiegel russischer
    gesellschaftspolitischer Diskurse
    Mit einem Vorwort von Margareta Mommsen
    ISBN 978-3-8382-0161-0

103 Ulrike Ziemer
    Ethnic Belonging, Gender and
    Cultural Practices
    Youth Identitites in Contemporary Russia
    With a foreword by Anoop Nayak
    ISBN 978-3-8382-0152-8

104 Ksenia Chepikova
‚Einiges Russland' - eine zweite
KPdSU?
Aspekte der Identitätskonstruktion einer
postsowjetischen „Partei der Macht"
Mit einem Vorwort von Torsten Oppelland
ISBN 978-3-8382-0311-9

105 Леонид Люкс
Западничество или евразийство?
Демократия или идеократия?
Сборник статей об исторических дилеммах
России
С предисловием Владимира Кантора
ISBN 978-3-8382-0211-2

106 Anna Dost
Das russische Verfassungsrecht auf dem
Weg zum Föderalismus und zurück
Zum Konflikt von Rechtsnormen und
-wirklichkeit in der Russländischen
Föderation von 1991 bis 2009
Mit einem Vorwort von Alexander Blankenagel
ISBN 978-3-8382-0292-1

107 Philipp Herzog
Sozialistische Völkerfreundschaft,
nationaler Widerstand oder harmloser
Zeitvertreib?
Zur politischen Funktion der Volkskunst
im sowjetischen Estland
Mit einem Vorwort von Andreas Kappeler
ISBN 978-3-8382-0216-7

108 Marlène Laruelle (ed.)
Russian Nationalism, Foreign Policy,
and Identity Debates in Putin's Russia
New Ideological Patterns after the Orange
Revolution
ISBN 978-3-8382-0325-6

109 Michail Logvinov
Russlands Kampf gegen den
internationalen Terrorismus
Eine kritische Bestandsaufnahme des
Bekämpfungsansatzes
Mit einem Geleitwort von
Hans-Henning Schröder
und einem Vorwort von Eckhard Jesse
ISBN 978-3-8382-0329-4

110 John B. Dunlop
The Moscow Bombings
of September 1999
Examinations of Russian Terrorist Attacks
at the Onset of Vladimir Putin's Rule
Second, Revised and Expanded Edition
ISBN 978-3-8382-0388-1

111 Андрей А. Ковалёв
Свидетельство из-за кулис
российской политики I
Можно ли делать добро из зла?
(Воспоминания и размышления о
последних советских и первых
послесоветских годах)
With a foreword by Peter Reddaway
ISBN 978-3-8382-0302-7

112 Андрей А. Ковалёв
Свидетельство из-за кулис
российской политики II
Угроза для себя и окружающих
(Наблюдения и предостережения
относительно происходящего после 2000 г.)
ISBN 978-3-8382-0303-4

113 Bernd Kappenberg
Zeichen setzen für Europa
Der Gebrauch europäischer lateinischer
Sonderzeichen in der deutschen Öffentlichkeit
Mit einem Vorwort von Peter Schlobinski
ISBN 978-3-89821-749-1

114 Ivo Mijnssen
The Quest for an Ideal Youth in
Putin's Russia I
Back to Our Future! History, Modernity, and
Patriotism according to Nashi, 2005-2013
With a foreword by Jeronim Perović
Second, Revised and Expanded Edition
ISBN 978-3-8382-0368-3

115 Jussi Lassila
The Quest for an Ideal Youth in
Putin's Russia II
The Search for Distinctive Conformism in the
Political Communication of Nashi, 2005-2009
With a foreword by Kirill Postoutenko
Second, Revised and Expanded Edition
ISBN 978-3-8382-0415-4

116 Valerio Trabandt
Neue Nachbarn, gute Nachbarschaft?
Die EU als internationaler Akteur am Beispiel
ihrer Demokratieförderung in Belarus und der
Ukraine 2004-2009
Mit einem Vorwort von Jutta Joachim
ISBN 978-3-8382-0437-6

117 *Fabian Pfeiffer*
    Estlands Außen- und Sicherheitspolitik I
    Der estnische Atlantizismus nach der
    wiedererlangten Unabhängigkeit 1991-2004
    Mit einem Vorwort von Helmut Hubel
    ISBN 978-3-8382-0127-6

118 *Jana Podßuweit*
    Estlands Außen- und Sicherheitspolitik II
    Handlungsoptionen eines Kleinstaates im
    Rahmen seiner EU-Mitgliedschaft (2004-2008)
    Mit einem Vorwort von Helmut Hubel
    ISBN 978-3-8382-0440-6

119 *Karin Pointner*
    Estlands Außen- und Sicherheitspolitik III
    Eine gedächtnispolitische Analyse estnischer
    Entwicklungskooperation 2006-2010
    Mit einem Vorwort von Karin Liebhart
    ISBN 978-3-8382-0435-2

120 *Ruslana Vovk*
    Die Offenheit der ukrainischen
    Verfassung für das Völkerrecht und
    die europäische Integration
    Mit einem Vorwort von Alexander
    Blankenagel
    ISBN 978-3-8382-0481-9

121 *Mykhaylo Banakh*
    Die Relevanz der Zivilgesellschaft
    bei den postkommunistischen
    Transformationsprozessen in mittel-
    und osteuropäischen Ländern
    Das Beispiel der spät- und postsowjetischen
    Ukraine 1986-2009
    Mit einem Vorwort von Gerhard Simon
    ISBN 978-3-8382-0499-4

122 *Michael Moser*
    Language Policy and the Discourse on
    Languages in Ukraine under President
    Viktor Yanukovych (25 February
    2010–28 October 2012)
    ISBN 978-3-8382-0497-0 (Paperback edition)
    ISBN 978-3-8382-0507-6 (Hardcover edition)

123 *Nicole Krome*
    Russischer Netzwerkkapitalismus
    Restrukturierungsprozesse in der
    Russischen Föderation am Beispiel des
    Luftfahrtunternehmens "Aviastar"
    Mit einem Vorwort von Petra Stykow
    ISBN 978-3-8382-0534-2

124 *David R. Marples*
    'Our Glorious Past'
    Lukashenka's Belarus and
    the Great Patriotic War
    ISBN 978-3-8382-0574-8 (Paperback edition)
    ISBN 978-3-8382-0675-2 (Hardcover edition)

125 *Ulf Walther*
    Russlands "neuer Adel"
    Die Macht des Geheimdienstes von
    Gorbatschow bis Putin
    Mit einem Vorwort von Hans-Georg Wieck
    ISBN 978-3-8382-0584-7

126 *Simon Geissbühler (Hrsg.)*
    Kiew – Revolution 3.0
    Der Euromaidan 2013/14 und die
    Zukunftsperspektiven der Ukraine
    ISBN 978-3-8382-0581-6 (Paperback edition)
    ISBN 978-3-8382-0681-3 (Hardcover edition)

127 *Andrey Makarychev*
    Russia and the EU
    in a Multipolar World
    Discourses, Identities, Norms
    With a foreword by Klaus Segbers
    ISBN 978-3-8382-0629-5

128 *Roland Scharff*
    Kasachstan als postsowjetischer
    Wohlfahrtsstaat
    Die Transformation des sozialen
    Schutzsystems
    Mit einem Vorwort von Joachim Ahrens
    ISBN 978-3-8382-0622-6

129 *Katja Grupp*
    Bild Lücke Deutschland
    Kaliningrader Studierende sprechen über
    Deutschland
    Mit einem Vorwort von Martin Schulz
    ISBN 978-3-8382-0552-6

130 *Konstantin Sheiko, Stephen Brown*
    History as Therapy
    Alternative History and Nationalist
    Imaginings in Russia, 1991-2014
    ISBN 978-3-8382-0665-3

131 Elisa Kriza
Alexander Solzhenitsyn: Cold War Icon, Gulag Author, Russian Nationalist?
A Study of the Western Reception of his Literary Writings, Historical Interpretations, and Political Ideas
With a foreword by Andrei Rogatchevski
ISBN 978-3-8382-0589-2 (Paperback edition)
ISBN 978-3-8382-0690-5 (Hardcover edition)

132 Serghei Golunov
The Elephant in the Room
Corruption and Cheating in Russian Universities
ISBN 978-3-8382-0570-0

133 Manja Hussner, Rainer Arnold (Hgg.)
Verfassungsgerichtsbarkeit in Zentralasien I
Sammlung von Verfassungstexten
ISBN 978-3-8382-0595-3

134 Nikolay Mitrokhin
Die "Russische Partei"
Die Bewegung der russischen Nationalisten in der UdSSR 1953-1985
Aus dem Russischen übertragen von einem Übersetzerteam unter der Leitung von Larisa Schippel
ISBN 978-3-8382-0024-8

135 Manja Hussner, Rainer Arnold (Hgg.)
Verfassungsgerichtsbarkeit in Zentralasien II
Sammlung von Verfassungstexten
ISBN 978-3-8382-0597-7

136 Manfred Zeller
Das sowjetische Fieber
Fußballfans im poststalinistischen Vielvölkerreich
Mit einem Vorwort von Nikolaus Katzer
ISBN 978-3-8382-0757-5

137 Kristin Schreiter
Stellung und Entwicklungspotential zivilgesellschaftlicher Gruppen in Russland
Menschenrechtsorganisationen im Vergleich
ISBN 978-3-8382-0673-8

138 David R. Marples, Frederick V. Mills (Eds.)
Ukraine's Euromaidan
Analyses of a Civil Revolution
ISBN 978-3-8382-0660-8

139 Bernd Kappenberg
Setting Signs for Europe
Why Diacritics Matter for European Integration
With a foreword by Peter Schlobinski
ISBN 978-3-8382-0663-9

140 René Lenz
Internationalisierung, Kooperation und Transfer
Externe bildungspolitische Akteure in der Russischen Föderation
Mit einem Vorwort von Frank Ettrich
ISBN 978-3-8382-0751-3

141 Juri Plusnin, Yana Zausaeva, Natalia Zhidkevich, Artemy Pozanenko
Wandering Workers
Mores, Behavior, Way of Life, and Political Status of Domestic Russian Labor Migrants
Translated by Julia Kazantseva
ISBN 978-3-8382-0653-0

142 Matthew Kott, David J. Smith (eds.)
Latvia – A Work in Progress?
100 Years of State- and Nation-building
ISBN 978-3-8382-0648-6

143 Инна Чувычкина (ред.)
Экспортные нефте- и газопроводы на постсоветском пространстве
Анализ трубопроводной политики в свете теории международных отношений
ISBN 978-3-8382-0822-0

144 Johann Zajaczkowski
Russland – eine pragmatische Großmacht?
Eine rollentheoretische Untersuchung russischer Außenpolitik am Beispiel der Zusammenarbeit mit den USA nach 9/11 und des Georgienkrieges von 2008
Mit einem Vorwort von Siegfried Schieder
ISBN 978-3-8382-0837-4

145 Boris Popivanov
Changing Images of the Left in Bulgaria
The Challenge of Post-Communism in the Early 21st Century
ISBN 978-3-8382-0667-7

ibidem-Verlag

Melchiorstr. 15

D-70439 Stuttgart

info@ibidem-verlag.de

www.ibidem-verlag.de
www.ibidem.eu
www.edition-noema.de
www.autorenbetreuung.de